SIGN

CW01024264

One Man's Scotland

By

Peter McManus

A catalogue record for this book is available from the British Library.

Hardback ISBN 0-9542912-0-4
Paperback ISBN 0-9542912-1-2

Published by:
M. E. P. Publishing
Newton Park Farm
Newton Solney
Burton on Trent
DE15 0SS
Tel: 01283 703280

Printed by Tranters, Markeaton Printing Works, Derby

To Jock Lamont

with good wishes

Peter McManus

To

My grandsons Adam and Clive hoping
that they, too, will experience and
appreciate the magic of Scotland.

About this book

The Highlands of Scotland have never lost their appeal for us, since we first took The High Road in 1954.

We have enjoyed marvellous days on the Hill and superlative hospitality in the glens. All this has inspired me to write this book.

My thanks to everyone who has made this book possible, many of whom have helped with information and photographs. My appreciation is contained in the text, but, in addition, I must particularly thank Margaret MacNally and her sons Lea and Michael for being kind enough to let me have so many of Lea's marvellous photographs, Ronnie and Margaret Ross of Braelangwell for their photographs and incomparable hospitality.

Thanks too, to my wife Edna, who made it all possible: She tramped the Hill with me, ran the lodges and typed the original manuscript. To my daughter Caroline and son Ross, good walkers and essential companions.

To my talented daughter-in-law, Stephanie, who tirelessly worked on the book, put the whole thing in order and acted as Editor-in-Chief.

To all whose hospitality we have enjoyed and appreciated in Scotland. To all stalkers, gillies and ponymen who have shown us the ways of the deer in every kind of weather and finally to all our guests who enhanced the pleasure of the Hill, the people in "The Glen", Strathcarron and not least, the Red Deer of Scotland.

Peter McManus

O Caledonia ! stern and wild..........
land of brown heath and shaggy wood
land of the mountain and the flood..........

Sir Walter Scott

Photographs

The photographs in this book have brought the whole thing to life. I am, therefore, most grateful to everyone who has been kind enough to supply them.

I must particularly mention Margaret MacNally and her sons Lea and Michael. They were kind enough to let me have Lea's remarkable wildlife photographs. All the wildlife photographs in the book, with the exception of the old Alladale stag, are by Lea MacNally.

Thanks to Marcus Munro who captured the moment when the old Alladale stag put his nose against my forehead. Marcus and Jennifer also let me have many other photographs including Cameron and the dinosaur.

Ross and Stephanie also provided a number of essential photographs.

Callum Campbell, at a bring and buy sale, picked up two volumes of photographs of the Debenham family in Scotland stalking and grouse shooting in the 1920's and 1930's. He was kind enough to lend them to me via Ronnie Ross.

Ronnie provided many of the photographs in the book including the remarkable one of his grandfather at Alladale in the 1890's.

The curator of Tain Museum who was most helpful and allowed me to use photographs from their extensive collection.

The District Library at Stornaway allowed me to use some of their photographs and others were from *Edwardian Highlands from old photographs* by Francis Thompson.

My thanks to everyone who was kind enough to help.

Contents

*"My heart's in the Highlands,
my heart is not here,
My heart's in the Highlands,
a-chasing the deer;
Chasing the wild deer and following the roe;
My heart's in the Highlands wherever I go."*

Robbie Burns

Chapter One
Scotland the Brave

SCOTLAND! A magical name with so many meanings, implications, emotions.

Without doubt it means so many different things for so many people but, surely, the overriding impression is of the wild high hills of the Highlands, the Red Deer, the turbulent history, the clans and tartans, Culloden, Balmoral, Scotch Whiskey, Harris Tweed, the Stone of Scone, Robbie Burns, the Loch Ness Monster, Bannockburn, the majestic salmon, prince of fish, the Red Grouse, the Golden Eagle, Killiekrankie, William Wallace and the whole Highland scene.

As a boy in the 1930's living in Rhyl, Scotland was a faraway place, imbued with mystery. Very few people we knew had cars in those days and the journey to Scotland either by rail or car, was a formidable venture. Not that we actually knew anyone who went on holiday to Scotland.

So childhood impressions reinforced my view of this magical, mysterious land: Firstly by reading about the exploits of the Red MacGregor in the pages of the *Wizard* (price twopence). These stories were set in a vague timescale, presumably the eighteenth century, where the brave Red MacGregor fought for right against the dastardly Sassenach oppressors.

Then, of course, Bonnie Prince Charlie. The gallant young Prince fighting unsuccessfully against all the odds to reclaim his rightful kingdom from the German usurper, King George. The disastrous defeat at Culloden Moor followed by his romantic flight through the Highlands with a price on his head, never betrayed by the poverty stricken but loyal Highlanders. His final escape helped by the never-to-be-forgotten Flora MacDonald.

That, surely, was romance and adventure enough but reinforced by reading *Kidnapped* by Robert Louis Stevenson. A tale set in the aftermath of the 1745 Rebellion with the brave David Balfour and the gallant but flawed Scottish soldier of fortune, Alan Breck.

Not forgetting the Loch Ness Monster. In 1931 the famous photograph appeared of the head and neck of the monster emerging from the loch. Fashionably debunked today but definitely not in the 1930's. So was there really a strange survival of a prehistoric monster in that huge, deep loch? It all added to the mystery.

There was, of course, much more along these lines, so the overriding impression of Scotland as a land of history, mystery and romance was indelibly stamped.

So when I eventually did go to Scotland, did it fully live up to my expectations? The answer is a resounding "Yes" as you will see from the following pages.

The Jacobite Memorial at Glenfinnan, where Bonnie Prince Charlie raised his standard at the start of the 1745 rebellion.

An eaglet feasts on the remains of a Red Deer calf.

Stephen Pilkington and stalker James Clark looking into Glen Alladale, with Carn Alladale in the background.

Chapter Two
Decision Made

In 1954 I bought a copy of *With a Gun to the Hill* by Stephen Pilkington: a purchase that was to make a far-reaching impression on my life. *With a Gun to the Hill* describes Stephen Pilkington's experience with rod, rifle and gun in Scotland during the 1920's, 30's and 40's.

Bodkin Adams, the doctor accused, though acquitted, of murdering elderly patients having persuaded them to make wills in his favour, claimed that *With a Gun to the Hill* was his favourite book and on his death it was put up for sale among his effects. No, I failed to buy it!

Stephen Pilkington and his brother Jim stalked throughout Scotland with their 7mm Mauser rifles. Little did I know at the time that I would stalk on a number of those deer forests and meet Jim Pilkington and many of the friends who had stalked with him.

During the 1930's they took the adjoining forests of Deanich (pronounced gee-a-nich) and Alladale. These forests comprised the main part of the old "Freevater Forest" i.e. "Walter's Forest", after Sir Walter Ross. Sir Walter was one of the only two Scottish nobles who fell at Bannockburn when practically every English noble family lost a husband, father or son.

The Ross family had held onto a huge tract of land known as the Balnagown Estate right through to the 1960's, finally in the ownership of Sir Charles Ross. Sir Charles was an incredible character! Legendary rifle shot and inventor of the straight-pull Ross rifle in which the bolt was operated by simply pulling straight back without the usual "door bolt movement". It was the standard rifle for the Canadian Army at the start of World War One but the Flanders mud defeated it.

Sir Charles lived at Balnagown Castle, Tain, Easter Ross now owned and restored at enormous expense by Mohammed Al. Fayed.

He was a *bon viveur* enthusiastically embracing wine, women and song, though he was, I understand, not much of a singer!

Although three times married he had no children and his last wife was his much younger secretary. On his death she inherited the estate and within the year married Francis De Moleyns, another *bon viveur.* Unfortunately she died shortly afterwards so De Moleyns copped the lot!

Sir Charles, like most of us, disliked paying Income Tax though in his case this dislike verged on paranoia! In his later years he lived in Canada and refused to pay Income Tax. On occasion he would pay incognito visits to the estate and hills he loved, secretly calling on his tenants and stalkers who never betrayed his presence to the police. When the pace got too hot he reputedly took to the Hill to avoid his pursuers like the fugitive Jacobites after the 1745. Eventually he would hop on a boat back to Canada but, like all mortals, he eventually had to slough off his mortal coil and, just as inevitably, the Taxman finally pounced!

Right! *With a Gun to the Hill* having decided me to head for Scotland to start stalking there were two essential requirements - a suitable rifle and somewhere to stalk.

For a rifle the clear choice was a new .303 BSA built on the superlative 1898 Mauser action. An excellent choice also used for the incomparable hand-built David Lloyd rifles at a later date. The price of the new BSA was £16.10s. How's that for value for money? This for a strong, well made, accurate rifle. I was delighted with mine.

The new .303 BSA rifle. Price £16.10s.

Switch. A good choice to cull.

Chapter Three
Where to Stalk

Next problem? Somewhere to stalk. 1954, however, was an excellent time to start stalking and this is why: Just after the war an ambitious scheme was put into effect to provide hydro-electric power throughout the Highlands. Suitable estates with ample water supplies were surveyed and these estates acquired by compulsory purchase where necessary. The dams were constructed, the hydro-electric plant installed and at the completion of it all the land round the dam and hydro electric plant was retained. The surplus land, i.e. the main part of the deer forest was sold back into private ownership.

In 1954, huge tracts of deer forests were Government owned so the stalking had to be let at what, in retrospect, were very modest prices. Just after the war the newly demobbed Captain Leslie Hunt and his wife Mary took over the tenancy of the Invergarry Hotel, Invergarry and made an excellent job of running it.

Leslie and Mary Hunt were the ideal pair to run a Scottish Country House Hotel, both of them remarkable people in many senses of that word. Mary Hunt was a superlative hostess who ran the hotel brilliantly with the hallmark of excellent cuisine.

She was the prime mover, without a doubt, with Leslie, a man of tremendous charm, helping to the best of his ability. He was the ideal "mine host": Not the "mine host" of a second rate pub but of the very best example of a Country House Hotel.

Leslie Hunt had attained the rank of Captain during the War and had retained his military title so he liked to be addressed as "Captain Hunt". It was not an easy war for him as he was captured and became a prisoner of war suffering many privations.

Many of his guests were upper class so Leslie, who spoke well enough as it was, had set out to acquire the supreme upper class accent. The result, sometimes, could be baffling! On one occasion he was complaining to the guests in the sitting room about the difficulties caused by lorks. The word lorks was new to us. He went on to explain, however, that if you were in a hurry to get to Fort William from Invergarry the lorks could cause queues and exasperating delays when boats came through and the road was temporarily blocked. Finally the penny dropped! "lorks" was his assumed upper class way of pronouncing locks.

At the other end of the social spectrum some of the female characters in Coronation Street, often talk about blorks. Another word that you may well find strange. What they mean are blokes. No doubt another variation on the rich tapestry of colloquial English. Though I cannot believe that lorks and blorks will ever become accepted to replace locks and blokes. If they do, as Sam Goldwyn might have said, include me out!

With so much stalking available the Hunts realised that there was enormous potential to extend the season and increase their profitability, so they leased the stalking on a number of estates: Invergarry North, Garrygualach (Greenfields), Levishie, Ceannacroc, North Dundreggan, Braeroy, Glengarry, Balmacaan, Corrielair and others. With all this stalking to offer their scope was vastly extended and they made very good use of it.

The Invergarry Hotel, then, was the obvious choice, so my wife Edna was reluctantly persuaded to make Scotland our holiday destination for August 1954 and accompanied by her brother Jim, who lived with us, we headed for Scotland in our 1949 Austin A90 Atlantic soft-top.

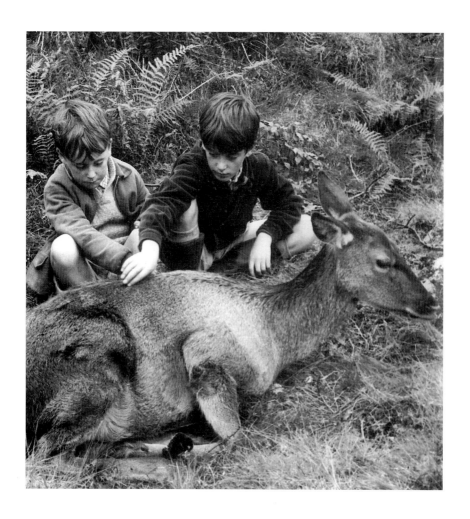

Michael and young Lea MacNally with their tame hind.

A good stag with hinds and calves.

Chapter Four
Deerstalking. Essential, or Cruel and Unnecessary?

If you are a countryman or countryman at heart, you will understand deerstalking and most readers of this book will fall into this category. What, however, if you are in neither category and are strongly opposed to hunting or shooting? Hitler, strangely enough, was opposed to both. You saw Bambi's mother shot by cruel and unfeeling hunters and ever since then you have been against shooting. Bambi, in any case, was a cartoon animal and real deer are far more beautiful. Can there be anything in nature more beautiful than a Red Deer calf?

It is worth mentioning that hunting with hounds and game shooting are entirely different subjects, worlds apart from deerstalking in Scotland and do not concern us here.

I would like you, for a moment, to put yourself in this position: Your Great Aunt Agatha has died, leaving you a Highland deer forest of 20,000 acres on the following conditions: You must manage the estate yourself with the welfare of the deer paramount. You are not allowed to sell all, or any part of it. Nor are you allowed to let it, other than for sporting lets.

If you are in breach of these conditions the forest reverts to your Aunt's estate and your interest ceases. If, however, you run the estate on the lines requested then, upon your death, it can be left to your family or anyone you chose.

The forest has an un-modernised lodge, a range of outbuildings and an un-modernised keeper's house.

So a lifetime of marvellous family holidays stretch ahead of you: You will be able to observe the wildlife, watch the deer calves frolic in midsummer, picnic by the hill lochs (Are you against fishing?) and walk through that magnificent country.

At last it is in your hands to help the deer and stop all shooting on your estate "with the welfare of the deer paramount". All this cruelty must stop so the now redundant keeper is dismissed. The deer are wild creatures, accustomed to living on the forest, so they are well able to look after themselves.

So for the first year things aren't so bad: Deer numbers build up, of course, but what's the harm in that? The snag is that there is no income from the estate to pay for essential maintenance as sales of venison and stalking rents have ended but, if you can afford it, so what? Another snag is that with the keeper gone there is an unwelcome increase in the amount of vermin on the ground and your neighbours will be none too pleased about that!

For the next year or two, however, the picture changes: You find out that the deer *cannot* look after themselves. You have completely overlooked the fact that nature is both cruel and ruthless.

Dead, dying and diseased deer litter the landscape. Calves lie dead against their mothers. The entire healthy stock of deer you inherited is now in a state of starvation and disease. As Germaine Greer said, "The amount of pain that any animal living in the wild is called both to inflict and endure is beyond our wildest dreams."

Your once admired forest is now a horrifying disgrace. The RSPCA are called in and you are asked to explain this dreadful state of affairs. You explain that you are an animal lover, opposed to the cruelty of shooting

"Cruelty!" say the RSPCA, "What do you call this?".

You go to see the old stalker and are amazed to find that his love of the Red Deer is no less than yours. "Then how can you tolerate the cruelty of shooting these lovely creatures?" You ask.

He explains that when he is hind shooting in the winter he gets no pleasure from the death of a hind, only the satisfaction of a good job well done. As for cruelty, death by a precisely aimed bullet from a high powered rifle is a quick and merciful end, bearing no comparison to leaving a poor hind to linger for months only to eventually die of disease or starvation.

He goes on to explain that the "real" stalking is done by the professional stalker shooting hinds in winter. He has carefully considered what cull must be taken, in this forest usually ninety hinds. His objective is to shoot the poorer hinds and calves that would never survive the winter anyway, always leaving the best stock. The sale of their venison contributes to the running of the estate and the cost of winter feed.

The kind of mid-winter stalking that few Sassenachs ever see.

Now that you fully understand the whole situation you may be persuaded; but what about stags? They are shot by "Sassenachs" who enjoy shooting. Cannot this be stopped and the shooting be carried out by the professional stalker as with the hinds? Well, yes, provided that you have unlimited cash to pour into the forest and are prepared to close your eyes to the complete picture.

"Sassenach" is often thought to mean "Englishman", but its true meaning is "stranger" i.e. anyone who is not a Scotsman.

The old stalker goes on to explain that to keep the numbers down to what the land will bear then about 75 stags have to be shot. If shot by the professional stalker the sale of the venison would help towards the maintenance of the estate, as with the hinds, but the greatest revenue of all, the stalking lets, would be lost.

With revenue from all sources: Venison and stalking rents, the place still cannot pay its way. The forest has been under the stalker's expert eye and that of his predecessors for generations to ensure that the deer stock has been maintained at the level the forest will stand. The problem is that in summer time there is enough grazing to feed a huge amount of stock, in winter the situation is entirely different.

Snow cuts off most of the 20,000 acres and even in the glens the deer are forced to survive by scraping through the snow with their hooves to get at the heather below. In any event, winter feeding has always been necessary to enable even the much lower stock levels to survive.

Now that you understand the necessity of controlling the total deer stock, what is so wrong with letting the stag stalking? Why is it so wrong for the well-aimed rifle bullet to come from a Sassenach rifle under the expert supervision of the professional stalker?

So it comes down to the fact that your only objection is that they would enjoy it, but isn't that objection now wearing a bit thin?

The Sassenach Rifle is not there merely to shoot the stag but to enjoy and be part of the whole Highland scene. To walk that magnificent landscape. To appreciate the pleasures and undoubted hardships of the stalk. To enjoy the expert companionship of the professional stalker. To experience the enormous pleasure of seeing the deer and the wildlife and, yes, at the climax of the stalk to have the satisfaction of a well aimed shot to bring the stalk to a satisfactory conclusion. By all means ensure that only competent shots are allowed to shoot.

Remember, too, that we are all hunters at heart, descended from ancestors who, for countless millennia, faced storm, tempest, cold, hunger, wild animals, every kind of hazard and threat to their very existence. If we can harness our inherited hunting instincts to the challenge of toiling up those high hills, battling with the elements and the humane pursuit of our quarry, surely this must be beyond reproach.

So you re-employ the old stalker, refurbish some of the old buildings for holiday lets and finally get the whole place on its feet "With the interests of the deer paramount".

But let Cervantes have the last word: in *The Adventures of Don Quixote*, Sancho said "What I mean is that I would not have kings and other great folks run into such dangers merely for pleasure; and indeed, methinks it ought to be none to kill poor beasts that never meant any harm."

"You are mistaken, Sancho" said the Duke; "Hunting wild beasts is the most proper exercise for knights and princes. The chase is an image of war. Besides, it is the peculiar sport of the great."

Nature: Cruel and ruthless. Deer killed by starvation towards the end of winter.

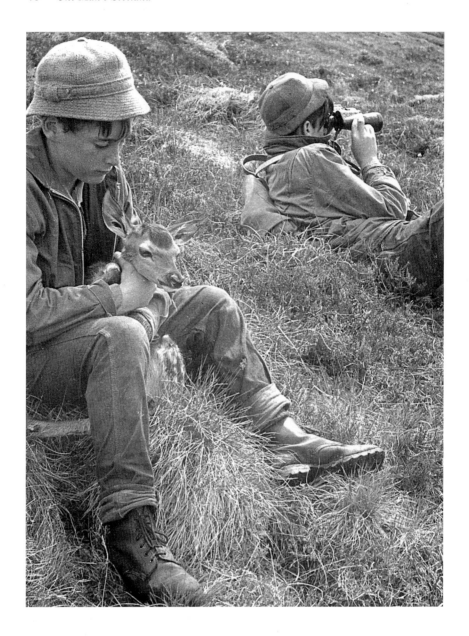

Young Lea MacNally on right and brother Michael calf tagging in June.
Lea spies for another calf.

Chapter Five
The Red Deer

The Red Deer are, without doubt, marvellous animals and on the Hill in Scotland they have their own social system. The hinds and calves live in groups of, perhaps, ten to fifteen animals and they stay together throughout the year. The leading hind is the most alert for any sign of danger and if danger threatens she barks in alarm and leads the rest of the group to safety. The trailing hind, too, keeps a rearguard lookout.

The leading hind always has a calf at foot but if she skips a year without a calf and becomes "yeld" (barren) she then loses her place as leading hind and another hind with a calf at foot takes over. Because of the harsh conditions of the Highland winters the hinds usually have a calf one year and then are not in good enough condition to conceive a calf for the next year. After this yeld year they will put on enough condition to bear another calf. Having said this, it is by no means unusual to see a hind with this years calf, last years calf and a three year old.

Stags do not stay together in the same kind of fixed groups but they can assemble in quite big numbers, on occasion, especially just before the start of the rut before they "break out" in their search for hinds.

If you want to baffle your friends, ask them the following question : Which animal has horns, four legs and barks like a dog? They will, of course, be baffled so you will say the answer is a cow.! "But what about that barks like a dog bit?", they will ask. "Why," you will reply, "I just put that in to make it more difficult!"

You will then, however, tell them that there really is such an animal.... a stag.... because if a stag is really startled he can, indeed, bark in alarm in the same way that a hind does. You seldom hear it but if you spend a fair amount of time on the Hill, observing or stalking, you are bound to encounter it.

Young Lea MacNally has located and captured another calf to tag.

At the onset of the rut, usually in late September, stag behaviour changes. The older and more mature stags "break out" from the stag groups they happen to be in and range across the Hill for miles, roaring as they go, looking for hinds. Their rutting fever is so intense that they cannot trouble to eat and this, exacerbated by their ceaseless search, means that they drop in condition.

When a stag does find a hind group he patrols round it to keep all the hinds together and to keep out any usurpers. Other stags will try to cut in and take some of his hinds but he will chase them off: He will often fight with challengers, a noisy affair of grunts and clashing antlers as they strain against each other, antlers locked in combat. It is very seldom that serious damage is done or a stag is killed as it is only the human species who kill each other!

The master stag will try to herd more and more hind groups into his circle, exhausting himself in this continuous attempt to round them up and fight off any intruders. Inevitably the whole thing eventually becomes too much to handle and he becomes so exhausted that a challenging stag takes over, chasing him away, so the whole process is repeated.

"I like September stalking", my friend Jim Pilkington used to say and there is a lot to be said for it *if* you are on a forest with plenty of stags. In September, before the rut, stags are more alert and usually in larger groups so it is much more difficult to stalk close enough to get a shot. There is, however, also the chance of a "right and left".

In October, however, the weather is worse. It will inevitably be colder and wetter so you will probably be wet and freezing but, on the plus side, everything is happening. The stags are roaring and on their ceaseless rounds. Easier to stalk, in a way, because the stag himself has all his attention on the hinds but all those hinds are keeping their eyes open for human intruders. A successful stalk is by no means a foregone conclusion.

If you are on a hind forest where the stags normally spend the summers on higher ground then stalking during the rut is your only chance. After all, your hind forest has provided the stag stock, now is the time to reap your share. For a hind forest, like Culachy for example, it would be no use trying to get a stag in early September as you would have no chance. You would have to wait until the onset of the rut.

Hinds at peace, for the moment, during the rut.

(Top) Our 1949 Austin A90 Atlantic outside the Invergarry Hotel. Edna in the passenger seat, her brother Jim at the wheel.
(Bottom) Our new 1958 2.4 litre Jaguar.

Chapter Six
We Take the High Road

The Atlantic was a great car, superbly styled. Fashionable for years to sneer at its "Brummagem styling" but now recognised at last. Powered by a two and a half litre four-cylinder engine and although nominally a four-seater it was really a 2+2 with little room for passengers in the back seats. The folding hood was electrically operated and in the "down" position it tucked away out of sight under a neat black canvas cover. It really could achieve 90 mph or more and in those days we drove along every road at the maximum possible speed. If a corner could be negotiated at 70mph, then that was the speed chosen, not 65.

A none too pleasant feature was its braking ability. The brakes were hydraulic front, mechanical rear. You could hurtle along a road at maximum speeds - say 85 mph on a short straight then brake for the next bend. This would be fine until the brakes got really hot and would suddenly decide not to work at all! So having raced along - straights, bends, straights, bends, you would come to the next bend, apply the brakes and nothing would happen: The car would continue into the bend with speed unchecked. This was a terrifying experience! So how did we survive? Down to a large slice of luck! We were very fortunate indeed. With experience you got to be wary of this peculiar characteristic and could tend to anticipate it.... most of the time!

The Austin A90 had a four-speed gear box with steering-column gear-change. The idea of a steering column change was excellent as it was absolutely to hand but, in practise, the lengthy linkage when worn could cause problems. I was always happy enough with the system on the A90 and on the Invergarry to Inverness run I would practise changing gear without the clutch, getting the revs exactly right.

In the 1950's we loved to visit Inverness which had changed very little over the years and must have been very much as it was three quarters of a century before. A lovely town of tremendous character and regarded as the capital of the Highlands. The gun shops were a delight with their displays of guns, rifles, and fishing tackle with shop fronts apparently unchanged for decades.

MacPherson's was probably the most famous but Grays and Grahams were equally worth a visit.

The legendary Mark VII Jaguar identical to ours.

In 1956 we sold the A90 (wish we had it now) and bought a 1952 Mark VII Jaguar with the legendary three and half litre twin-cam engine. How that car would go! Despite its size, which was huge by today's standards, and accompanying weight the acceleration was tremendous and its top speed was just over 110 mph.

As with the A90 it was always driven to the limit, as fast as any bend would allow and at the maximum speed possible. A motoring experience I wouldn't have missed, though petrol and oil consumption were frightening.

In the motoring press we saw a modification advertised to reduce fuel consumption. You fitted a third carburettor which, with an intake of only about one inch diameter, was about the size fitted to a large motorcycle. Edna and I bought this conversion and fitted it ourselves.

Starting away with your foot down, the throttles were opened on all three carburettors i.e. the twin SU's and the one inch bore carburettor. When you reached cruising speed and your foot eased off the throttle, the SU slides closed and you ran on the motorcycle carburettor.

The whole process was completely automatic, you simply drove the car and didn't have to think about carburation but the improvement in fuel consumption was dramatic, boosting fuel consumption to 25pmg compared to the normal 15mpg.

During the 1950's all sorts of older cars were still being used to travel to and from Scotland; everything from the huge old classics to humble Austin Sevens. On one occasion at the Tarbet Hotel when we stayed overnight we saw in the car park a 1920's Austin Seven with a canvas hood, an early 1930's Aston Martin, a four and a quarter litre Railton Drophead Coupe and a huge eight litre Bentley with a tonneau cover to keep out the overnight rain. Not a selection you would be likely to see in a hotel car park today.

Cars of the 1930's were very much part of the scene with Morris eights, tens and sixteens being frequently seen. Rolls Royces? Yes, a few, mostly modern but with a sprinkling of 1920's and 1930's models.

Petrol, of course, was very cheap by today's standards though we didn't think of it as particularly cheap at the time! Cruising speeds in general were very much lower than today. In the 1930's when the German autobahns allowed sustained high speed running, even Rolls Royces found it hard going! There were no diesel cars then and, in general, lorries were also petrol powered, not diesel. Some buses, however, had already switched to diesel engines.

In 1958 business was going well and we bought a new 2.4 litre Mark I Jaguar in Cotswold Blue. The 2.4 and 3.4 litre Jaguars in those days were considered to be among the most desirable cars on the road and even today they are still a classic design. So much so that the design of the latest Jaguar, as I write this in 2001, was clearly influenced by the design of the 1950's Jaguars.

So to drive a brand new 2.4. Jaguar was an absolutely

unforgettable experience: A super car. We drove to Invergarry in it for the stalking in 1958, the last year we were to stay at the Invergarry Hotel.

Although we were delighted with the 1958 model, in 1960 Jaguar improved it by producing the Mark II and we decided to change over to one. This time in Claret but we were able to specify a non-standard colour of upholstery. We chose black with red piping because we considered that black always looks well years later. An opinion that has proved to be absolutely correct as the upholstery still looks very good indeed over forty years later. We still have the car, now in honourable retirement.

From 1960 onwards, we have bought more modest cars and finally changed over to diesel. In 1983 we bought a Volkswagen 1.6 litre diesel Estate and we now have a turbo-charged version.

For that year, and many years afterwards we were, remember, driving with no speed limits on the open road as the only speed limits were 30 mph in built up areas. What a joy it was to be able to drive your car as you thought fit, without the imposition of speed limits. To make matters worse it was a Transport Minister who couldn't drive, Barbara Castle, who first imposed the 70 mph limit.

The first huge change on the run to Scotland was when the new Preston by-pass, Britain's first motorway, was opened. When we first hit this new high speed road Edna felt as if she had just passed the starter's flag at Brooklands!

The run to Scotland in the 1950's was very different from today: The major difference was the lack of motorways so the journey of about 400 miles from Derby to Invergarry took two days.

You had to go through the centre of all the towns on the way i.e. Ashbourne, Leek, Macclesfield, Manchester and dozens of small towns like Chorley and Whittle-le-Woods. Think of the enormous number of traffic lights there were to obstruct you: Lancaster, Preston, Penrith, then an unobstructed road at last, for about sixteen miles, from Penrith to Carlisle.

On again through more small towns and through Glasgow - a major task. North of Glasgow you were, at last, in the Highlands though the winding road round Loch Lomond side was a major hazard if you were in a hurry - as we invariably were.

We always stopped the night at the Tarbet Hotel, halfway along Loch Lomond side and were always thankful to pull in. A most welcome stop at this huge hotel; un-modernised then with bathrooms unchanged since the turn of the century or before. An excellent dinner, then fortified by a night's sleep and a good breakfast we were on our way again.

The winding run along Loch Lomond side behind us, then the climb up Black Mount and on to Rannoch Moor. The A90 given its head at last and we would hurtle along at 90mph or more. They were good roads, though not wide and, of course, much less traffic than today.

After this exhilarating run came the long descent into Glencoe, "The Glen of Weeping". The brooding, misty mountain tops still silently spoke of that infamous massacre. Then down to Ballachulish and its famous ferry.

Car ferries were the bane of motor travel in those days before they were superseded by bridges. It was a pleasure to take a slow ferry across the Kyles but not such a pleasure if you were in a hurry to get to your destination.

Once across, however, you again made better progress: Fort William was negotiated then the huge bulk of the lower slopes of Ben Nevis, Britain's highest mountain at over 4,000 feet, was seen for the first time. Next along the foot of the Great Glen, past the grimly named "Well of the Seven Heads" to our destination Invergarry and the Invergarry Hotel.

Our 1960 2.4 Jaguar which we still have.

Edna's brother Jim Andrews with gillie ready to start for the Hill.

Chapter Seven
We Walk the Hill

We hadn't booked our first days stalking for a day or two, planning to get in a few days walking first to acclimatise us to the tougher test of stalking itself. We walked up from the back of the hotel on the Invergarry North ground. Having successfully walked some distance we surmounted a small rise and there, below us, were four hinds. What an incredible sight - wild Red Deer - our first ever sighting. I have never forgotten the excitement of that moment. In those days we carried an 8mm cine-camera so the camera was quickly produced and that marvellous moment captured on cine film.

So the day quickly arrived for our first day's stalking. It was to be on Ceannocroc Forest (pronounce it Canna-crock) and our stalker was Donald Stewart. Our first meeting with a Highland stalker and Donald Stewart was a marvellous example: Diplomatic, well-spoken, immense general knowledge, vastly experienced and expert in his field. Guns, rifles, stalking, the deer and the Hill were all within his brief so it was a joy to be in his company. Unfortunately, however, the weather was unco-operative and having climbed up the ridge at Loch Cluanie, accompanied by gillie, pony and ponyman, we were marooned in the mist. It refused to lift so eventually we had to give up! A blank day!.

Next day's stalking was on the famous Glengarry Forest, again with Donald Stewart as stalker. This time the weather was favourable and we toiled up through the forest. Finally Donald Stewart spied a stag he deemed shootable so leaving Edna and Jim in a position to see the whole stalk, Donald Stewart and I crawled in together into position for a shot. Light good, stag within reasonable range, Donald got me into position on a knoll.

Careful aim, trigger pressed - and I clean missed that stag, to my absolute amazement. The situation was very different now: Before, it was a question of taking a shot at an undisturbed beast with no idea that it was in danger. Our only chance of another shot, however, was if he would stop in a position not too much further on to give the opportunity for a shot while still within range. Fortunately he did so and proved to be one of the best stags shot in Scotland that year, only two stags shot had longer horns at 34 inches. So the walk home with a stag on the pony was on winged shoes.

.275 (7mm) Rigby-Mauser. For half a century or more, the 7mm Mauser and the 6.5mm Mannlicher were the favourite choice for deerstalking.

The guests at the Invergarry Hotel were a remarkable crowd. In an earlier book I explained that if Noel Coward was asked to comment on an outrageous person or happening he would always say "remarkable". A word of consummate diplomacy. Did it mean remarkably good or remarkably bad? The word covers both extremes and could be interpreted by the listener exactly as he thought fit.

Most guests, of course, were "remarkable" in the very best sense of the word. Impossible to define them in any order of preference, but let's start with Miss Sopper. Miss Sopper was in her thirties, a confirmed bachelor girl though, to our surprise, she did get married at a later date. Well educated, a true extrovert and a thoroughly likeable personality. Hearing her speak she could well have been Penelope Keith's sister! On one occasion having crossed swords with Leslie Hunt over some minor matter, she made her peace by saying to him: "Oh, Leslie, I'm such a bitch!" Not true, of course!

"He (or she) is genuine" was a phrase frequently encountered in Scotland and we used to consider it to be an innocuous form of praise. After all, we reasoned, anyone can be genuine. Can be, no doubt, but so many people, we were to find, fall well short of this ideal, so the phrase then took on its true value. Miss Sopper, however, was as genuine as a 24 carat gold ingot.

She grimly stuck to her father's old clip loading 6.5mm Mannlicher rifle. This was made in the 1880's before the introduction of Mannlicher's incomparable rotary Schaunauer magazine. The clip loading idea became obsolete in the 1880's but before then it had been favoured by Mannlicher and others. You loaded a clip of five or six cartridges into the rifle and when the last cartridge was fired the used clip fell out to be replaced with a new, loaded clip. Miss Sopper's rifle was, by then, well worn and its performance had become erratic so there was often much wailing and gnashing of teeth when Miss Sopper returned from a day's stalking. Not, I hasten to add, every time because despite the limitations of her ancient rifle, Miss Sopper was often successful. Rifles used by the Invergarry Hotel guests were mostly 7mm Mauser though 6.5mm Mannlichers were also very popular.

An older man named Charles Tindall had a .308 by, I believe, Cogswell and Harrison. Westley Richards and 9.3mm Mannlichers were also used as were .303's. But, of course, iron sights were the rule i.e. a vee sight or an aperture sight, with telescopic sights very much in the minority.

.256 (6.5mm) Mannlicher. Beautifully made rifles; a pleasure to use.

The 7mm Rigby Magnum was another popular rifle and another guest, Cyril Butchart, had one. He was a very pleasant character indeed. He was a confirmed bachelor approaching middle age. Bachelors are inevitably different as they have no wife or children to consider or plan for. In any case why shouldn't they get married and suffer like everybody else! He was very proud of his Rover car with its virtues of quality and dependability which reflected his own status as a solid citizen.

An Irish couple of about thirty years of age were a very welcome addition to the company of guests. They brimmed over with Irish charm and sparkling conversation. He was a talented, witty and amusing raconteur who could always be relied upon to shine. Most of us were newcomers to stalking but he was an old hand, having stalked Red, Fallow, and Roe Deer in Ireland. He had a .300 Holland & Holland Rifle, an ideal rifle for deerstalking.

Mr and Mrs Robb were another charming couple. He did the shooting and his wife, an excellent walker, always accompanied him. A lawyer, he had written a book on "tort" (private or civil wrong) which is still referred to today. My son Ross has a copy and has found it immensely useful in his work as an agricultural consultant. Mr. Robb's *bete noir* was Government expenditure which had, in his opinion, been allowed to get far too high. I wonder what he would think today?

Mrs Mary Hunt herself was no mean stalker, making effective use of her traditional 6.5mm Mannlicher. Mr and Mrs Crossley were another charming couple and she, too, was an excellent walker who accompanied her husband.

In the late nineteenth century, General Hope Henry Crealock wrote and illustrated a magnificent book *Deer-Stalking in the Highlands*. Writing about the evening after a day's stalking, he wrote: "The entrance into the dining room of a stalking house is a critical moment in a day's sport. Mortification and vexation of spirit await the unlucky wight who has missed a good chance or, blundering his shot, has wounded and lost his beast.... Chaff is no name for what he may expect, and woe betide him if he tries to stammer lame excuses....

As the stalker of the day walks into the dining room all eyes are turned on him, and he is saluted with a general query from all: "Well, what have you done?" But the question need not be asked: You can generally tell by the way he comes into the room what has taken place on the hill.

If he has blood, triumph is in his eye, his gait is brisk and joyous, and he is full of chaff; while if he has failed, he has not a word to say for himself, looking very meek and "'umble".... The bachelor seems to me to have much the best of it when he misses; for he has not to undergo a certain lecture and chaff besides from the wife of his heart, and beyond his own mortification there is nothing to follow.

But the poor married man has, I suspect, a rough time of it.... for I notice the wife is as jealous of her husband's reputation and as keen for blood as her lord. How often has one watched the lady's manner on entering the drawing room! If her husband has missed, she comes in very quietly and is civil to everyone; but if he has killed a good stag, she enters the room with her nose en l'air, and an expression on her face of "Thank god I am not as other women are - my man don't miss." Then follows the smoking room ordeal, when you have to stalk your beasts over again and give all the details."

Over half a century later, much the same applied at the Invergarry Hotel.

To get a stag in a day was an achievement to which we all aspired. To get two would be a miracle! On one occasion the Crossleys got back to the hotel from stalking at Braeroy and when they came in to dinner we asked if they had got a stag. "Four" replied Crossley to our thunderstruck amazement! We felt like those people in an H.M.Bateman cartoon when one character, completely oblivious to the effect it would have, has committed an appalling gaffe and had astounded all the others. They all had faces contorted into surreal, outrageous disbelief. We all must have looked exactly the same!

Charles Martell was a man in his late thirties, unmarried then but to get married later. He shot well with his 9.3mm Mannlicher with telescopic sight. He and Miss Sopper were, at a later date, to take the Corriemulzie stalking. Corriemulzie in Sutherland marches with Deanich Forest.

Nigel Seligman shot well with his 7mm Rigby Magnum. Nigel was a charming extrovert with the ability to enliven any gathering.

Mr and Mrs Round from the Birmingham area were another pair of good walkers and very pleasant people. He had a Westley Richards rifle chambered for the .375 Holland and Holland cartridge. This is a big game cartridge considered too large a calibre for Red Deer but as different bullet weights were available he used a very light bullet. I remain to be convinced, however, that this was a very effective answer for stalking Red Deer.

A very experienced stalker was Charles Brocklehurst. He must have been approaching seventy years of age but he was a tall man and as fit as a fiddle. He had an estate in Kenya where trouble was just starting to build up, but he came back to the Invergarry Hotel every year in the stalking season to see, once again, the deer and the Hill. Another bachelor and a man who was immensely knowledgeable about the deer and the Hill and an enormous amount of other matters.

An ex. Naval Officer, Commander Campbell, was another experienced stalker. A big, powerfully built man and a competent shot with the stalking rifle. I remember him coming back from a rewarding but very tiring day on the hill and announcing in basso-profundo tones "I'll have a pint of beer in my bath!" Presumably this was intended for internal, rather than external, application!

The bar at the Invergarry Hotel was a cheery and convivial place but there was no heavy drinking. Good Scotch Whiskey, "The wine of the country" was a popular drink. I cannot claim to be a whiskey drinker, with a dram at New Year being my usual annual intake, but I do acknowledge its excellence.

At one time whiskey was just whiskey, but John Dewar of Perth was the first man to realise its potential. Careful blending was the key to quality, taste and consistency. On one occasion a lady who considered herself to be in the highest echelons of society introduced herself to him, saying "My name is Jenkin-Jenkin with a hyphen." Dewar replied, "and my name is Dewar Dewar with a siphon!"

My first stag. One of the best stags shot in Scotland in 1954. Edna with her brother on the left. Ponyman, gillie and stalker Donald Stewart.

No, not that fancy! King Alphonso of Spain in his stalking gear with the Duke of Sutherland at Dunrobin Castle.

Chapter Eight
Fancy Pants and Tweed, Glorious Tweed

When you first start stalking you are not going to wear any of that fancy gear! Deerstalker hats with ear flaps? Surely they are only worn by Sherlock Holmes and English sports car drivers? So you go to the Hill with your normal peaked cap. You then find out what the Highlander knows already: The rain, of which there is no shortage, goes straight down the back of your neck. You then give in and buy a deerstalker hat; not the Sherlock Holmes type, but one without ear flaps. This is what most Highland stalkers wear.

Neither are you going to wear a pair of those fancy pants. Surely plus fours became obsolete after having been worn by golfers in the 1920's? And as for knickerbockers? Not a chance! They went out with little Lord Fauntleroy! So you go to the hill in normal trousers, like any sensible human being.

You then experience the joy of walking through long, wet heather in the rain. Your feet are wet through anyway but now your trouser bottoms continually scoop up water and flap about your ankles depositing a constant stream of water on them. They are obstructive, uncomfortable, cold and totally impracticable. By the next year you have given in and bought a tweed suit with knickerbockers.

Now the rain drips off the turnups of your knickerbockers and in addition, you eliminate the flapping of soaking wet trouser bottoms round your ankles. I can still get into, and still wear, the tweed suit I bought for the 1955 season so how's that for value for money? True, it is not in use fifty two weeks in the year but during the last forty five years it has endured a tremendous amount of hard wear - many a glutinous crawl through peat hags and up stony Highland burns.

You quickly give in and buy a stick. Edna, Jim and I bought ours from Grays, the Inverness gunsmiths in 1954 for six shillings each, cut from the south side of Loch Ness. They, too, are still in use. The stick used for stalking has the root at right angles to give you an effective handgrip and these sticks are a tremendous help in both climbing or descending steep slopes.

So, once again, you have benefited from centuries of experience and realise that sticks are not exclusively used by old men on the way to their bowls club.

Nor this! A bit too extreme for most Sassenachs.

Tweed is, without doubt, wonderful stuff and ideal for wearing in the Scottish Highlands. Not only does it wear well but it has the amazing virtue of warmth, even when made soaking wet by the relentless Highland rain. The colours and texture too, blend in with the Highland landscape.

Of all the Scottish tweeds Harris stands at the peak. If haggis is the "Great Chieftain 'o the pudding race" (though I would submit Yorkshire as a worthy challenger) then Harris is the Great Chieftain of the tweed race. But what, exactly, is it?

It has been clearly defined by the Scottish Courts: " Harris Tweed must be made from Scottish wool, dyed, one hundred per cent spun and finished in the Outer Hebrides and hand-woven by the Islanders at their homes in the Islands of Lewis, Harris, Uist, Barra, and their several purtenances."

When wet it not only still gives the benefit of a degree of warmth but the bonus of its unique scent from the natural dyes obtained from the local roots, lichens and herbs.

It was originally brought to the attention of Sassenachs when Lady Dunmore brought it down to London in 1840 to sell it to her friends for the benefit of the crofters who made it. From then on its virtues were appreciated and its fame spread.

Still not quite right, but getting close. Doctor Samuel Johnson getting ready to tackle his Highland tour in the eighteenth century.

Stornaway is the capital of the Outer Hebrides and the headquarters of the Harris Tweed Association, whose head is traditionally a crofter and weaver from the community of about 400.

Weaving is combined with crofting on the Hattersley domestic loom (no relation to Roy!). This was, traditionally, the loom generally used and it was manufactured long before the days of "built in obsolescence". Many gave service for three quarters of a century and more. Sturdy, cast iron machines, pedal powered with their amazing cacophony of rattles, bangs, clicks, whirrs, and clanks.

The advantage of weaving is that it brings in some much needed cash when the horizontal Hebridean rain sweeps the Islands and work with the sheep or on the croft is impossible.

The Hattersley Domestic produces cloth thirty inches wide i.e. single width whereas the world standard today is double width i.e. sixty inches. About 1990 a new loom was brought in for evaluation, the Bonas Griffith Intermediate-Technology loom. Smaller, faster and quicker than the Hattersley and, most important, producing the sixty inch double width cloth.

There are also two large mills on the Islands. For these mills the wool is bought in at the Edinburgh Auctions already washed and cleaned. Back at the mills the carding, spinning, blending and dyeing are all carried out by modern methods so the traditional scent of wet Harris Tweed is no more.

But not everything at the mill is done by machinery: The spun yarn is "warped" by hand on a frame. This is the lengthwise thread. The "weft" yarn is woven horizontally across it. The cloth is then sent to the crofter for finishing.

When the crofter has done his work the completed cloth is sent back to the mill for final washing and finishing and the rolls of tweed are sent all over the world.

For wear on the Hill in Scotland we require the traditional "heavy" tweed but nowadays the mills also produce lighter weights for the fashion market i.e. lightweight, featherweight, and even gossamerweight. Even new colours are being designed and produced for fashion wear. All the industry now needs is for some famous, high profile people to start wearing it and get it noticed. Will Carol Vorderman and Madonna step forward, please!

(Top) Producing yarn 1890. Girl on right is "carding" using flat boards with steel teeth to comb straight the wool fibres. The woman in the centre is spinning from the card rolls. The woman on the left is winding yarn from the spinning wheel into hanks.

(Bottom) Weaving in Harris in 1910 with an old-fashioned wooden loom.

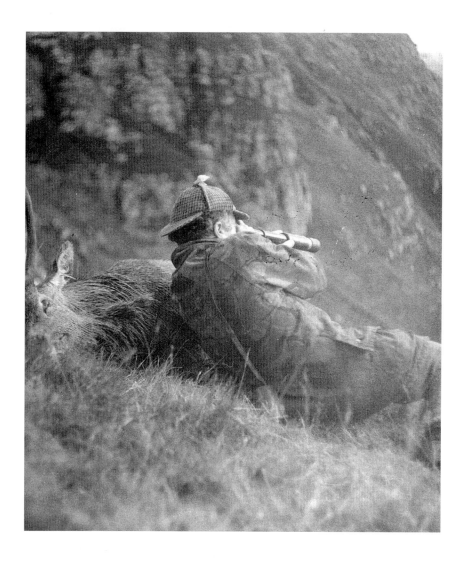

This photograph truly conveys the spirit of stalking. Lea MacNally spies for the next stag in Torridon's high hills.

Chapter Nine
The Stalker/Rifle Relationship

"For quite thirty years have I, in almost every county in England, been good friends with English game-keepers, and as a body, a more trustworthy, hard working, courageous, and civil set of men cannot be found. The whole thing is so different across the Border: For days together you and your stalker are alone, and a good one will, in a variety of small ways and good-natured little attentions to your comfort, make you feel quite friendly towards him; you cannot help seeing that all his thoughts and energies are directed to your sport and comfort."

So wrote Augustus Grimble in his book *Deer Stalking* in 1886.

For over half a century before that and over a century since, nothing has changed. The relationship between the Highland stalker and his Rifle has always been a very special bond. The Highlanders during the 19th century had little in the way of education but much in dignity, knowledge and humanity. Plus, of course, hardiness, ability to walk, run and crawl without ever seeming to tire. This in addition to an intimate knowledge of their forest and the deer.

Today's Highland stalker still has all those qualities but now with the benefit of an education denied to his great grandfather a century ago.

By comparison his Sassenach Rifle can match his stalker in few of those qualities: When it comes to walking the hill he is, in most cases, not in the same league! Yet regardless of this important discrepancy his stalker will make allowances and do all he can to see that his charge is shown the best possible route over the terrain, no matter how difficult it may be.

Many Rifles new to stalking will know very little about the whole thing and there is much to learn: Once again his stalker will be a willing tutor without a trace of superiority.

For his part it is up to the Rifle to make a determined effort to get into the best condition he can before making his journey to the Highlands. It is also up to him to know his rifle and how to use it. He may well never be able to match his stalker in the ability to climb that hill but he can ensure a satisfactory standard of marksmanship.

So the seasoned professional and the unseasoned Sassenach go to the Hill together to climb, crawl, stalk and shoot. Divided? No! United in their common purpose to successfully stalk the Red Deer.

So they *must* work together, *must* co-operate, *must* respect each others strengths and weaknesses. And the result? A special relationship that is hard to describe, harder still to duplicate anywhere else in the world. We Sassenachs are fortunate indeed to be accepted by the Highland stalkers.

The Rifle spies! Louis Pettit on Culachy forest. A Belgian who both looked and sounded like George Sanders.

With such a selection of forests there was, of course, a number of different stalkers to meet. All with their own methods and techniques but all conforming to the very best discipline of Highland stalking.

On Levishie the stalker was Jimmy MacDonnell. MacDonnell was a name local to that area before emigration had splintered the clans. Jimmy was a forthright character who would make up his mind on a plan of action and successfully pursue it

Stalking with him one day I had successfully got a stag with a steep downhill shot and we were making our way home through the birch woodland towards the foot of the glen. Suddenly a group of about five stags ran across in front of us. Rifle rapidly levelled and I shot the leading stag, quickly reloading in case a second shot was necessary. "One's enough, one's enough." shouted Jimmy anxiously, but my cine-camera recorded the stags as they ran out of sight. So two stags in a day - a marvellous moment and the highlight of my stalking career up to then.

A crofter and part-time stalker was Donald Campbell of Levishie and one day I stalked with him on North Dundreggan Forest, not the most popular of forests as you have a long walk to get high enough to have the chance of a shot and deer were very scarce. The pony's halter rope was far too short but we decided we would manage. We did get a stag, however, which we duly loaded onto the somewhat inexperienced pony but, at the last moment, something spooked the pony which shied away, wrenching the halter rope out of the stalker's hand.

We watched, dumbstruck, as the pony raced away with the stag on its back! Soon the weight of the stag caused the deer saddle to slip underneath the pony with the stag suspended underneath the pony's belly. Fortunately, however, it soon came adrift and no harm was done! What a relief!

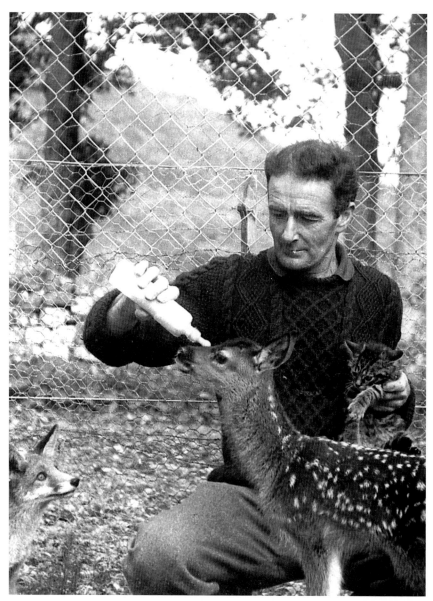

One of my favourite photographs of Lea MacNally. Feeding a Red Deer calf, holding a wildcat kitten with a fox looking on expectantly.

Chapter Ten
Lea MacNally. All-time Great

Lea MacNally was the stalker at Culachy Forest, Fort Augustus. This was not one of the Government owned Hydro-electric forests but was in private ownership. The owner was an old lady named Mrs Angelo. The Estate had been bought by her husband, many years ago. He was much older and had died a long time before.

Culachy is a "hind" forest. During the rut stags from the adjoining forests of Glendoe, Braeroy and Aberchalder come into Culachy in search of hinds and when the stag calves on Culachy eventually reach maturity they move out onto the higher ground of the neighbouring forests. As Culachy starts close to Fort Augustus the lodge is very little above sea level so the lodge, compact by Scottish Highland standards, has the benefit of a much lower elevation than most.

The lodge and nearby stalker's house had electricity provided by its own hydro-electric 110 volt D.C. supply. One of the first lodges in the Highlands to have electricity. This venerable system was still in use in the 1950's.

In the 1950's Scottish stalkers were paid very little and this applied to Lea, so with a wife and two small children to support, money was in very short supply.

We were not to stalk on Culachy until 1956 when Lea and I struck up an immediate rapport. Meeting Lea was an experience we were never likely to forget. An amazing man with a knowledge of the deer, the Hill and its wildlife that really astounded us. Lea had a lust to learn and to tackle his job with perfectionist zeal. As a stalker, he aspired to be the very best and this included the utmost consideration for we inexperienced Sassenachs. And Lea's wife, Margaret? Well, Ken Russell, the maverick film director, claims that somewhere among the teeming millions, there must be one's spiritual twin.....one's true soulmate, but the tragedy is that the chances of meeting such a paragon are millions to one against. At over seventy years of age and with three busted marriages behind him, he had clearly searched diligently, but unsuccessfully. He now claims, however, that he has at last, found his perfect soulmate via the internet!

But in Margaret, Lea had found that one in a million person....his ideal soulmate, so they were blessed with a marvellous marriage and two much-loved sons.

A day on the Hill with Lea was an experience to be truly valued; so much to see, so much to learn. As a Rifle, I am thankful to be able to say I never made a mistake with Lea as stalker, so he knew I was a "dependable shot".

Bridge built by General Wade's soldiers on Culachy after the 1715 rebellion.

Culachy was one of the forests leased by the Invergarry Hotel and on one occasion, early in the rut, stags were hard to find, (as Culachy is a hind forest). We had got in for a stalk on a good stag, near the Braeroy march. We moved into position for a shot, when a swirl of wind gave the deer our scent and they were instantly on the move, heading for the nearby Braeroy march.

"Try him!" said Lea as the stag started to gain pace. I swung the rifle ahead of the stag and fired, killing him outright as the bullet struck at the base of the neck. Success after what looked like total failure left us all delighted. My first running stag, too, so a notable personal milestone.

At that time, Lea was fortunate in having some really excellent students as ponymen and we usually asked them to carry a flask of tea on the pony for us. Having got a stag after a long day, that restorative cup of tea when the pony arrived was an eagerly awaited luxury.

"Where's the tea?" we anxiously asked on one occasion. The ponyman was taken aback for a moment, then, with a cheery smile, he replied, "The horse drank it!"

By the time I had met Lea, I had already acquired the nucleus of a collection of books on stalking and Lea was keen to learn all about stalking literature. This, remember, was before he had written an article or a book. I was able to tell him about the books I had acquired and advised him which books to read. The local library would supply them.

Among the books I recommended I remember putting at the top of the list *A Herd of Red Deer* by Fraser Darling. Fraser Darling spent about two years studying and virtually living with the Red Deer on estates on the west coast of Scotland. In addition I recommended a selection of other stalking classics.

This dedication enabled Lea to make a start by submitting articles on stalking which were very successful. Their success prompted him to write his first book and from then on he was on his way to a career as an author and authority on the deer, the Hill and the golden eagle.

He also became a dedicated wildlife photographer and his photographs were used to illustrate his books. All the wildlife photographs in this book, other than the old Alladale stag, are Lea's. Lea and I and our families became great friends and began a correspondence that was to continue until his death. He visited us on a number of occasions and we always called to see Lea and his family when we were stalking in Scotland.

Culachy, on the death of Mrs Angelo, was bought by Captain Usher who was not a stalker. He owned it for a number of years before it was bought by Ian Biggs, a keen stalker.

Shortly after Ian Biggs' purchase of Culachy, Lea left to become the Warden at the National Trust property of Torridon on the West Coast. Torridon is very different from Culachy: High hills, comprising a tumbled waste of boulders. A resident stock of deer, of course, but due to the harsh terrain, not as many as at Culachy.

Lea developed the Visitor Centre and, using his own photographs, incorporated a video show of Scotland, the deer, the Hill and its wildlife which was a great success with the visitors.

Lea with three hinds in the deer saddle.

Lea was a man of many talents but he would have been the first to agree that natural motoring ability was not included among them. He approached his career on the road with the same grasp of the subject as that of the Teletubbies to nuclear physics. By sheer determination he eventually became a competent driver but he would never have posed a threat to Michael Schumacher!

Living at Culachy with no personal transport of any kind was a problem, so we decided to solve it. We gave him a scooter as his introduction to the road. It had to be a strong, ruggedly built machine, not a toy, so we decided on a Zundapp Bella, 200cc as an example of well built German engineering. So Lea had his own transport at last. All he had to do was to learn to ride it!

The thought of changing gear was really daunting for him but it had to be faced.

After the abortive 1715 Rebellion General Wade was given the task of constructing a network of roads throughout the Highlands so that they could be effectively policed and one of the roads ran through the centre of Culachy ground up to the Corriearack Pass. This was an immense help for the stalking and an ideal place for Lea to learn to ride his scooter.

So Lea would start up and get away in first gear, screwing up his courage in readiness for the monumental task of changing gear. All concentration was devoted to this task but when he changed gear the Bella would instantly develop a mind of its own, leap off the road and go bounding over the heather! It would then be pushed back onto the track and Lea would try again.... with the same result!

Eventually, however, he did manage to master the beast and, for the very first time, he was on the road.

Having got used to riding the scooter he was finally able to buy a car and became a competent motorist. On one occasion he was driving with his wife as passenger on an icy road and in such conditions it is all too easy to lose control. It *could* happen to anyone but it *did* happen to Lea! The car shot off the road, somersaulting down into a ravine but by an amazing stroke of good fortune the car hit a tree which brought to an abrupt stop, the right way up! Lea and Margaret were shaken and stirred, of course, but escaped serious injury or worse. In Lea's later days at Torridon he drove the estate Land Rover as well as his own car.

As previously explained, on any Highland deer forest the deer numbers have to be controlled in the interests of the deer. Even forest owners with no interest whatever in sporting shooting recognise this.

An estate near Kintail had been left to the National Trust on condition that there was to be *no sporting shooting* and Lea was deputised to shoot there to keep the numbers under correct control.

To drive into the forest with his Land Rover he would utilise the hard gravel bed of the river and on one winter's day he did so to shoot hinds. The weather, always unpredictable, suddenly changed into a downpour of rain. By the time Lea got back to the Land Rover the river was rising fast into spate conditions. Lea loaded his hinds and started to drive back but the river rose with the rapidity that spate conditions can bring. The hill burns had been hit by an even greater downpour and discharging into the river, the huge volume of water created a veritable tidal wave that shot down the river and hit the Land Rover.

The Land Rover seats consisted of three "biscuits" i.e. thin, loose squabs. The huge wave hit the Land Rover and in an instant the squabs on the passenger seat started to float as the water level in the cab rose above seat level. The Land Rover then decided to stop!

Lea managed to get back to the bank safely but could do nothing about the Land Rover and when he returned next day with a tractor to salvage it he found that the Land Rover had been rolled over and over down the river and the roof was now level with the top of the steering wheel. Needless to say the vehicle was scrap!

Back from the Hill with four hinds to unload. Michael, aged fourteen, has shot one of them.

Lea became well-known in the world of deer and Prince Charles invited him to Balmoral. The Prince was a perfect host and made Lea most welcome. In a complete reversal of roles, Lea was the Rifle, Prince Charles his stalker and they got a good stag. Lea retained the antlers as a permanent reminder of a memorable meeting.

Eventually Lea returned to the Fort Augustus area and lived in a cottage on land that had once been part of the Culachy Estate, before dying of a heart attack when swimming with his grandchildren at Fort William. And although Lea is lost to us, his influence and his books remain and we have never lost touch with Margaret, young Lea and Michael.

Lea's sons, young Lea and Michael were to continue his interest in the deer and the Hill though neither became authors - or have not done so up to now.

Young Lea became a stalker on the famous estate of Glenquoich (pronounced Glen-coo-ich) and is now Head Stalker there.
Michael still stalks for guests on a part-time basis as time allows from his business as an agricultural contractor.

Lea's older brother, Hugh, has for many years arranged stalking for guests in the Loch Ness area.

So Lea has made an enduring impression on the world of stalking, Scottish wildlife, the deer and the Hill.

Margaret feeds the tame Roe Deer "Dainty" in the kitchen after an illness.

Going home from the Hill on Culachy Forest. A timeless scene that would have been the same 100 years ago.

Chapter Eleven
Jock Macaskill, Stalker
Extraordinary

A man whom I have always held in the highest regard was Jock Macaskill, stalker at the Invergarry Hotel. Whatever attributes you may consider essential in a Highland stalker, Jock had them all! First of all he knew his trade from A to Z. If anyone could conjure up a shot from apparently impossible terrain, that man was Jock Macaskill. He would always see that his Rifle was within reasonable range and in the very best situation for a shot.

In addition to all this he was a man of enormous charm and it was a joy to be in his company. Like all the very best Highland stalkers he could have any of we Sassenachs eating out of his hand!

Guns & rifles? What did you want to know? Whatever it was, Jock would have the answer - and that answer would be meticulously correct. The deer and the Hill? No stalker was more knowledgeable than he. Care and consideration for we inexperienced walkers? Not a universal attribute.... but Jock had it in spades.

Jock's father and grandfather had also been stalkers and their forebears before that. One of his forebears was, I understand, the subject of the following story: During the late nineteenth century when interest in stalking was at its peak and stalking was a very important part of the social scene, the owner of a large Highland estate had a very important guest and he was most anxious to see that this VIP got a stag.

This task was entrusted to his Head Stalker and under his supervision the guest was taken to the Hill. On the first day an excellent chance was obtained at a good stag. The distance was reasonable, and the guest in a comfortable position on a heather knoll.

"Bang" went the first barrel of the .500 Black Powder Express then "Bang" went the second barrel but neither bullet touched the stag.

"Bad luck" said everyone when the guest got back to the lodge. "No beginner is immune from a dose of stag fever, so next day will be better". But, unfortunately, the next day was not better, it was simply a repeat of the first.

After several days of this conspicuous lack of success the estate owner asked his Head Stalker to try the guest's rifle at the target and remember that in those days there was a wide gulf between master and man. A number of shots were fired, all perfectly satisfactory.

"Well" said the puzzled estate owner "Whatever is wrong with that rifle? Is it the sights?" "No, Sir," said the stalker "there's nothing wrong with the sights". "Is it the rifling, then?" he demanded. "No, Sir, there's nothing wrong with the rifling". "Is it the cut of the stock?" was the next question but, once again, the reply confirmed that this, too, was perfectly satisfactory.

"Well, what the Devil *is* the matter with the rifle?" demanded the now thoroughly exasperated estate owner. "I'm afraid, Sir," said the stalker hesitantly "it's not the rifle, its the afterpiece!"

So in our family "the afterpiece" is often named as the well deserved cause when things go wrong.

Roe Deer with fawn.

Last stag of the season 1966, shot by Lea MacNally. A good one to cull. Young Lea, (left) and Michael lead the pony.

Hunting scene on Shandwick Stone, Ross-shire ninth century or earlier.

Chapter Twelve
Hunting the Deer

Long before the introduction of firearms, deer were hunted in Scotland by tinchels: Tinchels were deer drives and could be modest affairs or huge gatherings.

In the earliest days deer were driven between long, converging stone walls into an enclosure where they were killed. The ring of men who drove the deer was the tainchell, a Gaelic word, later changed to tinchel which became to be known as this method of hunting.

Once trapped in the enclosure the deer were killed by swords, daggers or axes but dogs were essential to bring down the deer. At a later date shooting the deer with crossbow, arquebus or pistol was forbidden by law, though the law was often ignored.

For grander tinchels a large number of men would form a huge ring, perhaps miles in diameter, taking several days. The ring would then gradually close, driving the deer into ambush or to a chosen pass when the deer would be killed by any means possible.

Magnificent tinchels were organised for VIPs or Royalty: In 1528 the Earl of Atholl organised one for King James V. Many important people attended, even a Papal Representative. Of this incredible tinchel Lindsay of Pitscottie wrote: "They had all manner of meates, drink and delicates, that were to be gotten at that time in all Scotland....The King remained in this wilderness at the hunting the space of three days and three nights... I have heard men say it cost the Earl of Atholl every day in expenses a thousand pounds".

In 1563 Queen Mary was the guest of honour at Atholl and one of her courtiers, William Barclay, wrote: "Two thousand highlanders were employed to drive to the hunting-ground all the deer from the woods and hills of Atholl, Badenoch, Mar, Moray and the countries round about....they brought together two thousand Red Deer, beside roes and fallow deer."

A fourteenth century deer hunt.

"The Queen, the great men and a number of others, were in a glen when all these deer were brought before them. Believe me, the whole body of them moved forward like an order of battle. The sight still strikes me, and ever will, for they had a leader whom they followed wherever they moved. This leader was a very fine stag, with a very high head. This sight delighted the Queen very much, but she soon had cause for fear, upon the Earl saying "there is a danger in that stag, for if either fear or rage force him from the ridge of that hill, let each look to himself, for none of us will be out of harm's way; for the rest will all follow him; and having thrown us under foot, will open their passage to this hill behind us."

What happened a moment after confirmed this opinion; for the Queen ordered one of the best dogs to be let loose upon a wolf; this the dog pursues, the leading stag was frightened, he flies by the same way that he came, the rest rush after him, and break through the biggest body of the Highlanders. They had nothing for it but to throw themselves flat on the heath, and to allow the deer to pass over them.

It was told the Queen that several of the Highlanders had been wounded, and that two or three were killed on the spot: and the whole body had got off, had not the Highlanders by their skill in hunting fallen upon a stratagem to cut off the rear from the main body. It was of those which had been separated that the Queen's dogs and those of the nobility made slaughter. There were killed that day three hundred and sixty deer, five wolves and some roes."

This account must be taken with a pinch of salt: For example we know that a stag would not lead a huge herd of deer but, even so, this gigantic tinchel has never been forgotten. It is considered that it was held on the west side of what is now the Forest of Fealar with the deer driven into a steep pass on Ben-y-gloe. The Queen was stationed on a rocky outcrop overlooking Loch Loch, known to this day as Tom nam ban righ, "The Queen's Hillock".

Tinchels were often the cover for less innocent purposes: For example, Highland chieftains, under cover of a tinchel, would gather their men together for an attack on neighbouring clans. Sir Walter Scott in the first of the Waverley novels describes such a gathering set in the turbulent times of the Forty Five.

Castle Stalker, Argyll in its dramatic setting, under lowering clouds.

There was no need for fiction, however, in the tinchel at Invercauld, thirty years before. This gathering of chiefs, under the cover of a deer hunt, was to discuss and organise the ultimately abortive 1715 Rebellion. This was the attempt at an invasion by James,

Bonnie Prince Charlie's father. James was Jacobus in Latin, hence his followers were called Jacobites.

The Farquharsons of Invercauld had been there for centuries and are still there today. Farquharson is one of the most distinguished names in Scotland.

The great tinchels on Atholl forest are, fortunately, recorded at Blair Castle, home of the Dukes of Atholl. The organisation was meticulous and as early as August the Duke would send word to all the "fencible men" on his vast estates. Fencible men were all those between sixteen and sixty fit for military service.

They were instructed to turn up "in their best arms and apparell" with as many dogs as they could muster. Invitations would also be sent to the Duke's neighbours to attend "with some pretty men and with as many dogs as you can provide. You will be welcome."

On the given date all would assemble on a hill near Atholl Castle, Druim na H-Eachedra and the rules were read:

(1) That none shall offer to fire a gun or pistol in the time of the deer hunting.

(2) That none shall offer to break up a deer or takeout a gralloch except in His Grace's presence.

(3) That none shall be drunk or swear an oath.

"Whoever shall transgress any of the said rules shall be fyned and taken into custody, as His Grace shall appoint".

Although the important lairds were happy to organise tinchels they did not stalk deer themselves. This was done by the foresters: We would call them stalkers today.

The first time that the word "stalker" is recorded was in 1815 when John McIntosh of Atholl was instructed to kill twenty five beasts a year and Thomas Stewart, described as a "stalker", was instructed to kill twenty.

These early foresters had extensive powers to apprehend poachers and shoot any strange dogs on the forest. In addition they had to keep out or impound intruding sheep or cattle. They also had to keep down the vermin.

It would appear that to kill those twenty or twenty five deer, (no distinction between stags and hinds), the forester would stalk a chosen animal, fire at it with his primitive musket then release his deer hounds to bring down any beast not killed outright.

So it was the employees of the great estates who were the first "stalkers" in a sense that we would recognise today.

There were many clashes between foresters and poachers, some of whom were desperate and violent men. In many case the poachers were never apprehended as they would take to the hill and soon outdistance their pursuers.

The 1745 Rebellion smashed the Clan system and after that time few lairds could summon huge numbers of "fencible men" to a tinchel and by 1800 the day of the huge tinchels was over.

Although stalking, as we know it, did not really commence until the early nineteenth century, there were a few straws in the wind beforehand. Perhaps the first record of such stalking was at Atholl in 1832. Lord George Murray, younger brother of the Duke of Atholl, set up a summer camp in Glen Tatinich and sent back a supply of grouse and venison.

Eileen Donan Castle, ancient stronghold of the Macraes and one of the most impressive sights in Scotland.

Writing to his wife about his progress it is clear that spelling was not one of his greatest accomplishments, though his enjoyment of the sport is clear enough. He wrote: ".... There are plenty of moorfool (grouse) hereabouts so I really believe there is no day but there are five hundred deer within five miles of me.... we were disturbed by a dog running a fan (faun) and the hind not only defending her fan, but with great fury attacked the dog".

Although very few Highland chiefs were thought to have stalked themselves, Cluny MacPherson appears to be an exception. He was a Highland chief and member of the Clan Chattan, the Clan of the Cat. Motto: "Touch not the cat without a targe (shield)".

After the 1745 Rebellion he was preparing to flee the country to join Bonnie Prince Charlie in exile when he was seized with an overwhelming desire to take to the hill again for the last time and shoot his last stag.

Accompanied by MacDonald of Tulloch they went to Ben Alder Forest and proceeded to stalk a solitary stag. They were almost in position for a shot when the stag suddenly took off and ran for about two miles before coming to a stop. The stag then changed its mind and walked back the two miles to its original position when MacPherson killed it with a single shot.... or so the story goes!

Inverary Castle, Loch Fyne, Argyll. Ancient stronghold of the Campbells.

Colonel Thomas Thornton, sportsman extraordinary, with his multi-barrelled flintlock rifle.

Chapter Thirteen
Colonel Thomas Thornton

The first Englishman to discover Highland sport was reputed to be the Yorkshireman, Colonel Thomas Thornton. During the 1780's he made several expeditions to Scotland and in 1804 described his adventures in *A Sporting Tour through the Northern Parts of England and Great Part of the Highlands of Scotland.*

Thornton's physical prowess was legendary and the stories handed down about it take some believing! He was said to have covered four miles in thirty two minutes in a walking match. Jumped his own height of five feet nine inches. Jumped over six 5-barred gates in six minutes then repeated the feat on horseback. On one occasion he ran down a hare, on horseback, then picked it up in front of a large crowd of witnesses.

He was a good shot, an accomplished falconer and kept his own pack of foxhounds. Obviously not short of a few bob he was able to organise his sporting expeditions on a mammoth scale.

For one tour he charted a sloop, the *Falcon*, which sailed via Hull to the Moray Firth. At Hull his gear was loaded onto the ship. It included his pack of hounds, six hawks, four setters, six pointers, one deer hound, his armoury of firearms, eighty pounds of gunpowder, two small boats, portable kitchen and, of course, a housekeeper who was prostrate with seasickness throughout the journey!

The *Falcon* eventually docked at Forres where its contents were unloaded then re-loaded into forty-nine carts where they then proceeded to Raitts near Kingussie in the Spey Valley. Remember this when you are complaining about the amount your wife wants you to pack into the car for your annual holiday!

Thornton and his companions had travelled overland and this must have been a formidable journey on the roads of the day.

1 Langwell and Braemore	25 Strathconon	51 Balmoral
2 Borrobol	26 Killilan	52 Glenclova
3 Kildonan	27 Glencannich	53 Rothiemurchus
4 Badanloch	28 Glenstrathfarrar	54 Glenfiddich
5 Loch Choire	29 Fasnakyle	55 Blackwater
6 Ben Armine	30 Knoydart	56 Glenavon
7 Klibreck	31 Glenaffric	57 Glentanar
8 Dunrobin	32 Balmacaan	58 Ardnamurchan
9 Ben Loyal	33 Glenquoich	59 Ardtornish
10 Gobernuisgach	34 Achnacarry	60 Black Mount
11 Reay	35 Glendessary	61 Glenetive
12 Benmore	36 Glenkingie	62 Corrievarkie
13 Glencanisp	37 Culachy	63 Glenartney
14 Rhidorroch	38 Glendoe	64 Dougarie
15 Corriemulzie	39 Coignafearn	65 Brodick
16 Kildermorie	40 Conaglen	66 Braelangwell
17 Wyvis	41 Mamore	67 Amat
18 Braemore	42 Corrour	68 Alladale
19 Letterewe	43 Rannoch	69 Deanich
20 Fisherfield	44 Ardverikie	70 Glencalvie
21 Applecross	45 Benalder	71 Gruinyards
22 Coulin	46 Gaick	72 Forest Farm
23 Achnashellach	47 Glenfeshie	73 Former Langwell Forest
24 Kinlochewe	48 Atholl	74 Inverlael
	49 Mar	75 Strathvaich
	50 Fealar	

Key to the principal deer forests in Scotland and the Strathcarron Estates.

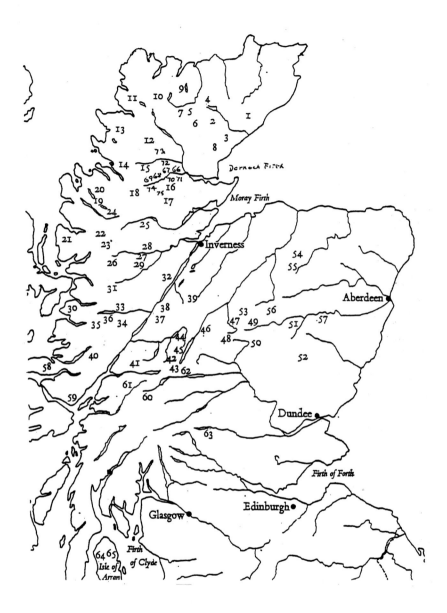

Some of the principal deer forests of Scotland and the Strathcarron Estates.

From his sporting base, Thornton set out on forays, shooting and fishing as he pleased, hawking for grouse and ptarmigan. He paid scant regard to where he was or on whose land, though he did get permission from some landowners, including Grant of Rothiemurchus. No-one challenged his right to be on any hill nor was any payment for the sport ever requested.

A Scottish wildcat snarls defiance from its bracken hideaway.

Despite having several rifles in his armoury he had no luck with deerstalking. In any case deer were very scarce at that time due to the revolution in farming in the Highlands. Crofters had been evicted on a gigantic scale to make way for the new Cheviot and Blackfaced sheep.

During those years deer stocks dropped to their lowest levels ever. By 1810 it was considered that there were only six forests left where deer were preserved: Atholl, Black Mount, Glenartney, Glenfiddich, Invercauld and Mar. In the Sutherland forests deer did, indeed, survive although not actively preserved.

In crofting days, before the invasion of the sheep flocks, the hill grazings were open to all: Children and the elderly would move out onto the hill grazings during the summer months to look after the cattle. They would live in tiny stone huts, often with turf roofs, some of which still survive. There was one sheltered by a fold in the hills at Braeroy in the 1960's: I wonder if it is still there?

Good stags at Glenquoich Forest.

"Man's inhumanity to man". A heartbreaking photograph of an eviction in North Uist as late as 1895.

Chapter Fourteen
The Highland Clearances

The Highland Clearances are often considered to be the result of sheep being cleared from the Highlands to allow deer to take over and provide deerstalking in the nineteenth century, but this was not the case. The notorious Clearances took place much earlier.

With the defeat of Bonnie Prince Charlie after the '45 the old clan system was effectively destroyed and the Highlands subjected to harsh oppression. In 1792 the Cheviot sheep were introduced to Scotland. They were a huge improvement on the native breed with something like twice the quantity of wool and twice the amount of meat. They were, moreover, just as hardy as the native breeds and were perfectly able to survive on the Scottish hills.

So here was a golden opportunity for the owners of Highland estates to make them much more profitable by clearing out the impoverished crofters and giving over the ground to sheep. So the Clearances were mainly the responsibility of Scottish estate owners rather than English because the huge takeover of Scottish estates by Englishmen, triggered by the later fashion of deerstalking, had not yet begun.

In Strathcarron, west of Ardgay, which we refer to as "Our Glen", the Clearances at Glencalvie even created an outcry at the time and *The Times* sent a correspondent to investigate... but more of this later. I suppose that the most notorious figure in the whole experience of Highland Clearances was George Granville Leveson-Gower, the First Duke of Sutherland.

He was, indeed, an Englishman whose example inspired the start of the mass emigration from Scotland unequalled by any country in Europe, even Ireland. This started in the late eighteenth century and had not ceased by the start of the twentieth.

The Duke of Sutherland had huge estates in Staffordshire and his marriage brought him about a million acres in Sutherland. To improve these huge acreages and make them more productive, the Cheviot sheep was the answer. But the downside was that to obtain this extra profitability the land had to be cleared of tenants.

Within the space of a decade he cleared out no less than fifteen thousand tenants. His willing henchman was his factor, Patrick Sellar, who later bought Ardtornish. In 1816 Patrick Sellar was prosecuted in Inverness for "culpable homicide" as a result of the clearances but, of course, acquitted!

A hard way of life.

So the remains of crofts and crofting villages can still be seen in the Highlands; melancholy monuments to another time and another way of life. Stalking at Levishie Forest in Inverness-shire we would drive up a steep hill and at the top see the remains of a complete crofting community, long since derelict, and this is repeated throughout the Highlands.

The crofting way of life was always poverty stricken and if conditions were made worse by, for example, potato blight or a drop in prices, existence was reduced to starvation level. An exodus from the Highlands was, no doubt, inevitable but the deliberate clearances were the most important factor.

Some Highland chiefs, faced with desperate conditions for their tenants, emigrated to Canada with them. The Earl of Selkirk took the nucleus of his clan to Canada and founded The Red River Settlement at a place that later became Winnipeg.

The MacNab of MacNab did the same, taking the members of his clan to Canada to cut down the timber in the wilderness and build a settlement two hundred miles west of Montreal. He attempted to subject them to the same feudal conditions as they had been obliged to endure in Scotland: An experiment that was destined to fail.

For many years I had the pleasure of owning the Joseph Manton flintlock double gun that was made for him in the early years of the nineteenth century and which he took with him to Canada.

From 1763 for a decade it is estimated that 20,000 people emigrated and throughout the nineteenth century the series of economic depressions continued this exodus. Even between 1901 and 1961 it is estimated that a further million and a quarter Scots emigrated. "Will ye no come back again?" is a Scottish saying to which the inevitable answer is, all too often, "No".

Deerstalking, as we understand it today, is comparatively recent. Since firearms were invented they have, of course, been used to shoot deer in the Highlands but not on a highly organised basis. The introduction of the railways in the mid-nineteenth century made the Highlands accessible and the lease of Balmoral by Queen Victoria in 1848 gave the Highlands instant desirability.

"Caledonia, stern and wild." was accessible at last and the rich and famous wanted a slice of it! It became fashionable to buy a Highland estate to indulge in the new sport of deerstalking. Scottish estate owners were only too pleased to accept the welcome windfall of English guineas.

The crofters had been ousted to make room for sheep at the end of the 18th century and less than half a century later the sheep were to be cleared away to make room for deer.

Climb onto a mountain top in the Highlands and look in any direction: Every acre you see is probably owned by an Englishman or a Continental. This, of course, is a legacy of the extensive land purchases in the mid-nineteenth century when deerstalking fever consumed the aristocratic and the wealthy and has been consolidated by the stock market boom of the 1980's and 1990's.

One stalker I know, but who will remain nameless, took a wealthy Englishman stalking for the first time in the 1990's. He shot two stags and thought that deerstalking was great stuff, so went out and bought a deer forest. Naturally he is far too busy to spend more than a few weeks a year there.

Not all Englishmen, by any means, are bad owners and many have made enormous improvements often, I might add, with the generous help of government grants; but if such grants are freely available who can blame them? In addition not all of them are, by any means, absentee landlords but the fact remains that to live in a country owned by the inhabitants of another country does seem bizarre!

Will the Scottish Parliament, new in 1999, change any of this? Well, as Chou-en-Lai was asked in the 1960's what effect the Russian Revolution of 1917 had had, his reply was "It's too early to tell". Perhaps, then, no changes will be made but to echo Chou-en-Lai: "It's too early to tell".

Considering, then, that Sassenachs own so much of their land we, and others like us, count ourselves especially fortunate to have been welcomed by the Highlanders with such marvellous hospitality. Yes, we have always valued and appreciated it.... and have done our best to offer hospitality in return.

Eking out a bare existence.

Coming in for a shot.

Chapter Fifteen
The Old Order Changeth

Just at the time that deer had reached their lowest ebb in the early nineteenth century, a new idea hit the Highlands: Why not charge to shoot over the Highland estates?

The signal for this remarkable change was in 1812 when the Duke of Gordon advertised the shooting on Glenfeshie forest. All sorts of replies were received, most from people who thought that the land could be farmed or ploughed but they were told that there was no lodge and no facilities. Only suitable for people "in the prime of life who could encamp for a few weeks among the hills during the shooting season"

No guarantee of sport was given other than that the ground marched with Mar and Atholl and would "soon be peopled with deer if preserved".

The forest was eventually taken by G. MacPherson-Grant of Ballindalloch who later bought it. It remained in the hands of the family for over a century.

So this was the start of the deerstalking that we would recognise today. Other shootings were then advertised or became known by word of mouth and the days of sportsmen like Colonel Thornton, wandering about to shoot where and when they pleased, were over.

Local lairds started to advertise in their local papers politely requesting that no-one should shoot over their land without permission. For example: "The Earl of Airlie requests that no Gentlemen will shoot or hunt on his estate of Auchterhouse during the present season. Strict orders have been given for the detention and prosecution of poachers and other trespassers".

William Coke, nephew of the famous Coke of Norfolk left his East Anglian pheasants and partridges to stalk in the Highlands. Thormanby in *Kings of Rod, Rifle and Gun* claimed that the "first man that went in earnest deerstalking in the Highlands was William Coke of Norfolk. He had a pair of corduroy breeches which Squire Osbaldeston declared he never took off for a fortnight. Crawling on hands and knees he was for a time being a separate Nabucadanezzar".

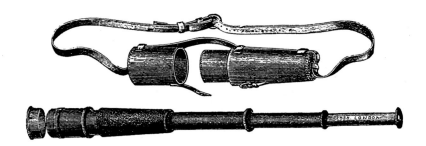

Ross telescopes 1895. Superb quality. Some still in use today.

The forest of Black Mount had held deer from time immemorial but at the beginning of the nineteenth century it had, like so many other forests, been turned over to sheep. In 1820 it was re-afforested i.e. the sheep were taken off and deer were allowed to return. Black Mount was one of the Breadalbane Forests and at the end of the century the Marchioness of Breadalbane became the most famous lady stalker of the nineteenth century.

Gaik in Inverness-shire had also been home to the deer until 1780 when it was let for sheep but this forest, too, was re-afforested in 1826. George Cupples in: *Scotch Deer Hounds and Their Masters* claimed that between 1811 and 1825 the number of deer forests was trebled from six to eighteen but by 1842 the number had reached forty.

So deerstalking had come to stay and from then on it was to go from strength to strength.

Scottish deer-hound from the early 19th century.

Modern Times! Opening of the Glasgow and Gainkirk railway 1831.

Chapter Sixteen
Lord Malmesbury

The second Earl of Malmesbury claimed that 1833 was the year that the invasion of the Highlands by Sassenach sportsmen really got underway. He wrote: "1833 was the first year that the Highlands became the rage and that deer forests were made and rented, but for prices not exceeding £300 a year. Sir Harry Goodricke, who was a leader in the young hunting men, hired Mar Forest and Lord Kinnard, Fealar in Atholl...I went later to the Isle of Skye and to Harris .....and the grouse, deer forest and fishing, all of which were first rate, were offered to me at £25 a year....at that time a stranger could fish and shoot over almost any part of the Highlands without interruption, the letting value of the "ferae naturae" being unknown to their possessors."

Lord Malmesbury rented Achnacarry Forest near Invergarry, Inverness-shire for fifteen years with the benefit of "Excellent ponies and very intelligent gillies ready to be engaged at five shillings a week and food".

In his memoirs he does not claim to be a superlative rifle shot and his rifle shooting let him down when he was invited to a deer drive at Balmoral in September 1852. Prince Albert had organised the drive and the rifles were posted in line. He describes his part in the drive as follows: "Two fine stags passed me, which I missed; Colonel Phipps (the Private Secretary) fired next and lastly the Prince, without any effect. The Queen had come out to see the sport, lying down in the heather by the Prince, and witnessed all these fiascos, to our humiliation".

At one time most Highland lochs were thought to contain a monster and Loch Arkaig was no exception. The locals were in no doubt about its existence and John Stewart, the Achnacarry stalker, had seen it twice. He had seen it basking, hollow backed and with an equine head, so it could not have been any kind of fish.

Lord Malmesbury wrote: "The Highlanders are very superstitious about this creature. They are convinced that there is never more than one in existence at any one time and I believe they think that it has something diabolical in its nature for when I said I wished I could get a shot at it my stalker observed very gravely: "Perhaps your Lordship's gun would misfire".

But, of course, the Sassenachs who came North to stalk needed experienced hill men who knew the deer and the Hill. Knew the ways of the deer and how to get the Sassenach "gentleman" into position for a successful shot. Knew which deer to shoot and which to leave. So the professional Highland stalker was born, or, to be more precise, evolved from the former foresters and shepherds.

So modern deerstalking was underway at last: The joys of the Hill were becoming more widely known but to get to the Highlands was a formidable task. The advent of the Railways was to bring sweeping changes, but for the Highlands, this was still some years ahead.

Deer at bay in a torrent - Scrope.

Before the railways came a journey from the south of England to the north of Scotland was difficult, uncomfortable, time consuming and expensive. By coach it could take two weeks and cost the substantial sum of £20: Multiply this by fifty to get some idea of today's values.

Alternatively the journey could be made by sea from London to Leith near Edinburgh and then on by a smaller boat or by coach. Another route was by sea up the West Coast and when the Crinan Canal linked Crinan Loch and Loch Fyne in 1801, this was a great improvement.

The Caledonian Canal, commenced in 1801, took about twenty years to complete and was another great improvement for travellers. Locks were built to link Loch Linnie, Eil, Lochy, Oich and Ness to make a navigable route from coast to coast.

Lord Malmesbury for his journey to Achnacarry, near Fort Augustus, used to travel by coach to Edinburgh, cross over to Greenock near Glasgow and then take a steamer for the rest of the journey. Why not a coach to Glasgow to avoid that long Edinburgh/Glasgow leg? Don't know! On one occasion his servants, making the journey by sea, were shipwrecked, losing all their luggage and some of his Lordship's too. Tourism, as we know it today, was not in existence in those days and the English traveller had to endure spartan conditions in the Highland inns where cleanliness did not come high on the priorities of the Highland innkeepers.

Joseph Mitchell, the Scottish engineer, in *Reminiscences of my Life in the Highlands* wrote of Donald Munro the landlord of the inn at Kinlochoilart describing him as "the worst of innkeepers" but "the most obliging and good-natured fellow alive". A huge, powerfully built man but with "truly Highland indolent tastes and habits. Salmon fishing, a shot at a stag or sleeping out on the hillside were more to his tastes than looking after his guests. Keeping a clean house or providing comfortable fare for his customers never seemed to enter his head nor did he consider it to be a necessary part of his profession".

For a woman to stalk in those days was almost unheard of and although a few did so, it was not until the 1880's when the Marchioness of Breadalbane became the most famous lady stalker of the 19th century, that women really started to stalk. It is, therefore, surprising that Lord Malmesbury mentions Lady Seymour stalking at Achnacarry in 1845.

Few women were game shots in the nineteenth century as aristocratic opinion was against it. Lady Randolph Churchill, for example, was not against ladies shooting but, even so, "did not admire it as an accomplishment."

In 1882 Queen Victoria made her opinion clear to her daughter, Princess Victoria, saying that although it was acceptable for a lady to be a spectator at a game shoot, "only fast women shot."

Even so, however, some women did shoot at driven game, fast or not! The women, not the game! Princess Radziwill, for example, was a frequent shooting guest of Sir Frederick Milbank at Barningham, though never a good shot.

The same degree of disapproval did not quite apply to lady stalkers because it was so different and required determination and hardiness even to attempt to tackle the high hills of Scotland. Even so, however, they were very much in the minority.

Lady Randolph Churchill, with the help of powerful field glasses, observed a woman stalking and wrote that first of all, accompanied by her professional stalker, she "crawled on all-fours up a long burn; emerging hot and panting, not to say wet and dirty, she then continued her scramble up a steep hill, taking advantage of any cover afforded by the ground, or remained in a petrified attitude if by chance a hind happened to look up."

Unfortunately the shot was not successful and the deerhounds had to be slipped on the wounded stag. Whether or not the stag was brought to bay so that the *coup de grace* was administered, we don't know, but Lady Churchill was obviously unimpressed!

Not only was it unusual for ladies to stalk it was equally unusual for them to accompany their husbands when stalking. Lord and Lady Ribblesdale were guests of the Duke of Westminster at his vast estates in Sutherland when to everyone's astonishment Lady Ribbesdale announced that she proposed to join him for a day's stalking. Bareheaded and with voluminous skirts and buttoned boots she was unsuitably clad for a day on the Hill. The Duke's sons predicted that the deer simply wouldn't stand for it and such a sight could well ruin the stalking for years to come!

In the event, however, all was well and "Contrary to all expectations, the Ribblesdales returned with a fine stag, though Lady Ribblesdale's hair was wringing wet, all the buttons were off her boots and her petticoat hung in shreds." The deer were not stampeded into the next county after all.

Lord Malmesbury was Foreign Secretary in 1852 and 1858. In 1844 he leased Achnacarry Castle and its adjoining forest for fifteen years, going there to stalk every autumn. He came to love Achnacarry and this is made clear in his autobiography "Memoirs of an ex-Minister."

There were many memories to record: Lord Elgin returned from the Hill one day none too pleased after his stalker had ordered him to crawl *up* a waterfall. Lord Edward Thynne killing a soaring eagle with a "rifle and single ball" and much more.

Lord Malmesbury described an encounter with a hind in 1849 as follows: "I had been out deer-stalking, and as I was returning home alone, and by bright moonlight, I saw a hind on the Hill a little above the road, and shot her, but just as I was stooping over her with a knife, she sprang up and struck me with one of her fore feet, hitting me in the forehead just between the eyes. The blow was so violent that it knocked me down and stunned me for a short time, and on recovering my senses I found I was quite blind, but this was only from the blood. Her hoof had cut a deep gash in my forehead and along my nose. The animal was lying quite dead by my side. I walked to the house, which was not far off, and the maid who opened the door was so frightened by my appearance that she fainted forthwith. This laid me up for a week but with no further consequences."

Lord Malmesbury left Achnacarry for the last time in 1859 with great regret. On October 2nd he saw a flock of wild swans flying south: " A broad hint to me to do the same." On October 25th he wrote:

"I beat the woods at Achnasoul and killed 6 woodcocks, 12 blackcocks, also a stag whose leg I had broken two days ago. This good day's sport and luck has closed my connection with Achnacarry, which has lasted for 15 years of the prime of my life."

He continued: "I rowed home from Moich with a heavy heart. Loch Arkaig was motionless and the colour of obsidian. The sun, after a bright day, had set behind a heavy mass of clouds, against which the mountains of Scaurnahat and Murligan looked ghostly in their garments of snow, whilst the northern slopes and corries of the Pine Forest retained every flake that had fallen. The stags, as usual in a hard frost, were roaring with redoubled passion in the wilds of Gusach and Guerraran. The herons were screaming as I disturbed them from their shelter in the islands; and then again the roaring of the harts re-echoed through the forest. As I landed at the pier a freezing mist fell over the whole scene, and thus we parted. Vale!"

Obsidian is not a word that trips frequently from the lips these days, but it means a dark, glass-like volcanic deposit.

For many of the new Sassenach stalkers grouse and ptarmigan were the main quarry before deer numbers had the chance to build up.

Glen Feshie was rented by the Ellice Family in the 1830's and huge bags of grouse were shot: 3,642, for example, in 1839 but only three or four deer a year. When deer were sighted the event caused quite a stir. On August 20th 1839 the entry in the game book was as follows: "Immense excitement occasioned by our being informed, after about two hours shooting, that some of Sir Joseph's deer were on the ground, (having come from the neighbouring forest of Gaik). Gillies, shepherds and dogs... started up the Feshie and found about fifty hinds and eight harts just crossing the burn to go home again. A well drilled volley at 300 yards brought down the best beast of the lot!" One shudders to think how many of the poor creatures were wounded!

Preparing the deer for being left on the moor - Scrope.

Alisdair Ranaldson MacDonell of Glengarry, who allowed the Sobieski Stewarts to hunt with deer hounds over his domain.

Chapter Seventeen
"Fings Ain't what they Used to Be"

So sang Lionel Blair in the 1960's and, come to think of it, they never were! Cicero, two thousand years ago, said much the same thing.

Bonnie Prince Charlie did not marry until late in life though that never failed to stop him having his fair share of "meaningful relationships"! Late in life, however, he married the young Clementina Sobieska, a descendant of the Polish kings, the Sobieskis. The marriage, however, produced no issue so there was no *legitimate* line of descent on the paternal side, but in 1848 two brothers claiming descent from Bonnie Prince Charlie appeared in the Invergarry area.

They were the Sobieski Stewarts and they lamented the passing of the old days in the Highlands. They deplored the new methods of deerstalking which the Sassenachs were introducing in the Highlands and wanted to go back to the traditional ways of deer hunting with deerhounds. They condemned the degenerative ways of the southern incomer who "nods in the heather or dissipates the vigils of his lodge in smoke and cards and whiskey" by comparison with the noble traditions of the old Scottish hunters "who beguiled the time with songs and traditions".

The brothers re-introduced the ancient hunts in the Glengarry area and also published the nostalgic *Lays of the Deer Forest*. In it they translated ancient Gaelic poems into English. The old Highland minstrels were highly esteemed for their poems, sung to a simple tune accompanied by a harp: Although these poems might have had their audiences rolling in the aisles in 1648 they were unattractively leaden in 1848, let alone today!

For the deer hunts dogs were the all important factor, not these new-fangled firearms. In *Lays of the Deer Forest* they say "No man went to the hill without greyhounds; they were indispensable attendants of deer-sport of every class....for it was justly thought not only a gross waste of venison, but a dishonour to the chase to allow a wounded deer to get away to die in the corries and be eaten by ravens." and we can, without doubt, agree with them on this.

By "greyhounds" they meant what we would call Scottish deerhounds: Big, strong rough-haired hounds, long in the leg, reputedly standing thirty inches high and weighing up to 100lbs. Different forests reputedly bred different strains and different colours; the Breadalbanes' Black Mount dogs, for example, were considered to have no equal in strength. The Atholl dogs were famous for their speed.

Young dogs could impetuously attempt to go for the stag's throat only to be impaled on the stag's defensive horns. The Sobieski-Stewarts described hunting in the old days at Glengarry in *Lays of the Deer Forest* as follows: "Two fine young dogs belonging to the late Glengarry were killed in their first run by a gallant stag, which they had driven down the dry channel of a mountain stream....and as they sprang at his throat from either side, with a rapid flourish of his horns, he struck them right and left and laid them dead among the stones. The experienced greyhounds rarely run at the deer's neck, but come up close by his flank, and shoot up at his throat too close for the blow of his horns, and to effect this they will sometimes for several yards run by his haunch, until they feel the favourable moment for making their launch at his neck."

In the book they also deplored the whiskey drinking in the Highland lodges but, nonetheless, considered a "dram" an essential stimulant on the Hill. They claimed that whiskey was buried at suitable locations ready for the hunters. It was considered that this helped to mellow the raw spirit. They describe the custom of burying whiskey by the Clach-an-t-Sealgair, the hunter's stone, by a burn.

"To show the trouble of conveyance and to improve the speed of the gillies, we had divers of these earth-sealed fountains; near customary trysts, or good passes, where the Deoch-Fala or blood drink might be wanted. More than once, however, we were disappointed on our dram by mice, who, mining over our bottles, found the corks; and probably mistaking them for the spungy stocks or roots and curious to taste some new kind of pignut at their feet; had neatly scooped them out of the glass; when, doubtless surprised with the potent whiff of the spirit within, they burnt their noses, with no less dissatisfaction to themselves than displeasure to us"

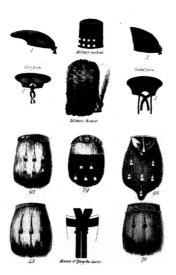

Some of the extraordinary dress styles from James Logan and Robert McIan's 1831 book Clans of the Scottish Highlands.

Glengarry Forest, it seems, had been afforested i.e. cleared of sheep and given over to deer in 1837 by a Sassenach tenant and without the competition of grazing by sheep the deer quickly colonised it. At the same time there was a tremendous attack on vermin and in the years between 1837 and 1840 the following were killed:

11 foxes	301 stoats and weasels.
198 wild cats	67 badgers.
248 marten cats	48 otters.
106 pole cats	78 housecats (gone wild)
27 white tailed sea eagles	3 honey buzzards.
15 golden eagles	462 kestrels.

This huge cull was even reported in the Inverness Courier.

Further along the glen, marching with Glengarry is Glenquoich, a famous forest whose head stalker today is Lea MacNally's son, "Young" Lea who carries on the family tradition. It is a well-managed forest in the hands of the same family for generations.

On one occasion a deer drive was organised for a very important guest, King Edward VII. The King was placed in a strategic position at the top of a pass and the beaters set out to drive the deer towards him. But you can't "drive" deer you can only "move" them. Once they think they are being driven against their will nothing will keep them going in the way you want and, regardless of terrain, the wind direction or whether or not Uranus is in conjunction with Capricorn they will break back and do what *they* want!

This was the case during this particular deer drive: The deer broke back and the drive was a failure. But the greatest exponent of deer driving of all time was the American millionaire Walter Winans.

He was, without doubt, a superlative shot at running deer and had the money to indulge in deer driving on a grand scale. In the late 19th century he leased a series of deer forests that almost stretched from coast to coast. A later chapter is devoted to him.

In the early days of the 19th century it was believed that deer lived to an incredible age and there was abundant "proof" to confirm this. In 1826 Glengarry himself shot a stag with a distinctive mark on his ear. Different foresters were consulted who confirmed that it was the mark of Ewan-Mac-Ian-Og, a forester who used to mark deer calves but had died 150 years ago. This confirmed that the stag must have been at least 150 years old!

This was not, by any means, the oldest "recorded" deer. Captain MacDonald of Tulloch who died in 1776 at the age of 86 had known "the white hind of Loch Treig" for the last fifty years but his father had known her for the same length of time and so had his grandfather before him! It was calculated, then, that the white hind was about 200 years old: A perfect example of adding two and two together and making thirty four and a half!

How experienced hillmen who had observed the deer for years

could be so mistaken, is beyond belief! They also thought that stags could travel enormous distances in a day. A distinctive stag would be seen one morning and the "same" stag observed sixty miles away that afternoon! There were many instances of such impossible journeys.

But if you ignore the nineteenth century stalkers' belief that stags could live impossibly long lives and travel enormous distances, their practical knowledge of the deer and how to stalk them was sound enough.

Sir Walter Scott's magnificent dwelling at Abbotsford.

The missionary's escape from the lion, from Livingstone's Missionary Travels.

Chapter Eighteen
Roualeyn George Gordon Cumming

Roualeyn George Gordon Cumming was one of the striking characters not merely in the Highland scene but in the wider world. As a young man he was a well-connected Highland poacher but later he became one of the first African white hunters. On a visit to the Duke of Atholl he couldn't resist poaching one of the Duke's deer on the way home and continued in the same manner.

He was the younger son of Sir William George Gordon Cumming Bart., of Altyre and Gordonstoun. Born in 1820 he was sent to Eton at the age of nine and even as a boy he was a first class stalker and salmon fisherman.

At eighteen he went to India as a Cornet (cavalry equivalent of second lieutenant) in the Madras Cavalry, then to Canada as an Ensign and finally, in 1834, to South Africa in the Cape Mounted Rifles. In South Africa, however, he resigned to launch himself into the unknown as a big game hunter. Nothing was known about it in those days and he was strongly advised not to go into the interior as it was "twenty to one against you coming back alive".

He was a tall, powerfully built man, impressively strong and with "the proud bearing of a Highland Chief and an eye bright and piercing as an eagle's". He wore Highland costume even in Africa, so he made a striking impression wherever he went.

His expedition to the interior was well planned with two wagons drawn by a team of oxen, and a staff of three natives and an ex-cockney cab driver! He was well stocked with provisions and all the gear he thought he might need. His armoury consisted of a single barrel 12 bore German rifle with which he had killed his first stag on Jura together with double rifles by Purdey, William Moore and Dickson of Edinburgh. The Dickson rifle had two grooved rifling to take a belted ball: "The most perfect and useful rifle I ever had the pleasure of using".

He got on well with the Boers though he described the Boer women as follows "their beauty, like that of Skye terriers I fear in most cases consists of their ugliness. They, however, sadly lack the "degage" appearance of the Skye terriers as their general air and gait might be more aptly likened to a yard of pump water"

Once into the interior he was amazed and delighted by the abundance of game: Vast herds of springbok as far as the eye could see. He met the famous Scottish Minister, Dr. Moffat with whom he was greatly impressed, describing him as "Minister, gardener, blacksmith, gunsmith, mason, carpenter, glazier". He continued on to meet Dr Moffat's son-in-law, unknown then but later to achieve greatness as Dr Livingstone.

Female elephant pursued with javelins, protecting her young, from Livingstone's Missionary Travels.

After being hospitably received by his fellow Scotsman he continued on into unknown country followed by an impromptu entourage of anything from 50 to 200 Bechuanas who relied upon him for meat. Whatever he shot was soon devoured by his hungry followers.

The kilt was not the ideal form of clothing for African conditions and his legs were inevitably cut and torn by thorn bushes. He shot giraffe, lion, rhino, and finally he came into elephant country. He described an encounter with a huge bull elephant: He had fired at the beast, hitting it in the shoulder and rendering it immobile but instead of immediately administering the *coup de grace* he decided to "devote a short time to this noble elephant before I should lay him low". He unsaddled his horses, made a fire, put the kettle on and made coffee. So he sat there drinking his coffee and contemplated the stricken beast. Finally the poor creature did succumb to a fusillade of shots from two of his heavy rifles: Not the kind of sportsmanship we would approve of today!

To finance his trip he traded flintlock muskets with the natives. He had paid £16 for a case of muskets, not a bad buy, and accepted £30 worth of ivory back for each musket, explaining to the buyers that the muskets were exactly the same as his own Purdey and Dickson.

But five years in the African Bush were as much as his health could endure and in 1849 he left Africa for ever to return to Scotland.

In 1850 he published his book *Five years of a Hunter's Life in the Far Interior of South Africa* which was a huge success and brought him instant fame. In 1851 he exhibited his trophies at the Great Exhibition. This was followed by a lecture tour during which he was splendidly attired in Highland dress and surrounded by his trophies.

In 1858 he returned to Scotland and opened a museum of his trophies at the side of the Caledonian Canal at the Fort Augustus locks.

In 1857 David Livingstone's book *Missionary Travels* was published to enormous acclaim. Livingstone himself confirmed that Roualeyn's book "Conveys a truthful idea of South African hunting" so this gave an important boost to Roualeyn's enterprise. During his last years, however, he became more reclusive and his fame decreased. He spent many hours wandering the hills and forests of the locality on his own.

He was always considered, by his fellow Highlanders, to have the gift of second sight and one day, apparently in excellent health, he ordered his coffin from the local carpenter with a request that it was to be delivered within four days. The coffin was delivered on time and 24 hours later, in March 1866, he was dead, shortly after his forty sixth birthday.

So did his gift of second sight provide him with a premonition of his death? What do you think?

Many others were to follow in Roualeyn's footsteps in African hunting but he was one of the true pioneers, one of the very first to step out into the unknown, defying that "twenty to one" chance of ever coming back alive.

Buffalo cow defending her calf, from Livingstone's Missionary Travels.

The travelling procession interrupted, from Livingstone's Missionary Travels.

The Prince of Wales firing a Maxim gun at Wimbledon in 1888.

Chapter Nineteen
The Tranby Croft Affair

Roualeyn Gordon Cumming was not the eldest son, but another Gordon Cumming descendant was to achieve notoriety a quarter of a century later and this is how it came about:

The Prince of Wales, later Edward VII, was greatly interested in horse racing together with a passion for gambling at cards. In September 1890 he and his friends accepted an invitation to stay as guests of shipowner, Sir Arthur Wilson, at his home, Tranby Croft, for the Doncaster races.

The party started on a discordant note when the Prince's current girlfriend, Lady Brooke, could not attend due to the sudden death of her stepfather.

Although Sir Arthur Wilson disapproved of gambling at cards, in deference to the Prince he raised no objection when a game of Baccarat was started with the Prince as banker. A fellow guest who joined the game was Sir William Gordon-Cumming, a Lieutenant General in the Scots Guards and a close friend of the Prince.

Sir Arthur Wilson's son was watching the game and he was amazed to see Gordon-Cumming surreptitiously increasing his stake *after* he had seen his cards. The boy later told his parents and another guest so for the next evening Sir Arthur watched carefully and found that Gordon-Cumming was definitely cheating.

The following morning, Lord Coventry and Lieutenant General Owen Williams confronted Gordon-Cumming who denied the charge but, even so, eventually agreed to sign a document promising never to play cards again. He was only too well aware that if he was publicly convicted of cheating, his army career would be at an end. In addition to that he would be excluded from his London Clubs and socially he would be cast into the "Outer darkness"!

In return for his undertaking, his hosts, the Prince and the other guests agreed to remain silent about the whole affair. This to protect not only Gordon-Cumming but to ensure that the Prince's gambling would not become common knowledge.

But, of course, "Two can keep a secret if the other one is dead" and news of the affair leaked out. In retaliation, Gordon-Cumming took legal action for "Seditious Libel" against his host's wife, son, daughter, son in law and Mr. Berkley Levitt, a fellow guest and a subaltern in his own regiment.

The trial began on June 1st 1891 and lasted over a week. The Prince of Wales was obliged to testify together with other witnesses but the jury found for the defendants, thus condemning Sir William Gordon Cumming of being guilty of cheating at cards.

The Times thundered: "He has committed a mortal offence; Society can know him no more".

So Sir William really was cast out into Society's outer darkness! Soon after the trial he married an American heiress and she did attempt to give house parties at their Scottish mansion, Gordonstoun (later to become a school attended by Prince Charles). But Society would have nothing to do with them and her efforts were doomed to failure. She turned to religion for consolation and Sir William turned to a pair of mistresses whom he installed at Gordonstoun.

Sir William was not alone in being damned by the affair: The Prince of Wales was, too. *The Times* was very put out indeed, saying that it was regrettable and that the Prince should neither have been involved in a lawsuit or "in the social circumstances which prepared the way for it" as the game had been played to please the Prince of Wales.

Referring to Gordon Cumming's signed declaration never to touch a card again they wrote: "We almost wish, for the sake of English Society in general, that we could learn that the result of this most unhappy case has been that the Prince of Wales has signed a similar declaration.

Apparently the Prince did give up Baccarat but he took up Bridge instead!

Burberry. What all the Best People wore in the 1890's.

The Prince of Wales, later to become King Edward VII stalking in the 1890's with his D.B. Black Powder Express rifle.

Chapter Twenty
Balmoral

It was Balmoral that gave the unmistakable stamp of approval to deerstalking. Queen Victoria and Prince Albert made their first visit to Scotland by sea in 1841: An excruciatingly slow journey. They started from London in the *Royal George*, a man-of-war converted into a yacht. It was considerably below the Queen's dignity to go by steamer so the *Royal George* was *towed* by a steamer, making a slow journey even slower!

Once in Scotland, however, they were captivated and from then on never lost their love of Scotland. They had a tremendous reception as they proceeded to Drummond Castle, family seat of the Breadalbanes. We were to see Drummond Castle, long derelict, when we stalked at the Breadalbanes' formerly enclosed deer forest, Drummond Hill, in the 1960's.

There Albert received his first taste of Scottish deerstalking, so very different from the driven roe and wild boar in his native Germany.

So both Queen Victoria and Prince Albert were hooked! Two years later they again sailed north to stay with Lord and Lady Glenlyon at Blair Castle, only five weeks after the Queen had given birth to Prince Alfred. In preparation for the Royal visit not a shot had been fired at stag or grouse for the whole season. After a day's grouse shooting Albert stalked the next day and shot three stags.

During the next week Albert shot two semi-tame stags from the dining room window with Victoria watching. Not the kind of "sport" very highly regarded in Scotland, then or now!

But after that it was back to the Hill for both Albert and Victoria; Albert to stalk and Victoria, accompanied by her lady in waiting, to watch. On their return she wrote in her diary "Lord Aberdeen (The Foreign Secretary) was quite touched when I told him I was so much attached to the dear, dear Highlands and missed the fine hills so much, there is a great peculiarity about the Highlands and Highlanders; and they are such a chivalrous, fine, active people. Our stay among them was so delightful independently of the beautiful scenery. There was a quiet, a wildness, a liberty and a solitude that has such charm for us."

Their next visit was in 1847. This time they sailed up the West coast, past Wales. They were to stay with the Duke and Duchess of Argyll at Inverary. Again they enjoyed a magnificent welcome.

They went on to stay at Ardverikie in the magnificent shooting lodge at Loch Laggan but this time the weather was dreadful and put something of a damper on the proceedings. The final result, however, was all to the good because in 1848 the Royal Physician, Sir James Clark, persuaded the Queen to lease a small castle named Balmoral on the drier, east side of Scotland. The Queen and the Prince took a 27 year lease of the castle and estate so the die was cast! Their first visit to Balmoral was in September 1848 and the Queen and Prince immediately felt at home. The delightful situation and the glen reminded Prince Albert of his beloved Thuringen, in Germany.

Queen Victoria with her personal servant, John Brown.

So at last they had a place of their own in Scotland, a very different proposition from staying as guests, no matter how welcome. They soon decided that they must buy the place and by 1852 they had bought the Balmoral Estate together with the adjoining estates of Birkhall and Abergeldie.

The next step was to build a new "modern" castle to replace the smaller old one and in September 1855 they moved into the new castle though the tower and one of the wings were still uncompleted. The Queen and the Prince put into effect a whole range of improvements to the Estate: New plantations, game larders and stables etc. When the time came to head south at the end of the stalking season she recorded how sorry she was to leave: "Every year my heart becomes more fixed in this dear paradise".

But their affection was not confined solely to the place itself but extended to their staff and, like so many Sassenachs before and since, it was the character of the Highlanders that was the most important factor in their enjoyment of the Highlands. The Queen wrote:

"The Prince highly appreciated the good-breeding, simplicity and intelligence which make it so pleasant, and even instructive to talk to them".

In return the estate staff greatly appreciated their employers. John Grant was the headkeeper when they first took over at Balmoral. Thirty-eight years old and: "An excellent man, most trustworthy, of singular shrewdness and discretion, and most devotedly attached to the Prince and myself. He has a fine intelligent countenance".

Another outstanding Highlander was John MacDonald, a Fort William man and "a jäger of the Prince" i.e. the Prince's personal stalker. But their most famous retainer was, of course, John Brown who started as a part-time gillie but in 1851 took over the leading of the Queen's pony and became a full-time member of the staff. He "advanced step by step by his good conduct and intelligence" to become the Queen's "permanent personal attendant".

It was with their Highland retainers at Balmoral that the Queen and Prince were able to enjoy as close a relationship as could possibly be attained between monarchs and commoners during that era. A relationship that was greatly appreciated by both sides.

The Prince, from the very start, was an enthusiastic stalker though never a very dependable shot. On one occasion he did, indeed, shoot five stags and a hind on Lochnagar. An achievement recorded by the Queen with great pride in her diary though you wondered how that hind was unfortunate enough to stop a bullet!

Prince Albert 1860. But how did he keep his knees so clean when crawling?

But her diary is by no means an unbroken record of successes, with misses and wounded stags occurring all too often. The stalkers and gillies had many long chases after wounded stags with their deer hounds and other abortive long chases after stags which Albert *thought* he had hit!

Although many of the stags had their weights recorded in the thirteen to fourteen stone class, as you would expect, others of only five or six stone were shot. Not mature stags at all, only "knobbers" i.e. young immature stags with only small horns; surely he had never actually *aimed* at such beasts and they were merely the unfortunate animals who stopped a bullet intended for a mature stag. It is out of the question that the stalkers would have pointed out such small stags for Albert to shoot.

Some writers, though unable to deny the Prince's erratic shooting, have put part of the blame on his "inaccurate" rifles, but this was *not* the case. Stalking rifles of the period were perfectly accurate, especially at the distances that the Prince would have been asked to shoot....no doubt 100 yards or less. Remember, too, that the Prince's rifles would be of the finest quality by the best makers. No, the poor shooting was due to the "afterpiece", not the rifles.

Prince Albert's results were recorded in a magnificent game book with covers of blue calf, gold lettering and silk lining inside. Even so, the record is surprisingly sparse. No details of heads are given, for example, only the weights. Even the "remarks" column tells us very little: No lengthy accounts of difficult stalks in the teeth of a gathering storm, only such remarks as "Shot in the presence of her Majesty the Queen and H.R.H. Princess Alice".

As well as stalking there were often deer drives in the Ballochbuie Woods when the Prince was often accompanied by the Queen. The Queen described a "little box, made of hurdles and interwoven with branches of fir and heather about 5ft in height" in which they sat while waiting for the deer to be driven or, more correctly, moved towards them.

On another occasion a drive was held in Corrie Buie and she described it as follows:

"At last the deer came out and straight upon us. It was the finest sight imaginable; there were about thirty or forty hinds with four or five stags, one, in particular, a magnificent one with fine horns. Albert aimed and got him. We went to look at him, and meanwhile Albert ran back to shoot another, which Duncan came to say was wounded. In running back after Albert, which I did very fast, I got such a tumble, falling my whole length on the heather, and I think on a stone, for I hurt my knee a good deal".

So their Balmoral holidays were a joyous time, far away from the affairs of State. Albert would shoot grouse and stalk the deer and both Albert and the Queen would go out to the Hill to observe and paint. They had a bothy built at Loch Muick (pronounced Mek) and on a number of occasions they would spend the night there, right out on the Hill.

It is a matter of conjecture what clothes the Prince wore when stalking. Landseer's paintings show him in clothes more suited to the drawing room than the Hill, but was this what he usually wore or what he chose to wear when posing for these paintings? We will never know but in those pictures he is shown dressed in a light grey, close fitting, frock coat, tight trousers and, believe it or not, spats! No, he was not wearing brown boots and a bowler! He wore a stiff collar with a choker tied outside it and, as a final touch, white walking stick and gloves. Remember, too, that this was the outfit he wore on the Hill, not merely standing outside Balmoral Castle, at least according to Landseer.

Balmoral Castle.

In 1856/7 the Queen and Prince set out by coach and horseback to explore the country beyond Balmoral. They headed out westwards, continuing to Glenfeshie. They stayed at country inns, dreadfully adventurous for the Queen of England! They were arduous journeys, covering over sixty miles a day over difficult terrain.

Sadly, 1861 was the last time Albert would stay at his beloved Balmoral because in the November he was struck down by typhoid and was dead within three weeks.

Although after Albert's death the Queen continued to stay at Balmoral and never ceased to love it, the unalloyed happiness of those years with her Prince Albert were never to be repeated. In 1862 she commissioned a cairn to be built on Craig Lowrigan in memory of the Prince.

For the following year she issued a memorandum edged in black, as follows:

"The Queen wishes that the Prince's forest should remain perfectly quiet this year. In future (if she lives) it is the Queen's wish that everything should go on as formerly - that Grant should receive his orders from *no-one* but the Queen *herself* (as he always did from the Prince) or from someone sent *specially* and *directly to him*, with orders from the Queen - this regards orders of every kind respecting the forest and all connected with it - the stalkers, keepers, dogs, etc., etc.

Respecting the grouse the same course as hitherto to be pursued. The gentlemen were always able to go out, without special reference to the Prince, excepting as regards the near and best ground. The Queen would also wish none of the nearest ground to be shot over as, both here and at Windsor, she does not wish any *real* shooting to take place this year - nothing, *in short* which could be at all considered as the Prince's ground".

Stag shot by Prince Albert in Corriebuie.

In time, of course, the grouse shooting and deerstalking returned to the normal pattern. It was said of Prince Edward, who was later to become Edward VII, that as a young man "You couldn't keep him from the Hill". A fit young man, a far cry from the corpulent character he became in later years.

I remember seeing a superlative .450 single barrel falling block rifle made for the Prince by Westley Richards in 1876.... the kind of rifle that a stalker, obliged to carry his own rifle, would have been proud to have chosen.

Now fast forward almost a century to 1932 when the writer George Scott Moncrieff coined the word "Balmorality". This was a disparaging description of Queen Victoria's enjoyment of Balmoral which he considered to be demeaning to the Scots and a wholly bad influence on Scotland. He was, of course, completely mistaken as the Queen and Prince Albert very definitely did *not* look down on their Scottish subjects, in fact quite the reverse. They regarded them as people to be admired and, as far as possible for that era, were on the closest possible terms with the Highlanders who served them so faithfully.

The Balmoral Stalkers in September 1858. Prince Albert's personal "jäger" pointing. John Brown, arms folded, next to him.

The way it was then. Stalking at Langwell, Ross-shire in the 1920's. A page from the Debenham family photograph album. In those days, Langwell was 18 miles long, but now broken up. Not to be confused with Langwell, Caithness.

Chapter Twenty One
Stalking at Glenshee and Drumchork

We had stalked at the Invergarry Hotel for five seasons - 1954 to 1958. In 1959 we decided upon a change of venue.

The Glenshee Hotel at the Spittal of Glenshee had some stalking ground so this was our choice. A different part of Scotland for us. In Aberdeenshire not far from the great estates of Mar and Balmoral, it was a very good Country House Hotel with excellent cuisine. The owner, Denis Winton, was a keen golfer who had laid out his own golf course in the grounds of his Hotel.

On Sunday mornings, guests, whether golfers or not, were dragooned into playing a round of golf. An excellent idea which generated much hilarity and enabled all guests to mix and get to know each other.

An amazing survival was its own railway! This had been laid down in the early 1920's and ran along the foot of the glen. You started out on a level track, then a set of points were manually activated to get you onto the next level and another set of points. From then on the railway ran on reasonably level ground to its "terminus" several miles up the glen.

The engine was, of course, petrol powered, not steam and I'm sure it was a huge single cylinder engine. Starting it was a truly man-sized job using a massive starting handle. There were two carriages, one with glass windows and the other with open sides. In addition there was a flat truck on which your stag would be carried - if you were fortunate enough to get one!

In the district were two Highland brothers named MacDonald, both lifelong stalkers. One was "Sandy" the other "Donald" and eventually I was to stalk with both.

It was not a huge area of stalking ground and when the east wind blew and the mist filled the glen, stalking was impossible. The mist simply piled deeper and deeper into the glen. Even so, however, we had good stalking and on the days we could get out we always returned with a stag. Sandy MacDonald was the very best type of Highland stalker and it was a great pleasure to be on the Hill with him.

We would frequently return on the wobbly railway which had not been terribly well maintained for decades. We would be in excellent spirits with a stag on the truck.

On the very last day I had a bonanza, returning with no less than three stags on the truck. First ever time I had shot three stags in a day and a notable stalking milestone.

On another occasion we took "Drumchork" (pronounced Drum-hawk) stalking with a bungalow for our accommodation. This was at the head of Loch Ewe.

Loch Ewe had been an assembly point for Atlantic convoys in both World Wars and was protected from submarine attack by a boom defence at the narrow entrance to this huge sea loch. There were also Naval Guns stationed by the boom defences. The guns had long gone but at that time the boom defence was still kept in working order and operated daily.

My brother, Brian, in his Merchant Navy days during the war, had on occasion started out from Loch Ewe on board the Atlantic convoys.

Again a delightful place for a holiday but deer were very scarce indeed. I managed to get just one stag!

Grouse shooting at Langwell, Ross-shire in the 1920's from the Debenham family album.

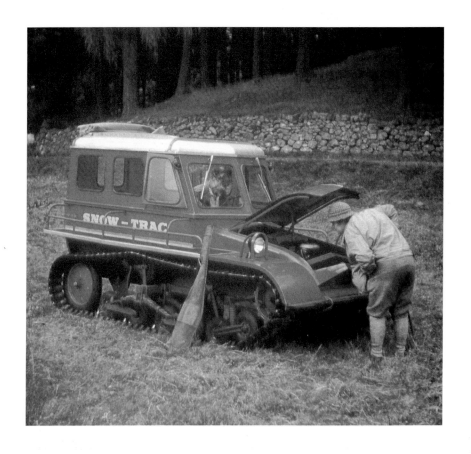

To the Hill in luxury.   Alec McLarty's snow-track at Aberfeldy.

Chapter Twenty Two
Off-Road Vehicles

For stalking in Scotland the problem of tackling the estate tracks on the deer forests was met at first by Ex-WD Jeeps or Land Rovers. Jeeps were a most welcome and comparatively inexpensive way of getting into the forests and they continued in use for many years after the War. The Land Rover, of course, was a great improvement and from their introduction in 1948 they continued for decades and in updated versions they do so to this day.

Neither the Jeeps or Land Rovers were economical but, of course, their four wheel drive was an enormous benefit. We were to cover many miles in them.

The Invergarry Hotel had a Land Rover and there was always competition to borrow it for the day. On one occasion we had managed to persuade Captain Hunt to lend us the Land Rover but he imposed the condition that we were to lend him our Jaguar. Our consent was reluctantly given as our Mark VII was a highly valued possession. On our return from stalking we had all gathered in the bar, as usual, to discuss the days stalking when after an hour or so Leslie Hunt said to us "Oh, by the way, I'm afraid that I dented your Jaguar when backing it out of the garage".

The polite response would, of course, have been "Really? No problem, it doesn't matter in the slightest!". Unfortunately, however, we did not possess such admirable supercool and expressed our concern with more force than diplomacy! The dent, fortunately was not too bad but was an inconvenience and expense we could well have done without.

The Jeeps and Land Rovers, excellent though they were, had to be driven on the estate tracks so ponies were used for collecting the deer and bringing them back from the Hill. There have been many attempts to produce a machine which would cross the terrain without resort to

estate tracks and one of the first was the Snow-track. These were tracked
vehicles with rubber tracks and were quite expensive. The driver and
passengers sat in a heated cab with a capacity for about six people.
They were powered by a Volkswagen engine and had huge front and
rear racks to carry the deer or other tackle.

Haflinger at Drumchork. Light, handy off-road vehicle.

A much cheaper alternative arrived later as the Argocat. It bore
no comparison to the Snow-track but was much cheaper and simpler.
It was rather like a plastic bathtub and although not a tracked vehicle it
had a series of low pressure doughnut tyres at each side.

The first ones had no cab so you were exposed to the elements
and they held about four people in extreme discomfort! They were
driven by simple motorcycle-type single or twin cylinder engines. A
long run back to the lodge in an Argo, wet through and in rain or sleet,
was a teeth chattering experience. Someone once criticised Henry Ford
for making "Second class cars" whereupon Ford replied "Second class
riding is better than first class walking", but I don't know which to
prefer....first class walking or third class riding in an Argo!

The enormous advantage of the Argo is that it does replace the
horse. Yes, I know that there is no more attractive sight in stalking than

to see the stag loaded onto the pony ready to head for the lodge, but maintaining a pony is a very different proposition from maintaining an Argo. In addition to that, a pony eats for 52 weeks a year and can suffer from illnesses or even die!

So although we all miss the link with tradition that the pony provided, we have been forced to accept the more modern alternative. What a difference from the early days of motoring when the acquisition of a model T Ford made the Hill so much more accessible. The model T on the estate tracks was an enormous advance compared to the pony, or pony and trap, that had up until then been the only way to shorten the walk when stalking.

I wonder, however, if all these changes really are for the better as far as the Sassenach stalkers are concerned? Yet for the professional stalker or estate worker, these changes are essential. Far less energy has to be used in tramping to and from the sections of the Hill where stags are to be stalked and the long walk back would have been very tiring indeed, especially when soaked to the skin after a long day's stalking. Could there be such a thing as having it too easy for the Sassenach? I am not thinking about older stalkers who simply could not tackle those very long tiring walks, but younger men and women who are perfectly capable of doing it. What do you think?

Macrae and Dick were the biggest garage group in the Highlands with large premises at Inverness and when we had occasion to use their services we found them both efficient and helpful.

In 1958 after the difficulty of borrowing the Invergarry Hotel Land Rover we decided to hire one from Macrae and Dick for the duration of our stay. This proved to be an excellent idea: No longer were we dependent upon the Invergarry Hotel's Land Rover and we had the enormous benefit of a Land Rover to use anytime we wanted it. We certainly made good use of it and found it well worthwhile.

Robert Tapp's brand new ex-American Army Jeep at Braeroy,
Inverness-shire. Author on left, stalker Neil Campbell in gateway.

The Debenham family head for the Hill at Langwell, Ross-shire in the early 1920's.

Our first view of Alladale Lodge in 1960. At that time, it had been unoccupied since 1939.

Chapter Twenty Three
Benmore Lodge and Alladale

After the death of Sir Charles Ross when the huge Balnagown Estate was left to Sir Charles Ross' wife, Lady Ross, the decision was made to create a large sporting enterprise. Braelangwell Lodge was converted into a hotel and a housekeeper and staff was installed at Benmore Lodge. The Manageress was a Mrs Attwood.

In 1960 we drove to Scotland: Edna, our daughter Caroline and I and Edna's mother, to take the stalking at Benmore Lodge for the latter part of the season. The only other guests were a husband and wife who were stalking at the other Balnagown forests.

We were superbly looked after with excellent cuisine and the stalking was of the same standard. The stalker was an old-timer named Donald Fraser. A man of enormous experience and it was a great pleasure to be with him on the Hill.

The hill of Benmore itself was at the end of a long glen and the snag was that you had to walk the length of the glen before you could start stalking. Inevitably the walk back seemed even longer! We also had a pony and ponyman.

One of the most famous books on stalking by Charles St. John, *Natural History and Sport in Moray* gives his account of stalking " The Muckle Hart of Benmore" and there were still good stags and good stalking to be had on Benmore. So stalking at Benmore was very successful and we had a marvellous stay.

The whole sporting enterprise on the Balnagown Estate was run by a very competent manager named John Hunter. Deer, grouse, ptarmigan, salmon and trout were all under his competent control. We were offered the opportunity of a day's stalking at Alladale and were delighted to accept.

In those days Alladale Lodge had been unoccupied since 1939 and it stood at the top of its brae like a sullen sentinel, though it has now been transformed into a magnificent house with a super complex of new buildings and new stalker's house.

The two young chaps in charge of the stalking were Brian Gibson and his friend Jim. Both bright-eyed, bushy-tailed and brimming over with enthusiasm. Brian's love for Scotland was never to fade and he eventually married a local girl and bought a croft at Brora. Sadly the marriage failed and he remarried, but despite marriage and health problems Brian's optimistic outlook remains unchanged.

Speaking recently to someone who has known him for years I said that I knew him when he was bright-eyed and bushy-tailed. "He is still bright-eyed and bushy-tailed!" was the reply!

With Brian and Jim we got in the Land Rover, drove down the Alladale Brae, round onto the curiously named Stranookie Hill, then down into Glen Mor where we stopped at the foot of the hill just before Eisen-yarn Corrie. A steep climb through a remnant of the old Caledonian forest, a mixture of Scots Pine and Birch, then along the Middle Ridge at the top of the corrie to Strone-gun-aran.

First shot at the target at Alladale, with Brian Gibson and Jim.

In Sir Charles Ross' time a guest was stalking a stag on Strone-gun-aran and was just preparing to shoot when a shot rang out and the stag fell, fatally hit. The guest and stalker were, understandably, amazed. The unseen stalker was Sir Charles Ross himself, shooting from a long way below them! Not the kind of stalking etiquette that would meet with approval then or now.

So Brian got us in for a shot but, as often happens in stalking, a swirl of wind suddenly alerted the deer to our presence and they were instantly on their way. Just as they were going out of sight they stopped for a moment to look back. The stag was still in sight provided that you stood up to shoot. Much further out, of course, but still within range.

I was instantly on my feet with the Mannlicher at my shoulder. A quick shot and we got the stag.

So a memorable first visit to Alladale. Little did we know, at that time, how important Alladale, Deanich and "The Glen", Strathcarron, would eventually become to us. That year had been a great success and another new dimension in stalking experience.

First stag at Alladale on Strone-gun-aran, looking down into Glen Alladale to the foot of Carn Alladale.

Charles St. John, whose account of the pursuit of The Muckle Hart of Benmore is part of stalking history.

Chapter Twenty Four
The Muckle Hart of Benmore

Charles St. John was one of the early 19th century stalker/naturalist/authors and he will always be remembered by his epic account of the stalk of The Muckle Hart of Benmore. He was born in 1809, grandson of the second Viscount Bollingbroke. He was a keen naturalist as a schoolboy, always with a collection of pets from stag beetles to squirrels.

He started work as a clerk in the Treasury but work was not his forté, particularly in London, and his stammer, though not severe, was a handicap in London Society. After four or five years he gave up work for good and went to Rosehall in Sutherland in the early 1830's. He was lent a house named Rosehall on the Oykel where he settled down to enjoy shooting, fishing and observing wildlife.

It was there that he met and married Anne Gibson who was not only of independent means but, according to his friends:

"as the lady with the true wife's devotion accommodated herself to her husband's taste and manner of life. He was enabled henceforth to live the life of a sportsman and naturalist in the Highlands which was only modified when the necessity of educating a young family induced them to draw near schools".

Margaret Ross' son, Steven, is a fishing gillie on the Oykel and has built a house at Rosehall. I have told him to take a leaf out of Charles St. John's book and choose a wealthy wife as he did. After all, as the Spanish say, it is as easy to love a rich woman as a poor one! Some might say, even easier! On the other hand it is also said that a man who marries for money earns it!

St. John wrote several books, the best-known being *The Wild Sports and Natural History of the Scottish Highlands*, in which he describes his epic pursuit of The Muckle Hart of Benmore.

There are other Benmores (Big Mountain) in Scotland but this one is probably the best known, Benmore Assynt in Sutherland. It was then part of the vast area of land owned by Sir Charles Ross' forebears, the same Benmore Forest that we were to stalk in 1960.

St. John seems to have enjoyed free range over huge areas of country, including Benmore, without having to bother about payment. There had long been stories of a huge stag and one Sunday evening in October 1833 a shepherd with a shieling at the foot of Benmore reported to St John that he had "crossed in the Hill a track of a hart of extraordinary size which could only be "The muckle stag of Benmore". St. John wrote:

"This was an animal seldom seen but (one) which had long been the talk and marvel of shepherds for its wonderful size and cunning. They love the marvellous and in their report the muckle stag bore a charmed life; he was unapproachable and invulnerable. I had heard of him, too, and, having got the necessary information, resolved to try and break the charm, though it would cost me a day or two".

Benmore from the drive to Benmore Lodge.

Early next morning, armed with rifle and shotgun, he set out for Benmore accompanied by Donald, his retainer and deerhound, Bran. St. John carried the single barrel rifle, Donald carried the double shotgun.

The pursuit of the Muckle Hart was to take six days but on the first day they saw no sign of it, ending up at the shepherd's shieling at the foot of Benmore, where they spent the night.

For the next two days they pursued the big stag, but never managed to get close enough for a shot. Nights were spent in a rock crevice with heather for a bed.

Benmore, head in the clouds, from the loch in front of the Lodge.

Still no luck on Thursday morning and by the evening the pouring rain made the prospect of another night in the open none too attractive. Suddenly, above the roar of a burn and the sound of the wind and rain, they heard what sounded like "the shrill treble of a fiddle."

Donald jumped for joy: "It's all right enough, sir; just follow the sound; it's that drunken deevil Sandy Ross; ye'll nae haud a fiddle frae him, nor him frae a whisky still". It was, indeed, the sound of Sandy's fiddle coming from a remote bothy, the den of illicit whiskey distillers.

At the foot of Benmore.

In the welcome warmth of the bothy the two were made welcome and the whiskey flowed freely. Too freely for Donald because by next morning he was incapable of continuing. St. John left him with the shotgun and Bran, the deerhound, to continue the search alone.

Another blank day until the mist came down, forcing him to make downhill but, again, he came across the footprints of the huge stag. A frugal supper, dining on a brace of grouse he had been fortunate enough to kill with a single shot from his rifle, then another night in the open on a bed of heather, taking what shelter he could between the rocks.

Dawn at last to follow the track of the Muckle Hart until the landscape opened up a wide landscape to spy. He soon located the stag and was able to calculate a wide detour to make his approach.

He made his final approach by crawling along the bed of a burn until he was within one hundred and fifty yards. Deciding to take the shot from there he crouched out of sight to put a new cap on the rifle nipple. When he looked up again, the stag was gone!

Scouring the landscape it was a great relief to see the horns of the stag again, walking away but still within fifty yards of the burn. Inching along the burn again he got within easy shot of the stag but the beast was lying down, facing the burn.

With cocked rifle at the ready St. John kicked a stone into the burn and at the sound of the splash the big stag was instantly on his feet but facing head on, presenting a poor target.

St. John aimed at the neck and fired and although the stag was hit, he was not killed and the stag made off uphill.... always a bad sign. The stag, however, was unable to continue uphill and turned back to the burn, tumbling into it, apparently dead.

Putting his rifle down, St. John took out his knife and approached the beast to bleed it. Seizing the deer's horns St. John had a tremendous shock when the stag reared up and hurled him to one side.

The stag was between St. John and his rifle, facing him like an angry bull, but St. John managed to get past and reached his rifle. Attempting to reload he found that the lead balls were for his shotgun and too large for the rifle bore. Nothing for it but to scrape one down to size on a rock. This finally accomplished and he was finally able to administer the *coup de grace*.

So the Muckle Hart of Benmore has gone down in stalking history as the most famous stag ever shot in Scotland. Surprisingly, however, St. John never recorded any information about it in his books. Its antlers were not, in any way, exceptional as it was only a nine pointer of no great length or thickness. Its weight, however, was a quite remarkable thirty stone.... amazing for a Hill stag. As it was shot in October its weight must have been considerably more before the onset of the rut.

In 1849 St. John had published A *Tour in Sutherland* describing his travels observing the wildlife of Sutherland.

In 1854, when only forty three, he suffered a severe stroke and two years later he was dead, but he achieved immortality with The Muckle Hart of Benmore.

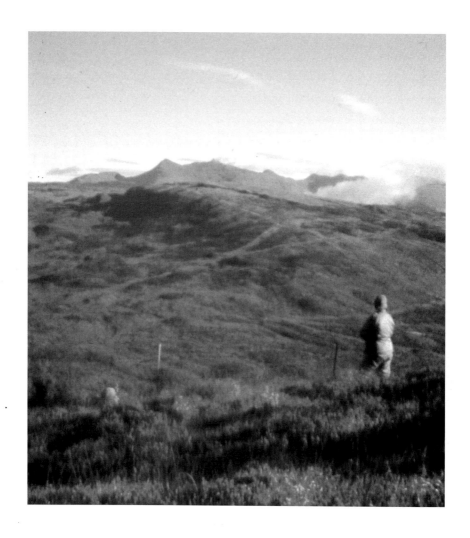

Looking back from the foot of Benmore.

That long walk back to the Lodge.

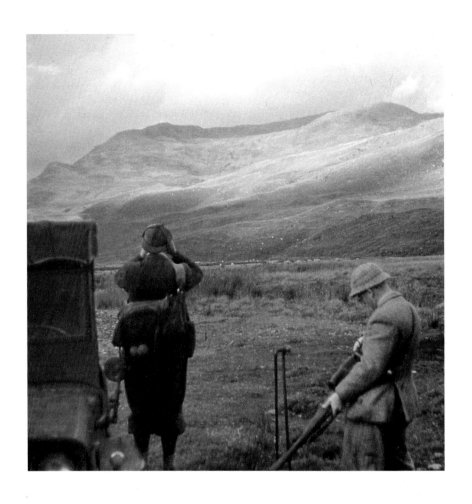

We spy from the Ex WD Jeep.

Chapter Twenty Five
The Braeroy Experience

In 1961, the Miss Mackintoshs at their Country House Hotel near Loch Awe in Argyll offered accommodation and stalking, so that was the choice and this time our small daughter, Caroline, aged two came with us together with Edna's mother.

New country for us again and delightful country, too. This hotel was very good indeed and the Miss Mackintoshs made an excellent job of running it, with imaginative cuisine. For example, there were "Devils on Horseback"; prunes surrounded with a curl of bacon - new to us and absolutely delicious.

There were very few deer on their stalking ground but we had a very pleasant stalker and enjoyed some exhilarating walks. If stalking was looking hopeless we would explore the surrounding countryside. I managed to get two or three stags and we had a very relaxing family holiday.

It was that year we commenced stalking at Braeroy, staying at the Letterfinlay Lodge Hotel for the first year and the Glenspean Lodge Hotel, Roy Bridge for the following two years.

To approach Braeroy Lodge from Roy Bridge you drive along a steep valley along which run the Parallel Roads of Glen Roy. The kings of Scotland were reputed to have driven along these roads to hunt deer at Braeroy.

The "Roads" are, indeed, parallel, running ruler straight along the hillside at different levels. In the ice age the foot of the glen was sealed by a glacier and a "road" would be formed by erosion of the water at the shore line. Centuries later the water level would drop due to melting of the glacier so another "road" would be formed. The process would be repeated as the glacier continued to melt.

Braeroy Lodge stands at the foot of two glens, overshadowed by towering hills. When we first went there it was jointly owned by

G. Y. Mackie, D.S.O. D.F.C. and Major Crighton Stewart, chairman of the Red Deer Commission. The forest was about 20,000 acres in extent marching with Culachy on the west side. It extended onto the lower slopes of Craig Megidh on the south side. Doctor Tom Patey, an experienced and highly regarded climber, was tragically killed in a fall when climbing Craig Megidh alone on a winter's day.

Craig a Chail "The best hill in Scotland" with Edna in foreground.

Braeroy was a superlative forest which, in the opinion of many experts, could be one of the best forests in Inverness-shire, given careful management.

Our stalker during the first year was George Grey. We had an excellent ponyman, Alec Morrison, two ponies, Sooty and Fly and an ex American Army Jeep which chugged along happily on three cylinders. Sooty and Fly had been on the forest all their lives and we pronounced them the funniest ponies in Scotland. Sooty would eat everything from venison sandwiches to plastic bags, if you would let him!

George was a good stalker but at the start he could not seem to find his form and for a day or two we did not manage to get in for a shot, despite no shortage of deer. Once he settled in, however, we never looked back and we soon had a day with four stags which included a right and a left and a running stag, so what could be better than that? From thence on we continued our success, ending the season with right and lefts on the last two days.

So at Braeroy we had really struck oil and looked forward to coming back the next year.

In 1962 the forest had changed hands and had been bought by Mrs and Mrs Robert Tapp, formerly fruit farmers from Kent. They were to stay there for many years until selling up in the 1990's. They were a charming couple with two small boys.

We also had a new stalker, Neil Campbell, who was not merely good but absolutely superlative: A truly inspired stalker and a joy to be with him on the Hill.

We would start the day by getting an early stag, if that was possible, and then we would declare "Now we can relax and start shooting", and this we did, with remarkable success.

Before we went to Scotland Edna would have been adamant that you could not shoot running stags consistently with a rifle but those years at Braeroy were to prove her wrong.

Neil Campbell and I evolved our own technique: By brilliant, careful stalking he would get us in for a shot at about seventy yards. Any closer was no good as the deer would so easily sense you. The first shot would account for the first stag. If they ran on and then stopped, so much the better. If not, I would shoot the next stag running. So to shoot two or three stags would usually be achieved. Four at times and on one memorable occasion I shot six!

We started off the holiday in splendid style with two stags on the first day. A day or two later we stalked a group of four shootable stags but could only get in to about 200 yards at the foot of a hill. The first shot got the first stag, then the other three beasts, confused as the sound of the shot echoed back behind them, ran directly towards us. All were accounted for with the next three cartridges. From then on, most stags were shot as right and lefts.

If we were into a position for a shot at a stag lying down we never waited for him to get up but shot him as he was. Conventional wisdom decrees a neck shot in those cases but this was not, by any means, always the case: It was a question of carefully considering the best position to place the bullet.

On the last day we decided on Craig a Chail "The best hill in Scotland", ending the day in splendid style with six stags which included two right and lefts.

I spy with my little eye.

So at what range was it possible to shoot a running stag? In my opinion about 120 yards, 130 at most. Beyond that distance I found the forward allowance impossible to judge for a running beast. So to shoot more than one stag without moving position had to be done before the stag groups dispersed at the onset of the rut. From then on when the stag was rounding up his hinds you could only get a shot at a single stag.

Bearing in mind that limitation it was, you will agree, remarkable that during my years at Braeroy over half the stags were shot as right and lefts, most of them running. No running stag fired at on Braeroy was ever lost wounded.

We would have a successful day, two or three stags, then on the way back Neil would stop and level his telescope at a distant stag. "I'm sure we would get in for a shot at that stag." he would say. "Too late," I would reply "time to head for home".

Will that stag on the skyline do?

On one occasion we were on the Culachy march, Lea MacNally ground. A good stag was just over the march "We can't shoot that stag." I said "He's not on our ground". "Just try your rifle sight against him and see how he looks." said Neil. But, no, I did not attempt to shoot that stag!

We were back again in 1963 with great expectations and we were not to be disappointed. Neil Campbell was in even more brilliant form, if that was possible and we now had the use of a brand new ex-American Army Jeep. So the mixture was as before, with rights and lefts predominating. Two, three and even four stags would be shot in a day and on one never-to-be-forgotten day I managed a triple right and left. We always fully loaded the Mannlicher's 5 shot magazine plus one cartridge in the breech.

So there we were, finally settled into a superlative forest with an incomparable stalker. We were set fair, so what could possibly go wrong? Well, life being what it is, something did!

Near the Lodge was an old keeper's house in poor condition having been empty for years. In 1964, a Mr Roadnight, having heard about the excellent stalking at Braeroy, approached Mr and Mrs Tapp and said that if he could have a ten year lease on the Braeroy stalking he would restore the keeper's house at his own expense, which would then revert to the Tapps at the end of ten years.

This was an offer they could not refuse.

When I heard about this I wrote to Roadnight and said that I had stalked successfully at Braeroy for some years and would it be possible to find me some stalking? I received a one line reply, signed by someone else in Roadnight's absence. The answer was "No"!

So that was the end of our stalking at Braeroy.

Kenny Kennedy owned a strip of stalking ground adjoining Braeroy at the Roy Bridge side. He was a superlative stalker and, by all accounts, a marvellous man. His father, long since retired, had been the Braeroy stalker for many years. I had the pleasure of meeting them both and found it an informative experience.

Kenny Kennedy was eventually to sell his strip of land to the Tapps and become a monk. Another of the amazing characters we met in Scotland.

Years later we were to obtain a day or two's stalking on Braeroy so that my son Ross could experience stalking on that unique forest. Ross did the shooting, Edna and I were the afterpiece's assistants.

By then the stalker was Gordon Addison, a friend of Lea MacNally and it was a great pleasure to meet him. There was, however, a tragic sequel.

One of his children was kicked by a horse on Braeroy and killed. At a later date Gordon was repairing the estate JCB when he needed it moving. He was underneath it and got his wife, who was completely inexperienced, to work the levers to move the machine. Something went wrong, the machine fell on Gordon and killed him. So Braeroy brought nothing but tragedy to the Addison family.

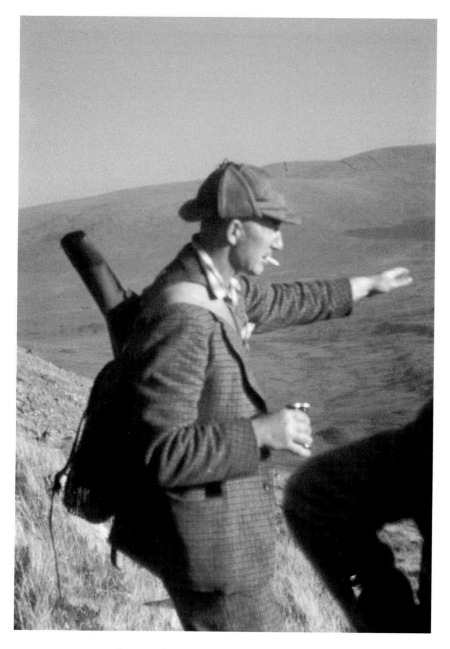

George Grey points out the next move.

The intrepid Marchioness of Breadalbane with her Head Stalker, Peter Grant.

Chapter Twenty Six
Drum Hill and the Marchioness of Breadalbane

The following year we went to Aberfeldy where J. Douglas M. MacGregor offered accommodation and stalking in nearby Drum Hill. Drum Hill was a real forest complete with trees whereas most Highland deer forests have little or no trees! They may well have been tree covered a thousand years ago before the destruction of The Old Caledonian Forest, the native woodlands that were predominantly a mixture of Scots Pine and Birch.

Drum Hill had once been an enclosed deer forest belonging to the Breadalbanes and was a small part of their huge estates. In the late nineteenth century the Breadalbanes were one of the largest landowners in Scotland with estates amounting to almost half a million acres. I believe I am right in saying that now it has all gone and in the 1980's the Marquis of Breadalbane was convicted of stealing groceries out of a woman's shopping basket in Earls Court, London.

The Marquis of Breadalbane's family name was Campbell, a name infamous in Scottish history for the connection with the massacre of Glencoe.

In the late 19th century the Marchioness of Breadalbane was famous as Scotland's leading lady stalker, writing a book about her experiences: *The High Tops of Black Mount*. Many years later, at Ardgay, Sutherland I was to meet Adam Henderson who had been the head stalker at Black Mount. He had been given *The High Tops of Black Mount* by the then owners. His copy was immensely interesting, containing numerous pencil notes by the family.

"Have you read it?" I asked. "I have read it *twice*" said Adam proudly.

The Marchioness of Breadalbane fully merits the description "remarkable". She was the former Alma Graham, one of the daughters of the fourth Duke of Montrose and endured the handicap of a fearsome squint. Despite this, however, she must have had charm because in 1872 she married Gavin, the seventh Earl of Breadalbane, for whom the marquessate was reinstated in 1885.

Her "fatal attraction" was horses! Not to ride, train, or eat, but to back! She was a prolific punter, thinking nothing of betting thousands on a horse and, like so many punters before and since, nearly always losing.

It is strange how gambling snares some people irretrievably. A Las Vegas casino owner was once asked if the punter could ever really win. "Well," he replied, "let's put it this way: When the lamb goes to slaughter the lamb might kill the butcher, but we always bet on the butcher!"

Although destined never to have children of her own the Marchioness was a kindly person who took a great interest in the tenants and their families on the Breadalbane estate, many of whom only spoke Gaelic. Unusually for an aristocrat in those times, she took the trouble to learn Gaelic so that she could speak to them in their own language.

It was most unusual for women to shoot in those days but she was determined to master it.

There is a photograph of her in her book wearing her long, heavy, tweed skirt, masquerading as a bell tent! It must have made stalking even harder when trudging through long, wet heather.

She also writes of the uplifting spirituality of climbing to the High Tops in terms that we would consider too sugary sentimental today but, yes, we know and understand what she felt.

The head stalker was Peter Grant and in her book she describes calling in at his modest home at the end of a hard day's stalking:

"What a bright welcome met us there! The cheerful, homely kitchen, furnished with a row of happy-looking little girls, standing large-eyed, like a flight of steps in age, and Johnnie, the one laddie, showing signs already of becoming a strong and active man for any kind of hill work. In the parlour was spread such a tea as only Clais-gobhair could produce - the home-made scones, butter and jam, milk which stood all cream in the jug, and Mrs Grant flitting around in her gentle care of every want. I am ashamed to say I drank seven cups of tea."

Then as now, sliding down a steep descent. It couldn't have been very practical for the Marchioness. Doesn't the Rifle's expression remind you of one of the Teletubbies?

So how did the Marchioness describe the appeal of toiling up the Black Mount hills in clothing that was far from suitable, to get within rifle shot of a stag? These were her words:

"The real enjoyment and pleasure consist in the close intercourse with nature - the solitude, the apartness, the constant variation of light and shade, the mystic vagaries of the fleecy clouds, the grandeur of the passing storms, the tender sadness of the setting sun leaving his last rosy kiss on the brows of the peaks and the quiet peace of the evening as we turn towards home."

Well, surely we can all agree with that!

She went on to say that it was often a battle to reach; "The utmost purple rim of the forest's high hills ..... can anything be more delicious than the sense of accomplished will? All trifling cares and troubles left far below, life seems altogether on a higher, nobler plateau; and the almost awe-striking realisation of the immensity of nature among the eternal hills fills the mind with solemn rest."

Again we can go along with all this, though the final sentence does go right over the top: "Here in these grand surroundings we may consciously feel God walks with Man."

Surely not when Man, or Woman, is carrying a stalking rifle!

But despite her cumbersome clothes she walked and stalked indomitably. She was so hardy that other than a short jacket and doughnut hat she disdained to use a waterproof or cape, merely relying on a woollen jersey carried in her stalker's pocket.

Although she waxes lyrical about the joys of the Hill and the magnificent surroundings she does not tell us of the final approach to getting into position for a shot. Like the rest of us she must have faced many a soaking, heart-bursting crawl along a peat drain or burn, but she never tells us about it.

She does, however, give a brief account of the climax of a deer drive on Aonach-mor on September 30th, 1897 when, accompanied by her stalker McInnes, she shot six stags with six cartridges. A remarkable stalking achievement that few people can ever have attained but she only devotes a few lines to it. She describes the increasing excitement as they watched the deer move up towards them but even then the shooting is only briefly described:

"Slowly I raise the rifle and cover him as he steps along. He stops a moment to look back at his neighbours and gets the shot in the right place. He is quickly followed by a fine ten-pointer a few yards further back. Two barrels have now accounted for two stags, and the rifle is quickly reloaded."

She writes of her introduction to the .450 Black Powder Express Rifle in the 1880's:

"A rifle was taken at haphazard from the gunroom ... in those days I had eyes to see through a stone wall, and fortunately a pair of arms long enough to get over most of the other difficulties. That rifle did not hide its light under a bushel... it bumped me on the nose, and kicked me in the shoulder till I was black and blue, and four or five shots at the target sent me home with a headache for the rest of the day. Its report was like a peal of thunder".

Towards the end of the 1880's the armies of the world were

moving over to the new magazine rifles with much smaller bores and cordite replacing the old Black Powder propellant. The British .303, the German .275 (7mm) Mauser and the Austrian Mannlicher of .256 (6.5mm) were ideal for deerstalking and the day of black powder was over after many centuries.

It was not until 1900, however, that the Marchioness bought a .303 double rifle by Purdey which transformed her shooting. She considered it to be: "For lightness, quickness in handling, and noiseless report, unsurpassed".

From then on the disadvantages of practising at the target were over: "For there is no recoil and no concussion to give headaches."

Douglas MacGregor's father had been a very successful game dealer at Aberfeldy when bags of over 500 blue hares were achieved in a day, not to mention grouse, salmon and deer. At that time Douglas was continuing the family business but I understand that it was eventually wound up.

The MacGregors lived in a Victorian house on the outskirts of Aberfeldy which they ran as a guest house and Douglas leased the Drum Hill stalking from the Forestry Commission.

The objective was the elimination of all deer from Drum Hill as the area had been fenced and re-planted with trees, but to wander through the thick woodland expecting a shot was a pretty hopeless task.

To successfully shoot deer there they would have to be driven so I never did get a stag on Drum Hill.

Douglas, however, was a marvellous companion. He had stalked all over the place and knew every forest and grouse moor for many miles around. A delight, therefore, to chat to Douglas and his friend Alec MacLarty, an agricultural contractor and keen stalker who lived nearby. There was much to learn from both of them.

Alec took us for a day out on the high tops in his Snow-track, a vehicle with rubber tracks and an enclosed cabin. It had huge racks back and front to carry deer or anything else. What luxury! I remember stopping for lunch at the top of a high ridge in the teeth of the wind. We took out our Thermos flasks, snug and cosy in the heated cabin. He let me drive this marvellous machine part of the way and I found it a delight. It was powered by a Volkswagen engine.

We were not stalking, only observing, but it was amazing to see a flock of Golden Plover trotting along in front totally undisturbed.

So we were to enjoy an excellent holiday but were not getting any stags, so what to do? Why not get in touch with one of the greatest of all Highland estates to see if a day's stalking could be obtained?

The estate was Invercauld in Aberdeenshire. Invercauld had been in the hands of the Farquharson family for centuries and the abortive 1715 Rebellion, thirty years before the 1745, had been planned there under the pretence of a deer hunt.

Invercauld marches with Balmoral and was owned by Captain Farquharson. His wife was an American. Douglas got in touch with the factor at Invercauld, a Mr Petrie, and stalking was available so we headed for Invercauld with great expectations - we were not to be disappointed. Grouse shooting is also excellent at Invercauld and American guests were a very important feature. Americans, I am told, are none too keen on walking so Invercauld had made a network of roads to keep walking to a minimum.

The stalker was Donald MacDonald, brother of Sandy MacDonald from the Glenshee Hotel and, once again, a Highland stalker *par excellence*. We had a gillie with us and a pony. Our first stalk brought us in sight of a group of about seventy stags: a sight that would be hard to match in any other forest in Scotland. There were some splendid animals: Good ten and eleven pointers, Royals, Imperials, the lot!

Donald studied them carefully with his telescope and finally said "There are three shootable stags there". In any other forest they would have said thirty three! So the stag selected was pointed out and shot - a fine eleven pointer "going back" i.e. he had previously been a Royal or Imperial but with increasing age he was producing less points.

My next stag of the day was in a small herd containing two or three shootable stags. I fired at the first stag and got it and as the other stags ran off I swung onto the second stag and fired. With my experience of shooting running stags at Braeroy I was completely confident. But my last shot at a running stag had been some years before and to my amazement I clean missed that stag. Donald was dumbfounded: Sassenachs just did not shoot at running stags and it was completely out of his experience. If I had made a clean kill, I would, no doubt, have been in order but to attempt the shot and miss was just too much. I was firmly told not to shoot at another running stag.

But the following days at Invercauld were quite incredible: An experience of a stalking lifetime. I did not blot my copybook again and as that was the only stag I missed I was forgiven! I would shoot two or three stags in a day.

One day another Rifle joined us to stalk on another beat at Invercauld. He was introduced as Captain Phillips and his rifle was a .240 Holland and Holland. This was the only time I saw one whilst stalking. Superbly made rifles very highly regarded by any Highland stalkers who had encountered them. The .240 calibre (6mm) bullet travelled at a tremendous speed at the time of its introduction in the mid 1920's and was not to be surpassed until the introduction of the newer 6mm cartridges such as the .243 over a quarter of a century later.

He told me he had not stalked for some time and whispered to me "How much do you tip these chaps?" I was delighted to be able to tell him!

On this beautifully maintained estate there were quite a lot of original Scots Pine surviving from the ancient Caledonian Forest. Many of them were superb specimens. The Estate had fenced off an area of about 200 acres to allow natural regeneration undisturbed by grazing deer. The whole area was at that time carpeted with self- seeded small trees, two or three feet high, so the experiment had been completely successful.

(Top) Although not designed for deerstalking, these 16 bore muzzle-loading rifles were the choice in the early nineteenth century. This example was made by the great Joseph Manton.

(Middle) An interim design, the capping breech loader. External percussion cap as in muzzle loaders, but the barrel slid forward to take a paper cartridge containing powder and ball. This rifle made by William Barratt and Son of Edinburgh.

(Bottom) The predecessor of the breech loading Black Powder Expresses. DB Muzzle loader by Williams and Powell, 40 bore (.500 calibre) with a large charge of black powder and slow rifling spiral to give a much higher velocity than the old 16 bores.

Chapter Twenty Seven
Black Powder and Onwards

In the early days of stalking, muzzle loading rifles of about sixteen bore firing a round ball were the weapons used. They were accurate enough at known ranges and, say, up to 100/150 yards. The necessarily curved trajectory, however, and the difficulty of accurately estimating distances on the vast Highland landscape made one shot kills the exception rather than the rule. Remember, too, that their striking power was very much less than the later Black Powder Expresses, let alone the cordite rifles that replaced the Expresses.

Deer hounds were essential for the stalking party to run down and bring to bay any wounded stag.

The advent of the breech-loading Black Powder Express rifles from the early 1860's soon revolutionised stalking. Make no mistake about it, these rifles shot very well indeed and the trajectory was much flatter than with the earlier muzzle loaders. In competent hands the Expresses were perfectly efficient.

Nowadays we think of Black Powder Expresses as breech loaders but the term "Express Train Rifles" was used by Purdey in 1856 to describe a new breed of muzzle loading rifles he had introduced in the early 1850's. They were 40 bore (.500 calibre) with a large charge of black powder and a slow rifling spiral to give a much higher velocity than the old 16 bores. They were soon to develop into breech loaders with their bottle-shaped cartridges, i.e. the Black Powder Expresses we recognise today.

An interim design between the muzzle loaders and the Expresses was the capping breech loader. In this case the rifles were, in effect, muzzle loaders with a percussion cap, but the barrel slid forward to load and a paper cartridge complete with lead bullet was put into the breech. The bullet would still have been a round ball and once the cartridge was loaded, the barrel was slid back and locked into position by a half turn of a bolt in front of the trigger guard. The cartridge did not contain a percussion cap and the charge was fired by a percussion cap placed on a nipple exactly as in a normal muzzle loader. Although it shot with the same characteristics as the muzzle loaders it was quicker to load.

After the capping breech loaders the next step forward was the advent of true breech loaders with pinfire cartridges. In this case a modern cartridge was fired by a pin sticking up vertically at the breech. The hammer struck directly down onto the pin to fire the percussion cap in the cartridge. The first breech loading Expresses were pinfire. The breech end of the barrel was slotted to accept the pin.

For stalking rifles the pinfire era only lasted a few years when it was finally superseded by modern centre fire cartridges and the Black Power Expresses really came into their own.

Many of these rifles were beautifully made by leading makers such as Purdey and Holland & Holland. Daniel Fraser of Edinburgh was one of the greatest Scottish gunsmiths and his Expresses had their lock internals gold plated to resist corrosion if water penetrated. No shortage of that on the Hill! The Black Powder Expresses were the limit of power and accuracy in sporting rifles before cordite.

The breech loading Black Powder Express rifles arrive. This is a .500 by Dickson of Edinburgh.

In the 1880's single shot military rifles were being replaced by magazine rifles with the new smokeless powders such as cordite. The new propellant made black powder obsolete at last and introduced the new small bores such as the British .303 or the Continental 6.5mm and 7mm's. These new rifles achieved much higher velocities so they shot with much flatter trajectories.

So now the limit for deerstalking was the human eye. The old rule was that if you can distinguish the stag's eye he is within 100 yards. Distinguish his ear and he is within 150 yards. Unable to distinguish his ear, then he is 200 yards out or more. But, like all generalisations this cannot be completely accurate due to the vast variation of light conditions in the Highlands.

So the development of the stalking rifle over about three quarters of a century showed the way design would go with even smaller bores and flatter trajectories such as the .240 (6mm) Holland & Holland of 1926. Though it was to take another quarter of a century before 6mm cartridges were to come into their own.

Up until the 1950's telescopic sights were unusual for deerstalking in the Highlands and it was not until later that they began to take over as did the new .243 (6mm) cartridge.

The .303 had a velocity of 2,200 feet per second, amazing for that time, but the .243 was almost twice as fast propelling the 100 grain bullet at about 3,500 feet per second, consequently having a much flatter trajectory.

Some of the younger Scottish stalkers are even improving on that: .308 military cartridges necked down to .22 and carefully hand-loaded can achieve velocities of up to 4,000 feet per second with hair-splitting accuracy.

When Lea MacNally eventually went over to a telescopic sight he chose a two and half power, reasoning that the far better sight picture was all that was necessary and a huge magnification was not required. In his case this was perfectly true because in his first season he shot eighty one hinds with eighty three cartridges.

The normal magnification today used by most stalkers on their .243 or 7mm rifles is 4X, but telescopic sights are being used by some fanatical enthusiasts with a power of 20X or more. With such sights and rifles of fantastically high velocity they will soon be able to fire at a stag from Sutherland and hit it in Caithness.

(Top) For the man who has everything. A cased S.B .500 falling block Express rifle complete with every conceivable extra made by Alexander Henry of Edinburgh for J.C.L. Kay of the 15th King's Hussars.
(Middle) D.B .400 Black Powder Express by Holland and Holland.
(Bottom) D.B .300 Black Powder Rook and Rabbit rifle by Holland and Holland.

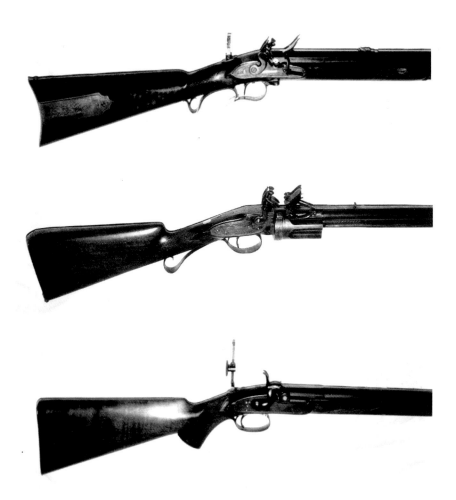

(Top) A Baker style military rifle made by John Manton for Lieutenant Allan McNab of the Queen's American Rangers and used in the American War of Independence. I wonder if he ever had a shot at a stag with it?

(Middle) Multiple fire arrives! Collier's patent revolving flintlock, though the practical application was still three-quarters of a century ahead.

(Bottom) .451 Gibbs of Bristol target rifle. The ultimate in muzzle-loading long range accuracy, still fired in competition at a thousand yards 150 years later.

Ardtornish House, Morvern, Argyll.

Chapter Twenty Eight
Ardtornish

In 1966 we stalked at Ardtornish on the Morvern Peninsular in Argyll on the west coast of Scotland. Morvern had not escaped bloody clan feuds in its long history, but worse was to happen in 1746 in the aftermath of the '45. Two government ships, one ominously named "Terror", anchored at Loch Aline and the sailors together with soldiers of the Royal Scots Fusiliers landed with orders "to burn the houses and destroy the effects of all such as were out in the rebellion."

The captain of the second ship reported that "near 400 houses amongst which were several barns filled with corn, horses, cows, meal and other provisions were destroy'd by fire and firearms."

In addition to this, fifteen crofting townships along the coast received the same treatment.

Robert Louis Stevenson had seen the Morvern coast when, as a teenager, he had accompanied his father on a inspection tour of the western lighthouses. Evictions were still continuing at that time as thirty families were being evicted on the orders of Ardtornish's new owner.

In *Kidnapped*, he wrote "and there began to come to our ears a great sound of mourning, the people on board and those on shore crying and lamenting to one another so as to pierce the heart." Many more people were destined to leave the port of Loch Aline for America, evicted from their homes.

The notorious Patrick Sellar, factor to the Marquess of Stafford, who cleared Strathnaver and Strath Helmsdale, Sutherland of its crofters with ruthless efficiency, bought the Acharn Estate in Morvern, evicted over two hundred people and stocked it with sheep. Six years later, he bought the nearby Ardtornish Estate, having first instructed the existing owner to clear out all the people before completion of the purchase.

In the early nineteenth century at the start of the deerstalking era, the dreadful events of 1746 were only a distant memory, almost impossible to imagine. The world had moved on and Loch Aline had become a place of leisure and pleasure for the moneyed inhabitants of Ardtornish House and their equally affluent guests. This leisured existence would continue unchanged until that dreadful date with destiny in 1914 changed everything.

Before the arrival of the railways, a journey from the south by road would have been long, inconvenient and uncomfortable so the little port of Loch Aline really came into its own for Ardtornish House guests. Some of them fully experienced with rod, rifle and gun in Scotland together with newcomers looking forward to fishing for salmon and trout after the Hampshire chalk streams, shoot grouse after Southern pheasants and of course, experience the achievement of getting their first stag.

A paddle steamer from the 1860's on the Caledonian Canal.

The lovely side-wheel paddle steamers would arrive from Greenock to disembark their passengers together with all their impedimenta: Trunks, valises, hatboxes, fishing rods, cased guns and rifles, everything necessary for a fishing, grouse shooting and stalking holiday. Excited children with their governesses, husbands and wives and young men new to the Highlands. The pier-master's house and ticket master's office were transformed into a hive of activity. A piper in Highland dress from Ardtornish House would be waiting to greet the guests together with horse-drawn gigs and carts to transport the guests and their luggage. So from the start of stalking through to 1914 this privileged life would continue unchanged.

By the mid-nineteenth century, Morvern had passed into Sassenach hands. But did Patrick Sellar or the Abel-Smiths build Ardtornish House? I don't know, but as Mr Sellar's name appeared below all the bells, it would appear to have been Patrick Sellar.

Ardtornish House was built in the early part of the 19th century as a huge shooting lodge, an incredible structure in yellow stone.

You drove into the enclosed courtyard which, as far as I remember, never saw the sun. Cars parked there overnight could be the very devil to start at the end of the season in cold and damp conditions, so we were told, but we were fortunate and had no trouble.

Ardtornish belonged to the Abel Smiths, a family long famous for its success in the City of London and has remained in their hands for many years. We made all the arrangements through Mrs Faith Raven who was, presumably, an Abel Smith before marriage.

The ground floor was huge and contained many rooms, all unused. All sorts of things were stored in those rooms - a boat in one of them! One room was "The Music Room" beautifully panelled in pine with carvings of musical instruments. Another room was the library containing all the fishing and stalking classics: *The High Tops of Black Mount* by the Marchioness of Breadalbane. *The Art of Deer-Stalking* by William Scrope. *Deer-Stalking in the Highlands of Scotland* by Lt-General Henry Hope Crealock. *The Moor and the Loch* by John Colquhoun and many others were all there. They were worth a lot of money then, goodness knows what they would be worth today .... if they have survived! There was also a ballroom on the ground floor.

The House had no less than three separate electric supplies: 110 volt DC from an ancient Hydro Electric system, 240 volts AC from a diesel generator and 240 volts mains AC. All were in use when we were there.

A panel of bells manually operated by wires was next to the original kitchens. Each bell had a hand painted slogan by it so that the servants could see which room was ringing the bell.

The bells had many labels including "Mr Sellar's Study", "Mrs Sellar's Flower Room" and many more. On one occasion in the middle of the night during our stay, one of the bells rang. Could it have been operated by Mr Sellar's ghostly hand? No-one volunteered to descend into the dark stairwell to investigate!

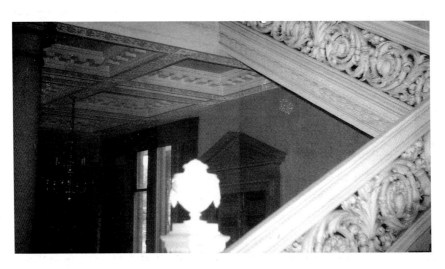

The ornate staircase at Ardtornish House.

The second floor was reserved for the Raven family so we occupied the third floor. In addition to the stairs there was a lift: A true hydraulic lift as it was operated by water power, not electricity. When you looked down from the ground floor into the lift well there were all sorts of hisses and gurgles caused by leaking water due to lack of maintenance. The lift was not considered safe for people by then, but was a great help for hoisting luggage up and down.

You entered the third floor into a huge high gallery around the central stairwell. The walls were lined with portraits of the Abel Smiths going back to the 1840's. The living room overlooked Loch Aline and the view was magnificent. In the evenings the setting sun turned the surface of the loch into molten gold. It was a huge room and I once asked everyone to close their eyes, visualise the room and say how many tables were in it. No one guessed a large enough number but there were no less than seven. The room, however, was so large the tables were lost in it.

There was a large kitchen, plenty of bedrooms and two bathrooms on that floor. The bathrooms were half lined in marble. There was also a nursery complete with a huge brass cot.

As it was October we asked the factor if we could have the ancient central heating on. It was a huge coke fired furnace. He agreed provided that we paid for the coke. "How much does it use?" we asked. "About a ton a week." he replied!

As the forest came down to sea level, the deer fared far better than those on a normal forest and there were some huge stags. 15 stone would be considered big on most forests but on one occasion I looked at a 17 stone stag in the larder hanging next to a 19 stone beast. The 17 stone stag was dwarfed by the 19 stone monster.

Fishing catches were recorded in the game books from 1853 and in the early days were mostly trout. Salmon catches did increase and thirty were caught in 1863 going up to fifty two in 1864.

There was another stalking party at the same time as us. They occupied a house on the estate and were completely self contained. They used an Allen garden tractor to haul the stags to the nearest track or road. The first time we had seen an Allen garden tractor used in stalking and were never to see one again. On many forests, of course, the rough terrain would have defeated it. We would share out the stalking beats with them as there was plenty of room for both of us.

Ardtornish was another forest blessed with a network of private roads. In the 1920's a fleet of about a half a dozen Austin Sevens were purchased to enable the guests to tootle round the estate. The garages had survived but not the cars!

We had two splendid ponies at our disposal and after the day's stalking the ponies would be unsaddled and allowed to run home on their own. After a few days when we had been stalking successfully our stalker, Jim Thornber, suggested that after dinner we could go out to try for another stag. They come down off the Hill towards dusk so you could cut them off for an easy shot with very little walking. What a great idea, I thought, but after a couple of times I decided against it as it was not real stalking. On a poor forest with this method being the only way to get a stag, fine, but on a good forest it was not necessary.

As Ardtornish was right down to sea level on the west coast, warmed by the Gulf Stream, the gardens contained many flowering shrubs, some still in glorious flower in October.

There was an estate motor boat that took guests round the peninsular for a picnic during the summer or for stalking during the season. Sadly the boat had been laid up for the winter by the time we arrived so we were never able to have a boat trip.

The road along the north side of the sea loch was the one along which David Balfour walked with the blind fiddler in *Kidnapped* by Robert Louis Stevenson. Despite being unable to see he ominously carried a flintlock pistol in his pocket.

That was not the only literary association with Ardtornish: The estate was bought in 1845 by Octavius Smith, a London distiller. He was, I understand, the ancestor of the Abel Smiths.

Loch Aline. David Balfour and the blind fiddler in Kidnapped walked along the far shore.

The great Derby philosopher, Herbert Spencer, was a friend of Octavius Smith and was among the guests at Ardtornish.

Spencer was one of the great philosophers and thinkers of the nineteenth century with a formidable literary output. His importance in the evolution of English thought was as the philosopher of the great scientific movement of the second half of the nineteenth century. He was a firm believer in the progress that was leaping ahead in that era.

Spencer welcomed Darwin's "Origin of Species" in 1859 which inspired him to coin the phrase "The survival of the fittest", still not forgotten today.

He visited Ardtornish for the first time in 1856 and a fortnight after his arrival he sent a letter home dated August 16th. He enjoyed the whole Scottish scene and wrote: "Fishing, and rambling, and boating, and bathing form the staple occupations; varied, occasionally, with making artificial flies and mending fishing rods."

He was clearly a most welcome guest and was invited to extend his visit to six weeks. The carefree days continued with picnics, boating, sketching and catching trout and sea trout on the River Aline and Loch Arienas.

There was another famous literary association with Ardtornish when John Buchan, author of *The Thirty-Nine Steps*, stalked there in the 1920's, as you will see in the next chapter

So we had good stalking at Ardtornish in country that was entirely new to us: A memorable addition to our stalking experience.

Now that's how to handle a rifle. A Highland stalker demonstrates.

One of Lea MacNally's favourites. Photograph of a limited edition print by W. Forbes.

Chapter Twenty Nine
John MacNab

John Buchan was a successful author who later became the Governor General of Canada and in 1925 he published the famous novel based on deerstalking, *John MacNab.* John Buchan was a tremendous walker, good rifle shot, a keen stalker and an accomplished fisherman. Most years he would stalk at Ardtornish alternating with Glen Etive, so he was well qualified to write about stalking.

John MacNab is the story of three men living in London and bored with life. Lord Lamancha was a Cabinet Minister; Sir Edward Leithen a wealthy city Lawyer and John Palliser Yeats, a Banker.

To add a dash of excitement to their lives they evolved a plan: They would adopt the name of John MacNab and under this name would issue a challenge to the Highland landowners. They would write to the chosen owner and tell him that within a period of 24 hours on a given date they would poach a salmon and a stag from the estate but, as they were honest men, they would return the stag and salmon to the estate owners.

So the three characters had a marvellous time outwitting the owner's defences to achieve their objective. The Hill and the stalking are well described by the author who really did know what stalking was all about, and fishing, too. There is even a map of the fictitious forest which takes Ardtornish as its inspiration. This is almost certainly the case because the book is dedicated to Rosalind Maitland, sister of Gerard Craig Sellar, owner of Ardtornish where Buchan had so often been a guest. The very Gerard Craig Sellar whose ghostly hand had rung the bell in the night during our stay!

In the book the idea of John MacNab was inspired by a fictional character named Jim Tarras who had an estate somewhere in Moray and had shot big game in Africa as a young man. Jim Tarras was reputed to have written to estate owners saying that he would poach a stag and return the carcass to the owner: So was there a real life John MacNab? The answer is "Yes". The real-life character was Captain Jimmy Brander Dunbar, a well known poacher who had a small estate near Pitgavenie near Elgin. Jimmy Brander Dunbar, however, was not a romantic poacher who warned owners that he was going to poach on their land..... he just poached!

The story is told that when he was about ten years old Jimmy's father gave him and his brother Archie .410 shot guns and a box of cartridges. The boys, to decide the effective range of their new guns, fired alternatively at each others rear ends, only protected by their kilts.

This was done at decreasing ranges until they were knocked over by the impact of the pellets. Having then decided the effective range of their guns they set to work on feathered targets. Jimmy shot his father's pheasants in short time and sold them in the local town to finance the purchase of new cartridges.

Yes, I agree, its seems a peculiar and singularly ineffective way of establishing the range of a .410 shotgun but that's the legend so I simply pass it on unchanged!

Lovely, but deadly. The Scottish Wildcat.

Turning his father's pheasants into cash, without permission of course, gave him his introduction to poaching and after that start he shot on other peoples' land exactly as he pleased. That was fine for him but not the other way round! He hated the idea of anyone trespassing on his own ground.

Seeing a stranger fishing from a boat on his loch he fired at him with a .22 rifle and knocked the pipe out of the intruder's mouth, only to realise that it was a local solicitor to whom he had just let the fishing.

On his 3,000 acre estate he only employed illiterates to whom he paid minimum wages. He quarrelled with everyone and had a shocking reputation as a neighbour. He did get married to a lovely woman but she eventually left him taking their two daughters.

Over his front door was the skull of a German sniper whom he claimed to have killed in the First World War and in keeping with this grotesque greeting the interior of his house was said to be filthy. As a form of indoor sport with an air rifle he would sit in his armchair and fire at flies on the walls: Good practise for more serious work, no doubt, but not so good for the decor.

But was there a closer connection to the fictitious John MacNab? There seems to be no hard evidence of this, though in advancing years, he did tell all sorts of yarns. One of them was that during his Army career he accepted a bet in the mess for £20 to shoot a stag in any forest he chose in Scotland and did so at Inverlochy; but whether true or legend we don't know.

What we do know is that he used to rent small crofts in deer country and shoot anything that moved on, in or around them. Everything from deer to salmon were shot or caught.

John Buchan really did meet Jimmy Brander Dunbar when he was getting on in years and considered him to be a loveable reprobate. So it appears that whiskey-induced tales of sport in the Highlands inspired John Buchan to create John MacNab. A novelist of John Buchan's ability would easily be able to flesh out the stories he was told to give us the immortal fictional character of John MacNab.

Looking down on Alladale Lodge.

Chapter Thirty
We Take Alladale Lodge

In 1967 we took Alladale Lodge and its stalking for the last two weeks of the season, to form an association with "The Glen", Strathcarron, that continues to this day.

What we didn't know at the time was that the two forests of Alladale and Deanich, the old Freevater Forest had been taken for some years by Jim Pilkington. For 1967, however, the estate had doubled the rent to a figure that looks like peanuts today, but Jim, in protest, had refused to take the forests for 1967.

Jim and his party had stayed at Alladale Lodge which had been re-furbished, though not modernised, in 1961. Deanich Lodge, however, had lain empty since the Pilkington's last took it in 1939, so both Deanich and Alladale forests were stalked from Alladale Lodge.

In early October we headed for Scotland: Edna and I, Edna's mother and Elsie Grattidge who helped with the children, Caroline aged eight and Ross aged four. I drove our Jaguar (which we still have) and Edna drove our 1966 Mini with as much luggage as we could cram into it and kept it spinning along at 70/75 mph in glorious autumn weather.

We stopped for the night at the Sharrow House Hotel just short of Penrith where dinner, bed and breakfast for the whole party cost £15.19.d which we thought was expensive! How inflation has changed our perception of money since then.

We flew along next morning still in glorious weather, stopped for a picnic lunch north of Glasgow then that glorious run along Loch Lomond side to Ballachulish Ferry, surely one of the most scenically attractive roads in Britain.

Our intention was to stay the night at Inverness but we were making tremendous time along the Great Glen to Loch Ness. "Do you think we could make it to Alladale tonight?" said Edna.

Even if we could get in would Edna agree just to get in, put the children to bed and not want a full-scale "settle in" with cars unloaded and everything put away? Edna agreed she would!

We arrived at Ardgay at about 6pm and rang the factor, Mr Hickley. at Glencalvie. His wife told us that if there was someone in at the annexe we could get in: If not, we could not! It was about a 45 minute drive to get to Alladale Lodge she told us, so it would mean arriving at dusk.

The start of the Alladale woodland. Not a bogle in sight at that time of day!

Down "The Glen" and onto single-track tarmac roads. Past Braelangwell Lodge then left at The Craigs telephone box, past Amat Lodge and past the Glencalvie Lodge turn. Here the single track tarmac road ends and you are onto an estate track to Alladale and Deanich.

A wild, eerie drive in the gathering dusk through one of the northernmost remnants of the Old Caledonian Forest, a mixture of stunted Scots Pine and Birch. Trees covered in moss, festooned with dripping lichen with as many dead trees as live ones! The whitened dead branches making a surreal, impossible tangle and the road a waste of water filled potholes. The cars bumped along raising spray like motor boats. If there really are bogles or goblins, we decided, this eerie, desolate landscape would be their chosen habitat! If Bill Shakespeare had seen it he would gladly have swopped this location for that blasted heath!

Finally after what seemed an interminable drive the road wound steeply upward, up the "Alladale Brae". As we swung finally up the drive to Alladale Lodge we saw a figure dart back from one of the darkened windows. One of those goblins? No, Rosie Munro the stalker's wife!

We had arrived in the middle of their daughter's seventh birthday party which they were holding in the huge dining room in the lodge as we, of course, had not been expected until next day. We assured them that this was fine with us, as long as they didn't make too much noise after midnight!

Rosie Munro, who was in her late twenties, insisted on showing us round the lodge despite our insistence that she should go back to the party. We were then invited to join them for a cup of tea and cake.

So then we started the marathon task of tackling up the lodge! No electricity or telephone so Calor gas lights lit, fire started in the sitting room, children fed, beds switched round and made, children put to bed then, despite Edna's assurance, the cars completely unloaded and everything put away.

We were all absolutely whacked after all this, especially Edna, who had done the lion's share! Finally we sat down to a scratch meal at 9.30pm!

Alladale Lodge is well described by Stephen Pilkington, who stalked there in the 1930's, in his book *With a Gun to the Hill.* Look out of the living room window and the landscape must have been much the same as it was a thousand years ago. You could have been in 1967 or 1897 as the furniture and decor were unchanged.

"The lodge stood high above the junction of Glen Mor and Glen Alladale on the north side of the foot of the glen from which it takes its name, facing south-west and looking over a glorious view of woods and hills, at its best in the autumn when the birches and rowans were one mass of flaming orange and crimson against the dark contrast of the occasional old scots firs ...... The best room in the house was the large sitting room, with huge windows commanding the whole of the view, in which we always had tea when we were from the Hill in time and watched the sun setting over the hills, their tops turning to fire as the sun sank in the west and the green evening light paling as night reached upwards from the shadows of the glen".

The lodge was not built in Scottish Baronial style but simply as a large, stone built, Victorian country house, about as big as a small hotel. There were three bathrooms plus several toilets. Two of the bathrooms just as they were in 1900 with one "modern" bathroom which we chose to use. There was no shortage of bedrooms, for a much bigger party than ours.

The kitchen spread over three rooms! The main kitchen had two Calor gas stoves with sink and draining board, storage cupboards and work surfaces. The next room was a "washing up room" or still room. The final room with an Ideal Boiler made a magnificent drying room.

From this room there was a door to the annexe: First the Gun Room, then other odd rooms and finally the self contained stalker's quarters in which Richard and Rosie Munro lived with their daughter Morvern. Richard was the Deanich stalker.

Whoever had been responsible for the decor loved pictures but hated colour! All were either black and white or sepia. They mostly depicted 18th century ladies but were mixed with a number of dreary black and white landscapes.

The living room was complete Victoriana. There was a 19th century cast iron fireplace with green tiles and pine surround. In front of that was a huge brass surround about 10 inches high. There was a huge double panelled door and pine skirting about a foot deep with a massive pine architrave.

There was no shortage of chairs, settees and occasional tables. There was a corner bookcase, a Victorian bureau and a massive, tall sideboard with multiple drawers. The whole thing was inlaid with marquetry....a Victorian delight! Lighting was by two Calor gas lights on the fireplace wall and two on the opposite wall. In short, the perfect example of a traditional Highland shooting lodge.

By next morning, after a good night's rest, we were ready to go and delighted to meet Donald Clark, the Alladale stalker and Jim Stephenson who was to be our ponyman. We instantly liked the look of both of them, not realising at the time that we couldn't have wished for a finer stalker/ponyman combination in the whole of Scotland.

Snow on the tops.

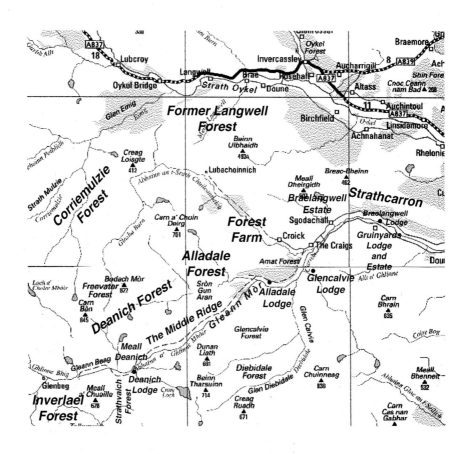

The principal estates of the Strathcarron area.

Chapter Thirty One
First Week's Stalking with Donald Clark

Donald Clark, despite his English sounding name, was as Scottish as a Burns Night haggis and was the same Donald Clark who, aged twenty, had acted as gillie for Jim Pilkington and his sister Anne when they took Alladale in 1930, 37 years before.

His father, James Clark, had been the Alladale stalker and Donald was the Deanich stalker when Stephen Pilkington took it in 1938. Donald, however, was unmarried so there was no young Clark coming along to succeed him.

Our ponyman, Jim "Steve" Stephenson, was a Zoology student from Dumfries-shire. He was due to start work for the Nature Conservancy that November studying fresh water mussels in Loch Leven. We did not know it at the time but this was his first ever season with the deer yet a man with a lifetime's experience couldn't have done a better job. He had, however, driven grouse and had taught fly-fishing to youngsters all over Scotland for, I believe, the Society for Physical Recreation. The youngsters stayed in Youth Hostel accommodation.

I had brought my .303 BSA now with telescopic sight and the .256 (6.5mm) Mannlicher with its aperture rear sight and tried both at the target. As I shot just as well with either I elected to stay with the Mannlicher, a wise decision as it happened as so many shots were to be taken in conditions of dreadful light...rain, mist, sleet and snow. The telescopic sight would have been a considerable handicap.

Glen Alladale runs roughly east/west. On the south is the Middle Ridge, a huge mountain mass running for five or six miles. On the north side is Carn Alladale. At the head of Glen Alladale lies the steep face of Legorme. At the forked burns you come to Fouran, the Hill of the Springs and one fork takes you to the huge steep corrie of

Glasha, the north shadowed by the mountain mass of Bodoch Mor.

On the south side of the Middle Ridge lies Glen Mor, the Big Glen, which eventually comes to a huge T- junction in the hills. Before that you have reached Deanich ground and Deanich Lodge is situated at the junction. Straight on you would continue into Glen Beag, the Little Glen. The larger part of Deanich Forest lies to the north with Inverlael ground on the south side of Glen Beag.

For our first day's stalking Donald decided to climb to the top of the Middle Ridge from the south side, taking the same route that we took seven years before with Brian Gibson. A stiff climb for a start through the Old Caledonian Forest with Eisen-yarn Corrie ahead of us. To the top at last and once at the top walking is comparatively easy.

On past Strone-gun-aran where we got a stag with Brian Gibson in 1960 then further on we heard a stag roaring below us. Glen Alladale was filled with mist rising and falling but it fell enough to give us a brief view of the stag before the mist obscured him again.

Finally we got into position for a shot. By now the stag was lying down facing towards us uphill. It was quite bare ground so I crawled on alone with the rifle. Lea MacNally, as mentioned earlier, had a cat-like patience. He could wait for ages for a stag to rise and come broadside to present an excellent target, but cat-like patience is something I lack! In addition I find that if you lie for a long time, wet and cold and usually in the teeth of the wind, you get colder and colder and then a shot taken with freezing fingers loads the dice against you. So, wherever possible, I weigh up the chances and take the shot as it is offered.

Sideways at an angle down the slope with one elbow in the air and with only the head and neck for a target, I took careful aim and made no mistake.

"A good shot and a long shot, too." said Donald delightedly. Edna said later that before I took the shot he had his cigarettes and matches out of his pocket....a sure sign that the stalker knows his Rifle is going to miss! The cigarettes, however, were quickly put back in his pocket and down he went with a springy step to gralloch the stag, i.e. remove the entrails

It was only about 12.30pm so Donald said we should try for another stag. About an hour later we were again in a position for a shot but the mist had lifted from the glen, partially obscuring the stag. Once again, however, the Mannlicher made no mistake so we were delighted to start with two stags on the first day.

The descent is "steep but not dangerous" said Donald but when you dislodged a stone it went bouncing downhill for 500ft or more! It was the longest, steepest descent we had ever experienced up to that time and I used Edna's method of sliding down on my bottom for the steepest stretches.

Donald handled the stag and, on occasion, the carcass would slide and tumble down a tremendous distance. At the bottom our ponyman was in sight so we were able to load up and start the long walk back to the lodge. The first stag was left out for collection the next day.

We were back at 5.30pm, soaking wet and tired with the inestimable luxury of a hot bath followed by a meal that the finest hotel in Europe couldn't surpass.

After dinner, round the blazing log fire in the lodge, we were able to relax and re-live the day. There is surely no more comfortable spot on the planet than the fireside of a Highland lodge after a hard day's stalking.

Roe doe in Autumn.

That first week we enjoyed magnificent stalking; the kind of stalking that could not have been bettered in any forest in Scotland. The weather? The worst that we had ever experienced! They were long tiring days, too, often not arriving back until after dark.

Shots were almost invariably difficult including several neck shots and often taken in the rain. One stag missed: a neck shot in the rain with teeth chattering after a long wait: Mine, not the stag's! The kind of shot you either clean kill or clean miss. No wounded stags were lost.

A good Roebuck.

One blank day in shocking weather with all the luck against us we were returning home empty handed. No problem because, as Jim Pilkington would have said, that was the day the deer won! Coming back through the Alladale woodland as darkness was falling we were startled by an unearthly scream... the whistle of a rutting Sika stag. To hear this unexpectedly at close hand really is blood curdling.

The stag stood and watched us as we came to a halt. Donald quickly slipped the rifle out of its cover and handed it to me....but I couldn't shoot that stag: It was not "stalking". I was far happier to go home empty handed.

On Saturday, the last day of the week's stalking, we were on the Middle Ridge and saw a stag with hinds below us on the face. We managed to circle round and get into position for a shot. Creeping to the edge of a crag Donald indicated for me to join him and whispered "He's fifty yards away directly below you." Hanging over the edge with Donald holding my legs I fired at the stag and got him. Turning to Donald I said "That's something I thought I would never see on this forest." "What's that?" asked Donald. "An easy shot" I replied!

So the best week's stalking ever and the worst weather. The next week was to be better and worse!

A Roe fawn suckles.

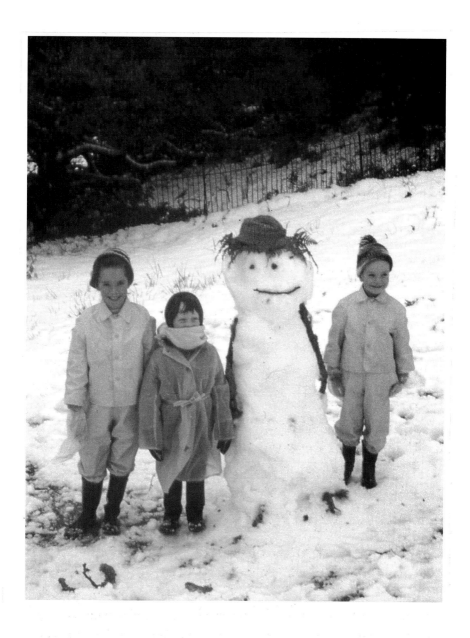

Caroline, Morvern and Ross with their snowman.

Chapter Thirty Two
Shooting in Sunshine and Snow

We did not see much of the Deanich stalker Richard Munro that season of 1967, but we did see quite a lot of his wife, Rosie, who looked after the lodge. Rosie had been born on Ardtornish at Beach (pronounced Be-ach), a remote shepherd's house. I got my first stag at Ardtornish within sight of that house. She was a cheery character always happy to chat away. Never a dull moment when Rosie was around.

At old Highland lodges like Alladale there is no shortage of "things that go bump in the night" and when the gales tore at the lodge, every window rattled and every door creaked. The wind howled, whined and moaned. You would lie in bed and hear the eerie whistles of the rutting Sika stags: Three notes, high, medium and low. A pause then they would be repeated. Hard to believe that such a sound was produced by a living creature.

In the evenings at Alladale sitting in front of the fire in the living room, Edna would suddenly feel a draught across her legs and she knew instantly that a "presence" had entered the house. Ghoul, Ghost or Goblin? No, it was Rosie Munro coming in from her quarters to borrow a saucepan, mincer or kettle and of course, take the opportunity for a chat!

Things would mysteriously disappear from the lodge but just as mysteriously reappear. A bed would disappear then, a few days later, reappear again; Rosie's sister had been to stay! Her sister, Bridget, was about thirteen years old so Ross and Caroline would play with her and Morvern. Ross and Caroline had settled in wonderfully well at Alladale and would go to bed without trouble...far better than at home! At home Ross could go to bed and shout for Edna several times but at Alladale he might shout once, just to show us who was boss, but then would soon be fast asleep.

Richard and Rosie had two cows as there is no milk delivery at a place as remote as Alladale. Ross and Caroline enjoyed watching Rosie milking her cow. She gave them milk to drink warm from the cow. Ross didn't like it!

Rosie supplied us with milk but the quantity was always unpredictable. The milk jugs would disappear and reappear always with different quantities of milk!

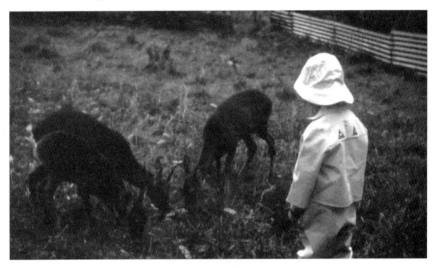

Ross feeds Lea MacNally's tame Roe deer.

So Alladale Lodge suited us all very well indeed... Edna and I, Caroline and Ross, Edna's mother and Elsie: We all voted it far better than staying at any hotel.

On one Sunday we all went over to see Lea and Margaret MacNally and family; a long haul. We started at 9.30 am and arrived at Culachy at noon. It was always a great pleasure to see them again. Lea had been suffering with a run of erratic shooting by his stalking guests, leaving six stags to get in the week ahead... the last week of the season.

His tame Roe Deer doe, "Dainty", was three years old accompanied by last year's faun and this year's twin fauns. When she had reached maturity she had disappeared for about ten months back into the wild. Lea never even caught a glimpse of her. She returned just as unexpectedly and within two weeks her first faun was born. Surely this must be unique for a Scottish Roe Deer? From then on she only disappeared for a day or two at a time. Caroline and Ross enjoyed feeding her with leaves.

Margaret had prepared a lovely meal for us despite my having diplomatically told her beforehand that a bowl of soup would be perfectly adequate.

So lots to talk about at Culachy: The deer, the Hill, rifles, forests, cabbages and kings! The clock raced round until we reluctantly had to leave.

The next week's stalking had to start without Edna as her heels were rubbed raw. While we went off to the Hill, Edna, Elsie, Caroline and Ross went Sika stalking in the woodland. Stalking and crawling they managed to get into the middle of a herd of Sika, a wonderful experience for them all.

On the same day we had a long, long walk, getting to the tops in magnificent weather. Hardly a breath of wind and finally with a mixture of snow patches and heat haze we tramped to the roof of Scotland. From the same spot we were able to see the sea on the east and west coasts with the mountains of Sutherland to the north: A wonderful moment. We eventually managed to get into position for a shot at a good stag facing head on. I made no mistake and found that he had the longest horn of any shot to date at twenty seven and a half inches.

So was this glorious weather a portent of things to come? No, it wasn't!

The next morning we woke to find a light fall of snow with even the comparatively low hill in front of the lodge snow covered. It was a fine morning, however, so we decided to stalk the Middle Ridge: Steve to go along Glen Alladale and meet us at 3pm. We were to climb up on our usual route on the Glen Mor side through the Old Caledonian Woodland with Eisen-yarn Corrie to our left.

We were almost out of the wood and we heard a deer bark: "Red Deer hind." I thought. "Jap Stag." said Donald. A moment later and we saw two Japanese Sika stags running across the clearing in front of us and there was a mad scramble to get the rifle out of the cover. The stags had halted as they saw us, then ran on strongly. Swinging the rifle ahead of the leading stag I fired, with the roar of the Mannlicher much louder than on the open hill.

I was sure that I had hit that stag but he didn't appear to flinch, neither did either Donald or I hear the distinctive smack of the bullet, though a lot depends on the acoustics of the place.... sometimes you hear the bullet strike, sometimes not!

"They can go on like that with a heart shot." said Donald, then added doubtfully "But he was running so strongly". Although I felt I had made no mistake, on those quick shots it is all too easy to snatch the trigger and get a clean miss.

We went on to the edge of the clearing where he had gone out of sight and there he was, stone dead, shot through the heart. A good six point Sika stag. We pulled him onto a knoll to be collected later.

We started again along the Middle Ridge with Eisen-yarn Corrie on our left when it started to snow. we were warm enough and enjoyed the sensation of battling with the elements as the dry snow rattled against our waterproof jackets.

We crossed over to look on the Alladale side but the fierce north wind meant that there was little shelter there so we zig-zagged along the top of the Middle Ridge looking alternately into Glen Alladale and Glen Mor. There were heavy snow showers with clear intervals.

Finally in one of those intervals we saw deer high up on the Middle Ridge on the Glen Mor side. A long detour along the ridge would keep us out of sight so we started out but then it began to snow in earnest.

The snow was driven at tremendous speed by the north wind on our right. Visibility was soon down to little more than 100 yards, then to less than fifty yards. Never have I seen snow behave like it other than on films or TV. For about four feet above ground level the snow blew like a sandstorm, with amazing density: The surface of the snow-covered ground was scoured smooth by the snow like a torrent cascading down the bed of a river.

Every step showered a plume of snow as we gasped against the biting, snow filled, wind. On the windward side the snow stung like stinging nettles.

I glanced at Donald and was amazed to see the windward side of his face was solid with ice! Reaching up to my face I found it was the same! I had to scrape the ice off with my fingers only to find that the ice quickly formed again.

Caroline and Ross slide down the Alladale Brae.

The driving snow got so bad that we stopped and lay down for a rest and I watched, fascinated, as the snow quickly drifted over my Brinylon waterproof and bridged across to make an unbroken layer of snow. Yet, believe it or not, I wasn't cold! My feet were wet through and freezing, as could only be expected, but my body was quite warm. The snow was surprisingly dry and my clothes underneath the waterproof were dry: We had been much colder during those soaking days last week. I could even joke with Donald about the possibility of seeing a St. Bernard dog turn up with a small barrel of brandy under his collar!

The snow covered us more and more deeply converting us into replicas of the Babes in the Wood but covered with snow, not leaves. It made me understand how travellers, caught in these conditions, could fall asleep, never to awake.

Finally those freezing feet urged us to start walking again. On we went with the storm, if anything, getting even worse, and at last, we started to get cold. But we continued on the seemingly endless detour.

Finally when we were getting really cold Donald halted in a small hollow, peeped over the edge and said "The stag is about 100 yards in front of us lying down". Only a man who knew every inch of the Hill *in all weathers* could possibly have done this: Made a long detour with visibility down to zero at times yet end up within shot of a stag.

Donald unhitched the rifle and put it down in the snow with the cover unfastened. Within minutes the snow had drifted over the cover!

So we waited and waited getting colder and colder and although the blizzard varied in intensity it showed no sign of stopping. We continued to wait until both Donald and I were shivering with cold with our teeth chattering like demented castanets.

I decided that we could wait no longer: Either we would have to give in and go home or shoot in the snowstorm. I decided to shoot! I told Donald that we could wait no longer as I would be too cold to hold the rifle. I would have to shoot now. Donald agreed.

I slid into position to the edge of the hollow to see the deer in a cleft running down the hillside with the stag lying down in the snow with his body hidden in the snow, as Donald had said. I then realised that he was not lying down after all: He was standing up with his whole body encrusted with snow though, strangely enough, his head and neck were not.

How's that for a target? A snow-covered stag in a snow-covered landscape against a snow-covered bank in a snowstorm!

It was uncanny to lay the foresight against the snow covered side of the stag and estimate the correct place for a heart shot. It was still snowing, of course, as I pressed the trigger and heard the smack of the bullet. The hinds streamed out of the cleft but the stag stood motionless... a sure sign of a fatal shot.

"Put in another bullet to make sure." said Donald, but I, with supreme self confidence replied "No, he's hard hit".

At that instant the snowstorm intensified and blotted out all sight of the stag, bringing it home to me that Donald had been absolutely right. Even if fatally hit the stag could possibly go on for, say, seventy yards and in those conditions we would never find him.

In a few moments the snow thinned and the stag was visible again in exactly the same place so I was able to fire again. It wasn't necessary as it happened, but Donald had been right to make absolutely sure of the stag.

We walked towards the stag and I worked the rifle bolt with freezing fingers to extract the cartridges only to drop the rifle in the snow! Donald couldn't gralloch the stag without swinging his arms and beating them against his torso to regain some semblance of warmth.

We dragged the stag onto a smooth section of the hillside and let go... The stag slid down the snow-covered slope unaided for about 500 feet.

Never had we deserved a stag more, we decided, and we were certain that no stalker/rifle combination in Scotland could have done better than us today. Certain, too, that no neighbouring forest would have got two stags that day.

We were almost at the Deanich march on the Middle Ridge: It was difficult getting down that steep, snow-covered slope though the stag got to the bottom practically unaided! A long walk back to the Land Rover but a pleasure after walking the high tops in that snow storm. It was still snowing but we were sheltered by the Middle Ridge.

We went back to the Land Rover then up the hill to drag down our Sika stag, load it up into the Land Rover then head back for home. We were back at the Lodge about 5pm, not nearly as wet as those days during the week before.

But what about poor old Steve who had been waiting in Glen Alladale without a sign from us? Donald said that I was not to worry as Steve had instructions that if there was no sign of us by 4.30pm he was to make for home. To our great relief he arrived back about 5.30pm with our flask of tea unopened...This after hours of waiting in the snow. I resolved to tell him to drink that tea in future if we were not back on time.

Donald was always to maintain that this was the worst weather in which he had every stalked stags (not hinds) during his lifetime of stalking. It was, however, entirely his own decision to keep going through that snow storm. Had he suggested turning back I would have agreed without demur.

There was more snow in the night and the next morning it was impossible to get out onto the high ground so we decided to start at about 2pm along Glen Alladale with the hope of a shot. During the morning we made a fine snowman for the children: Dead bracken for his hair with my Deerstalker on top. Stones for buttons and a bent twig gave him an ear splitting smile! Henry Moore would have approved!

We started about 2pm, this time joined by "Silver" the Deanich pony. He had jumped the gate from the paddock to join his pal, our pony, Tommy! Despite the late start we did manage to get in for a stalk and the shot was successful. Delighted we loaded the stag onto the pony and headed for home. The bitter weather had driven the deer down to the foot of the Glen by the time we were getting back to the Lodge so we clattered along, three men and two ponies.

Suddenly, Steve stopped and pointed. Little more than 100 yards ahead of us was a shootable stag lying down with his back to us at the side of the path. The wind was blowing towards him too! Why he had failed to pick us up I'll never know!

"He's safe enough tonight" I said to Donald "too easy". "But he's awful handy" said Donald wistfully. Between then and home we could have shot two more stags, none more than 120 yards from the path. If you ever miss a stag do you get such a chance on your way home? Never! For good measure a Japanese Sika stag was only 50/60 yards from the track in the Alladale woodland.

We arrived back home at 7pm in the dark after a good day.

For the last day's stalking we decided we would take Steve with us to climb onto the Middle Ridge and leave the pony behind. If we were fortunate enough to get a stag we would drag him down either to the foot of Glen Alladale or Glen Mor.

So off we went and we did have one or two attempts to get within shot of deer but without success. Finally we got into position for a shot at a stag lying down a fair way out and the shot was brought off successfully.

On we went and finally got into position for a shot at another

~ Continued on P209

Lea MacNally spies for an Autumn stag.

Golden Eagle with chick.

Japanese Sika stags in their red summer coats.

Japanese Sika stags in their dark winter coats.

Hind with calf.

A stag roars defiance in the rut.

Stags fighting in October.

Stags boxing in the spring. One has already shed his antlers.

The spirit of stalking. One stag culled, now Lea is spying for another.

One of Lea's favourite photographs. Winter stags against the dramatic backcloth of Ben Tee in the Great Glen.

Sunshine, shadow and snow in the Highlands.

A switch - very long in the horn.

Summer stags untroubled by rutting fever.

Lea MacNally homeward bound with three hinds on the pony.

Narcissus.

Is there anything more beautiful in nature than a Red Deer calf?

Winter hinds.

Eisen-yarn Corrie in the snow. Edna, the author, Richard Munro.

Fox and badger.

Crawling through the snow for a shot at a hind.

Looking west from Deanich Lodge.

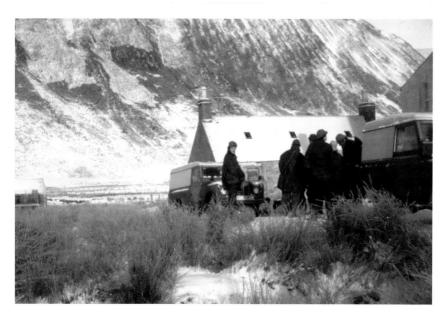

The stalking party start out from Deanich Lodge. Ross, Richard, Larry, Bill.

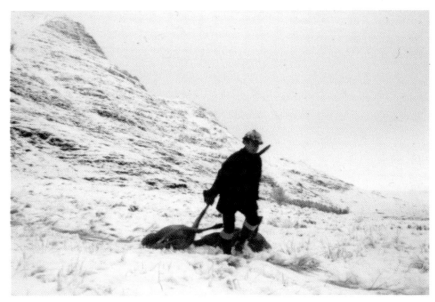

Lea dragging two hinds in bitterly cold winter weather but with the prospect of a blazing fire and magnificent meal ahead.

On the roof of Scotland. Richard Munro and Mr Bagel spy above the Glasha Burn.

Richard Munro spies at Alladale.

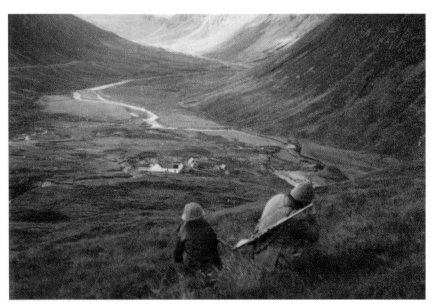

Richard Munro with his son, Marcus, spies westward along Glen Beag above Deanich Lodge. Meall Deanich on the right.

Larry Weare with the big stag he shot at Alladale. Note the tremendous spread of the antlers. Marcus Munro right, Adam Ross left.

Ronnie Ross spies at Braelangwell.

The Hornpipe beats into the wind.

Preparing for landfall. Ross on left, Bill Auden right.

Bill, right, Ross, left, fish from the Hornpipe. Ted holds his head!

Nigel delightedly shows his fish.

stag almost vertically below us at about 120 yards. Those steeply downhill shots are all too easy to miss but we managed to bring it off.

We were back home late that evening about 7pm. A hot bath, a magnificent meal, then for the last time we chatted away round the roaring log fire at the lodge. Rosie Munro nipped in for a final chat and I wrote up my stalking diary for the last time, finishing it as the last dying embers glowed in the grate.

A wonderful time for us all: We would be back next year, we decided.

Hauled back up again.

George Ross, Ronnie Ross of Braelangwell's grandfather who was the Alladale Stalker in the 1890's. Not the George Ross of Corriemulzie.

Chapter Thirty Three
The Remarkable Rosses

Ronnie Ross is the stalker and river keeper at Braelangwell, Strathcarron. You will meet Ronnie in the following pages. Ronnie's grandfather, George Ross was born in 1848 at an address given as "The face of Glencalvie." This, of course, was *after* the Glencalvie clearances which were on Corrievalachie, not the face of Glencalvie.

His brother Hugh was born at the same address and became the Deanich keeper, living in the old keeper's house, which was still there until recently demolished.

George became the Alladale keeper and lived in the old keeper's house, which still survives in Glen Alladale. He had eight children, six boys and two girls. Four of the boys served in World War One as snipers in the Lovat Scouts. One of the boys, also George, was Ronnie's father, born in 1888 and he won a Military Cross.

His brother, Donald, Ronnie's uncle, was also in the Lovat Scouts. He was born in 1884 and was the keeper at Rhidorrach for over 30 years.

Ronnie's father was the keeper at Coulin, Wester Ross, then at Langwell, Ross-shire (not the Caithness Langwell). In the 1920's Langwell stretched for 18 miles on "The other side of the hill" from Deanich / Alladale, but it has since been broken up. The lodge, however, survives. Ronnie's father eventually became keeper at Gruinyards opposite Braelangwell.

Langwell was owned by the Debenhams....yes, the Debenham Debenhams of stores fame. Rhidorrach was owned by the Roses, of Lime juice fame.

Corriemulzie marches with Deanich on the north side and Alladale on the west. The huge, steep sided corrie, Corrie Mor, was Deanich ground originally but in recent years has reverted to

Corriemulzie. Just as well, perhaps, as those steep sides are virtually impossible to stalk from Deanich ground.

Donald Ross, the Rhidorrach stalker, with his wife, before World War One. Son of George Ross of Alladale.

From 1872 to 1905 the Corriemulzie stalker was George Ross who kept a diary of those years. (Sorry to confuse you with all these George Rosses but as far as we know, George Ross of Corriemulzie was not related to the Rosses of Strathcarron, though they would have known one another.) The diary has never been published and the original has been lost but, fortunately, a copy survives in the hands of Niall Graham Campbell who was the Deanich and Alladale factor during our early days there. Niall is an extremely pleasant character with, as factor, the unenviable task of diplomatically dealing with owner, shooting tenant, stalker, Uncle Tom Cobleigh and all!

Corriemulzie is reached from the Bridge of Oykell and in those days the track was in shocking condition. The lodge was in such a state that, according to Grimble:

"A sportsman of the new school who went to inspect the place came away declaring he would not put his servants in such a hole!"

But regardless of the condition of the lodge, Grimble recorded that "The ground always yields some heavy stags and good heads".

George Ross required the patience of the proverbial saint to endure the shocking shooting of so many of his stalking guests. Some later writers have blamed the inaccuracy of the Black Powder Express rifles, but this was definitely not the case. The Expresses were perfectly accurate, look how they performed in the hands of stalkers like Horatio Ross. All they required was a competent "afterpiece"! But despite numerous disappointments with easy shots missed, time and time again, Ross accepted it all with surprising tolerance.

Sometimes sportsmen managed to lose deer without even firing a shot: In the 1873 stalking season Ross got two of his "gentlemen" into position for a shot on some flats by the march. The idea was that both should fire together, a not unusual practice in those days, in the hope that a volley would be sure to hit *something*. In this case, however, despite "a good chance" neither fired a shot due to "some misunderstanding between them."

George Ross, Ronnie Ross' father, Gruinyards keeper in the 1950's. Also son of George Ross of Alladale.

One of his "gentlemen", only described as "Mr Eddie", sorely tried his patience in 1872/3. On September 24th 1872 he stalked for Mr Eddie and Mr Davys above Keas Wood but despite having "a good chance" they fired four shots each and missed with every one. Following the same herd to the march they again got into position to shoot. Mr Eddie fired three shots and managed to kill a "heind", not a stag. Mr Davys fired four shots, all under fifty yards range, but missed with every one.

On September 19th 1877 Mr Eddie killed a stag at 200 yards at the back of Mealan-na-mohr and missed another despite firing two shots at it. He then got in for a shot at another group of deer, fired three shots and wounded two stags. Next day he fired at a stag lying down - and missed, shot at a running stag but wounded this, too, and lost it.

Ronnie Ross of Braelangwell in contemplative mood.

Ross' diary gives a fascinating picture of how deer forests developed during the final part of the 19th century. At first, when the sheep had been taken off and the ground afforested, it took time for the deer stock to build up and in the 1870's only about a dozen stags per season were shot. No doubt the ineffectual shooting, too, helped deer stocks to build up! By the 1890's however about thirty stags per season were being killed on Corriemulzie, plus a few hinds.

The shooting, however, still remained abysmal and in 1883 only one stag and one hind were killed. On October 10th the Rifle missed three chances and two more the next day. Surprisingly, despite the excellence of the rifles of the day, some "gentlemen" turned up with "Pea rifles" (small bore rifles, unsuitable for deerstalking) and simply wounded the beast which, of course, got away. Towards the end of the century collies were used to track wounded stags and bring them to bay, so this was a welcome improvement.

In 1895 the forest was sold and the new stalking tenant was Sir Arthur Chichester who, on his third day out stalking, turned up with a 12 bore gun fitted with sights and, presumably, firing a solid ball. They stalked four small stags; Sir Arthur fired at one and hit him on the shoulder but he went off wounded. He then fired at the next stag and hit him five times without killing the poor beast. Ross had to administer the *coup-de-grace* with stones and "the gun was condemned right out there".

At the end of one season the total bag was four stags but Ross did record that "Mr Wigston missed fully twenty stags". In 1902 he said that Mr Pease was "the hardest miser I ever met".

In 1874 he reached his literary heights and this is clear in his description of a day's stalking on September 24th:

"Directly on the sky line on the east side of the cory, we had to take the knee walking for fully a mile distance, and in some places we had to belly-sledge it, for hundreds of yards, till we passed most of the heinds....then there was not too much time to lose, in a second bang goes the Martinni from the gentleman's shoulder and after going a few paces this beautiful animal fell full length sideways on the ground, after re-scenting our breaths with real mountain dew and as usual making the animal lighter (gralloching) for the homeward journey, we steered our course for home, which we reached at a rather late hour".

So poor George Ross had a very difficult time, stalking for so many shocking sportsmen who could not hit the proverbial barn door and, as were most stalkers in those days, only paid a pittance, no doubt less than £40 per annum. Living, too, in harsh conditions with no amenities.

Yet his diary, despite all disappointments, is not bitter. It is, in fact, a cheerful record of his time as a stalker during that important period of deer forest development.

Ronnie Ross and Glencalvie stalker, John Gordon, share a joke during a day at the foxes.

A page from the Debenham family's photograph album grouse shooting during the 1926 season at Langwell, Ross-shire. George Ross, Ronnie Ross' father was the keeper there before World War Two.

Looking west along Glen Beag from Deanich Lodge, Meall Deanich on right. Inverlael ground on left. Far peak is Strouban, the black cliffs of Inverlael in the distance.

Chapter Thirty Four
In the Kingdom of the Deer at Deanich

For 1968 we had expected to be back stalking at Alladale as we had so enjoyed our stay in 1967 but by then Jim Pilkington had regretted his decision to give up the two forests and had decided to take them both again.

So were we out on our ear again a la Roadnight? No! Jim Pilkington was a true gentleman so he was *not* prepared to kick us out. Deanich Lodge had been empty through the War years and beyond: Walkers would find shelter there for over a quarter of a century but in 1968 the lodge had been made habitable again and was available for the end of the season with the Deanich stalking. If we would like to take it for our usual period, that would be fine. In any case we had a much smaller party so the larger Alladale Lodge would be more suitable for Jim Pilkington and his guests, most of whom had stalked with Jim and his brother at Deanich and Alladale in the 1930's. We were to have the pleasure of meeting most of them in that and subsequent years.

The run along Glen Mor from Alladale to Deanich was fine for a Land Rover but very hard going indeed for an ordinary car. It had been notoriously bad in the 1930's and was worse in the 1960's. The low slung Jaguar used to take some punishing knocks on its underside and the Mini would arrive with its exhaust pipe nearly flattened.

Deanich Lodge must be one of the most remote inhabited dwellings in the British Isles. Once there you are in the Kingdom of the Deer. This is their territory, you are the intruder. There are deer to be seen from the lodge at any hour of the day and when you lie in bed at night you can hear the clatter of their hooves on the drive when they have descended from the high tops.

Opposite the lodge on the north side towers Meall Deanich at the west end of the Middle Ridge. The long glen, however, continues from Glen Mor into Glen Beag. Beyond the lodge it is all Deanich ground on the north side but at the junction of the glens the glen at right angles to Glen Mor and Glen Beag runs south into Strathvaich ground. (Strath Rannoch at this end, all part of Strathvaich).

Beyond the junction on the south side of Glen Beag is the remaining part of Inverlael ground owned by Dr. Whitteridge and, after his death, owned by his wife.

A Hydro Electric road runs along the foot of the Inverlael Hill to a dam where the water from the hill burns and the River Carron is diverted into a tunnel cut right through the hill to Loch Vaich so, strictly speaking, the very narrow strip of ground between Deanich Lodge and Inverlael is their ground, not Deanich's. On the other hand the Inverlael stalking parties drive along their section of the Hydro Electric road then cross onto Deanich ground on the north side of the river to continue along the Hydro Electric road to get to their stalking ground.

So as they use the road on the Deanich side surely it is fair if Deanich use the stretch of Hydro Road on their side but this has been the subject of dispute.

Small in the saddle! Ross with the author and Caroline.

Richard Munro constructed a "home made" road from Deanich Lodge to the Hydro Electric road on Inverlael and we had not been in Deanich Lodge for many hours that first year before Dr. Whitteridge turned up at the lodge with his stalker to tell us we had no right to use that home made road. Obviously we knew nothing about any dispute and pointed this out to him saying that we would talk to the Estate about it. We did, however, continue to use the road and it is still in use by Deanich to this day but, from time to time, the dispute breaks out again.

But Deanich Lodge suited us down to the ground and we were to spend many happy days there in future years stalking, fishing for salmon and trout and plinking with the .22 rifle.

Although we had met Richard Munro the year before at Alladale we had never stalked with him so now we had the pleasure of getting to know him. Richard was a first class stalker. A small man but with a tremendously long stride. If Richard couldn't get you in for a shot then no other stalker in Scotland could. It was always a pleasure to be on the Hill with Richard.

Deanich is not an "old man's forest" and there are no easy stalking beats. Whichever way you decide to go it is straight uphill! I suppose the easiest beat is the "South Side", though easy is a relative term. This is the ground that lies on the South Side of the river from the Alladale ground up to Deanich lodge. We were to get our first day's stalking on the South Side and have stalked it on many occasions since.

On that first day we managed to get into an easy stalk and were back home early: This suited us very well indeed with the children back at the Lodge with Edna's mother and Elsie, but on many occasions we were to stalk the South Side in very different weather conditions.

We would usually be stalking stags on the north facing slope above the river in a north wind and it could be bitterly cold with, all to often, a touch of sleet or snow, especially if we had to wait for a stag to rise.

The deer would chose a place sheltered from the wind and we would invariably be in the teeth of the wind with no shelter. Your feet are always wet in your walking shoes when stalking in Scotland, other than in the very eastern forests where you can walk dry shod. In the west, however, you walk in water filled shoes. When you are walking your feet warm the water in your shoes and socks but if you lie waiting for a stag to rise for any length of time the heat exchange reverses and the cold water in your shoes transmits the cold to your freezing feet. Waiting for a shot on the south side we would often wonder if the deer could hear our teeth chattering!

When we eventually got back to the lodge, freezing cold after a long day on the Hill, a restoring cup of tea would be the first essential followed by a hot bath..... bliss! The bath followed by a hot meal that the most competent chef in the finest hotel couldn't surpass. After the meal the events of the day would be dissected and lived again.... The solitary hind and calf that made the hoped for approach impossible..... The knobber who caught a glimpse of you from afar..... The leading hind that caught a puff of your wind and took the whole group away.

There is no doubt in my mind that a Highland shooting lodge on an October evening in front of a blazing log fire with a few companions to share the experiences of the day is the most desirable place on the face of this planet.

Richard Munro unloads a good switch.

Most of the Deanich stalking was, of course, on the north side of the glen where most of the ground lay. The Land Rover would take you up to the lower slope of Meall Deanich on the west side then you would start the long climb up the Allt na Veggerish path. At the top, ahead of you to the right lies a large rocky outcrop, "Pilkington's Knoll" as we were to christen it. We got quite a few stags around that knoll.

At the top of the path we would stop for a "spy". Richard with his telescope and we with our monoculars. For stalking you *must* use a telescope, not monoculars or binoculars. Admittedly you can see deer well enough with them and a monocular has a tremendous advantage in being so "handy" as you can slip it in and our of your pocket in an instant. To really identify a stag, however, and to see exactly what his horns are and whether he is shootable or not, you must have a telescope.

Much to my regret I never did become proficient at using a telescope but my son Ross started out with one so it is second nature to him. Yes, he also uses a monocular for a general view but the telescope is supreme.

When I started stalking, the three draw Ross telescope with two and a half inch lens and aluminium construction was the perfect instrument but they were always rare and expensive. Lea MacNally had a superlative aluminium Ross which he had restored but it was eventually stolen from his car by a thief who would, no doubt, never again use it for its proper purpose. Donald Clark had a wobbly old brass Ross telescope with only a small object lens but, to everyone's amazement, he could see wonderfully well with it.

Grays, the Inverness gunsmiths, were later to introduce a superb two and a half inch three draw telescope with aluminium construction and bloomed lenses which were superior to the Ross and it is a Grays telescope that Ross uses.

There are many stalking beats at Deanich. Continuing along Glen Beag you would climb up the Strouban Path at the top of which, in the 1930's, the sweltering Michael Wroughton in the Pilkington party, would gulp down draught after draught of spring water in an attempt to cool down. At the top of the path ahead of you lies Loch Strouban which contains large trout but not many of them! Beyond the loch the ground rises until you come to the steep cliffs plunging down into Corrie

Mor on the Corriemulzie ground.

This used to be part of Deanich but as the sides are so steep it is virtually impossible to stalk from Deanich Lodge. Stephen Pilkington describes driving the corrie to rifles stationed above it in the late 1930's but Jim Pilkington told me that this was the only time, in his experience, that it was ever driven.

Away to the left of Loch Strouban is the Strouban Ridge and beyond that the Reedy Loch and the White Stone. Beyond that again the land slopes up to the delightfully named "Window of Douchary".

Swing to the left to overlook Glen Beag again and you are now at the "Green Face". Before the stags break out at the start of the rut there are always stags on the Green Face and if you are ever there looking down on the deer and find a 6 x 30 Zeiss monocular please let me know as I lost it there in the 1960's!

Get a stag on the Green Face and it is an easy drag down to the floor of the glen and if your preparations have been correct the pony and ponyman will soon be there to take the stag home.

All you have to do is to walk back to Deanich Lodge, but what a walk this is! For a start there is no path so you struggle along on broken ground, in and out of deep peat hags. So you give up and walk along the side of the river only to find that the walking is even worse with your route often blocked by overhanging banks!

Back again up the bank and into the broken hags. By the time you finally reach the lodge you're whacked!

Beyond Deanich in Glen Beag past the dam where the Hydro Electric road ends there is an old ponypath on the Inverlael side of the glen and miles along it is an old corrugated iron bothy. This is maintained by the Mountain Bothies Association to provide overnight accommodation for the hardy souls who brave walking in the most remote areas of the Highlands. Irreverently known as "Bothy Buggers"!

The bothy had not been used by Inverlael for stalking for many years as it is about twenty miles from the lodge. But in the past, before motor transport, a stalking party would set out from Inverlael Lodge with a string of ponies and ample supplies to stalk this remote part of the ground, staying at this isolated bothy for three or four days and making the best of the primitive accommodation.

Beyond this bothy there is, to my knowledge, no path or track but hardy walkers, often from Germany, would call at Deanich Lodge on the way to taking this route and crossing to the west coast of Scotland at Ullapool..... rather them than me! On one occasion a young German called at Deanich Lodge and when I answered the door I said to him "Are you Dieter or Wolfgang?". "Dieter". he replied!

One January when we were hind stalking a young Dutch couple, experienced at walking in the Highlands, went by heading for Ullapool, carrying a tent and gigantic rucksacks. It was snowing hard and they were bare headed. I often wondered if they made it successfully. Even if they did, it must have been a wet, cold uncomfortable night in their tent. But having said that, full marks for effort for the young people who are prepared to tramp from coast to coast in the Highlands, enduring such weather.

So at Deanich there are a wide variety of stalking beats all enjoyable in their own way.... as long as you remember that it is not an "old man's forest"!

That first year at Deanich was a resounding success. We got every stag we fired at, got to know Richard Munro, met Jim and Sue Pilkington and as we went over to join them a few times, we got to know them too.

Crawling into position for a shot, overlooking Glenmor. Alladale Lodge in view behind the middle ridge.

(Top) Glen Beag.
(Bottom) Edna, Caroline and Ross spy.

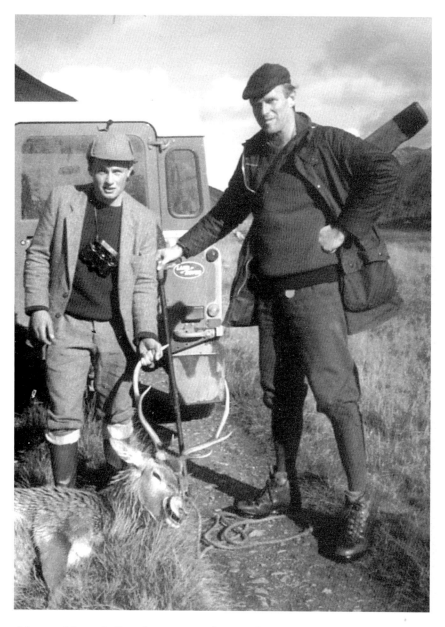

Marcus Munro's first day as a professional stalker, 1984. His guest was 6 foot 9 inches tall.

Ross with the two salmon he caught on one August morning at "Caroline's Pool", Deanich.

Chapter Thirty Five
Lazy, Hazy Days of Summer

Now we had found a forest and lodge that suited us down to the ground we were to return year after year, always with Richard Munro as stalker, Johnny Murray as ponyman and using the 6.5mm Mannlicher with its aperture sight.

Richard and Rosie Munro next had a son, Marcus, and we had the pleasure of watching him grow up. Later another son, Richard, was born though we were not to know him as well. Sadly Rosie was to die when Marcus was only about eight years old and he can barely remember his mother.

We eventually took Deanich Lodge for two weeks in August as well as for the end of the October stalking. In August it was our summer holiday when we would fish the hill lochs for trout and the river for trout and salmon. We would also shoot the odd stag. Marcus would join us for many of these fishing and stalking trips and right from the start he was a truly remarkable young man.

Marcus and his father had a marvellous *rapport* and could communicate effectively without exchanging a word. It was always a great pleasure to see them together. Off to the South Side to fish Crom Loch, Marcus would always be the first there, the first to cast a line and the first to catch a fish. Always a marvellous walker he said to us, when he was quite small: "In walking your brain is your greatest power. If your brain tells your legs to walk, *they must walk!*" Edna replied: "My brain tells my legs to walk *but they take no notice!*"

Marcus was driving the Estate Land Rover off-road when he was too small to look through the windscreen. He managed by opening the vents below the windscreen to look through those! When he was about ten he dearly wanted to ride a motorcycle and by then we always took two miniature Kawasakis with us for Caroline and Ross to ride.

So Marcus asked what it was like to ride a motorcycle. "You can drive a Land Rover" I said "it's just like that". So I showed Marcus the controls and off we went with me on the pillion. He managed without trouble but after about a mile he turned his head to me and shouted "It's not like driving a Land Rover!"

Marcus was to go on to become a superlative motorcyclist and could make a motorcycle do anything but talk. He has always had a motorcycle since owning his first 50cc machine at sixteen.

Marcus would usually join us on our stalking and fishing expeditions at Deanich. Stalking with a large party, we would usually choose a sheltered place in a deep peat hag, where we could observe Richard and the Rifle as they set out on the stalk.

Marcus, during the wait, would then enact many roles! With his stick, he would become a champion snooker player, potting all balls with unerring accuracy. He would then transform into an award winning golfer; his stick changed from snooker cue to golf club. Next he would slip into the role of fearless swordsman, taking on the dastardly Guy of Gibson, Robin Hood's sworn enemy,....and so it would continue!

A salmon in "Caroline's Pool" almost ready for the landing net.

Marcus was an excellent rifle shot as soon as he could hold a rifle and he shot his first hind when aged seven. Now he has raised rifle shooting into an art form. No iron sights or 4x telescopic sight for Marcus! His stalking rifles have telescopic sights of 20x power. Hinds are not shot in the traditional spot behind the shoulder, but through the neck or head and at twice the usual distance, too. Three hundred yards is normal for Marcus.

Ammunition? He loads his own to precise measurements and has developed rifles with a huge cartridge case necked down to take a .22 calibre that shoots "flat", without any appreciable bullet drop, from here to eternity. Hill foxes are shot at night by spotlight with these space-age rifles.

Marcus is now married with a wife and two children. They live in a superlative stalker's house, newly built by today's owners of Deanich and Alladale Mr and Mrs Macaire. It is some distance behind the Lodge in an elevated position, enjoying marvellous views of the glen.

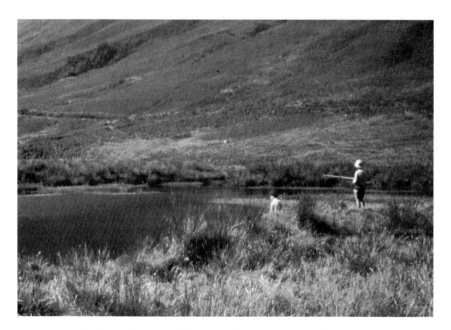

Fishing for those big, but elusive trout at Strouban.

(Top) Hooking a trout at Crom Loch.
(Bottom) Young Marcus Munro fishing at Loch Pollaig, Alladale.

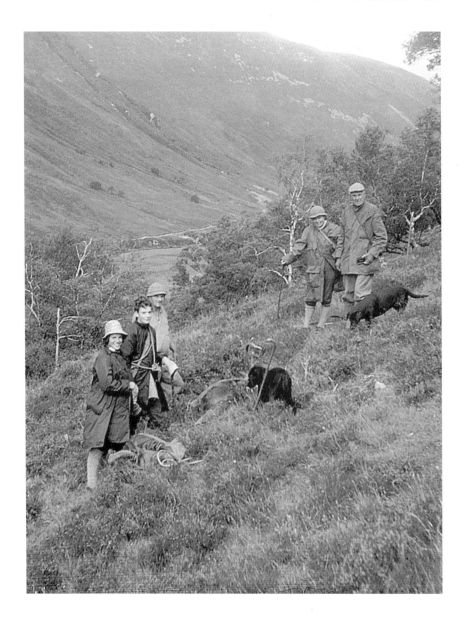

August stalking. A stag above Beach Wood on the Middle Ridge. Caroline, Ross, Richard, Edna, Jim Pilkington and his Labradors.

Ronnie Ross of Braelangwell, diplomat extraordinary, relaxing during summer trout fishing at the Braelangwell loch.

Chapter Thirty Six
Elusive Salmon and Hungry Trout

Although we were primarily stalkers we thoroughly enjoyed summer days fishing. When fishing Crom Loch on the South Side we would take a picnic and a tiny camping ring on which we would make lots of tea! Enjoyable relaxing days with a good catch of trout.

On sunny days you were not troubled by midges and by the time of October stalking the frosts have killed them off anyway but in August, on overcast or muggy days, the midges could be a menace! All sorts of repellents were tried.....Autan, Jungle Formula etc. but they were only partially effective. The high hills of Scotland may well be considered to be an earthly paradise but Satan has his say with those midges!

The River Carron, which continues to the Kyle at Bonar Bridge, is a good salmon river right up to the Glencalvie Falls. On the north side of the river it is Amat ground and on the south side, Glencalvie.

The Glencalvie Falls, however, are an almost insurmountable barrier for the salmon so they are either trapped in the large pool below the falls or have to divert up the Blackwater, a Carron tributary.

The falls are very steep and narrow indeed so other than in very dry weather the salmon cannot get past them. If the falls were to be blasted with explosives to create a channel wide enough for salmon to negotiate, they could get up and would be able to spawn in the burns of Alladale and Deanich. With so many extra fish breeding in the river, returning to the sea and then coming back again, the fishing on the whole length of the river would be vastly improved. Unfortunately, however, agreement cannot be reached with all proprietors.

The falls, in fact, must have altered over the years because in the two stalking "Bibles" in the 1890's and 1920's the salmon fishing at Deanich was described as reasonable but little or no salmon had been caught at Deanich in the years leading up to our time there.

Salmon are peculiar creatures: Trout eat because they are hungry but salmon do *not* eat in fresh water so why, you may well ask, do they take a fly? The short answer is that they don't! Or, to be absolutely correct, not until they feel like it and that is only when conditions are absolutely right: That means when the river is rising or just starting to fall. Not forgetting the vital question of water temperature. Want to know all about water temperature? Ask Ronnie Ross of Braelangwell!

Ronnie Ross of Braelangwell is a superlative fisherman: Salmon, trout, Artic Char, Ronnie is the man to ask. Flies, weather conditions, water temperature and everything else. Ronnie's vast experience encompasses them all.

Ronnie Ross with Jockey Ross (no relation!) and friends fishing for trout at the back of Benmore.

But why do the salmon take a fly if not to eat? It must be some kind of instinctive reaction when, as I have said, the river conditions are absolutely right.

One year at Deanich the flow of water in July over the falls was much less than it had been for years so some salmon had managed to get over the Glencalvie falls and up into the Deanich water. Driving back to the lodge with Richard Munro in the Land Rover one day we came to a stretch of water with a pool at the head of it. "Do you think it would be worth trying for a salmon there?" I asked Richard. "The water conditions look right with the river rising".

No salmon had been caught there before but we decided to give it a try and very soon after first casting into the pool Caroline hooked and caught a salmon. By the end of the morning Caroline and Ross had caught four salmon and from thence on the pool was named "Caroline's Pool".

Ronnie Ross and friend head across the Torridon moonscape to fish for Arctic Char.

So for that year we struck a bonanza and caught a number of salmon, more than had been caught at Deanich for years. It was just as well that we took advantage of this opportunity because it was not to be repeated the following year. About half way between Alladale and Deanich there is a huge, long pool and you would often see salmon jumping in it but although many a fly was cast over them no salmon ever took a fly in this pool, which we called Jim's Pool. Jim Pilkington, who was an expert salmon fisherman, said that the only chance of catching a salmon in a large, still, pool like this was if there happened to be a breeze to create a ripple on the surface of the water but although it was often fished in those conditions the pool never yielded a salmon.

As long as fishermen have ever fished for salmon there has always been earnest and often furious discussion on the virtues of different salmon flies. One man would swear by a Jock Scott another would champion a Hairy Mary.

In the 1920's a keen fisherman expounded a heretical theory: The type of fly or even its colour didn't matter! What mattered was getting the fly *down* to the fish. In that case, he was asked, are you saying that a trout fly such as the March Brown would catch salmon if fished deeply enough? He agreed that it would and when asked to demonstrate he, sure enough, caught salmon with a March Brown. As a young man Jim Pilkington had met him and found him a fascinating character. Jim had never forgotten the advice to *get the fly down to the fish.*

Marcus Munro with his son Cameron fishes in Glen Alladale by the old keeper's house.

The greatest revolution in salmon flies, in recent years, were the tube flies invented by Richard Waddington. We were to meet him later at Deanich and Alladale and I will describe those flies then.

To non-fishermen the appeal of salmon fishing appears baffling but it is, without doubt, a fascinating business. For a start you are fishing in delightful surroundings and, unlike coarse fishing, you are constantly on the move: Casting on different pools, working along the river, enjoying the sights and sounds of that magnificent landscape so even if you catch nothing you are rewarded by the pleasure of the whole scene.

If you *do* hook a salmon you, too, are hooked because the salmon is a tremendous fighter and to successfully land it is an achievement. Once hooked it then has to be played and kept out of any situation where the line can be tangled or snapped. So although we never became experts, or anything like it, we did thoroughly enjoy salmon fishing.

Trout, of course, are a very different proposition because they eat when they are hungry so they will take the bait much more readily. Once again, there is a wonderful range of trout flies at your disposal with all sorts of unusual and exotic names from the Black Pennel, an excellent fly, to the Welsh Coch-y-Bondhu. (All right, anglicise it to Cocky Bundy!)

Opposite Jim's pool is the Blown Wood on the South Side of the glen. Japanese Sika in August lie up in a sheltered place during the day in a suitable hollow in the woodland but with a view below them so they can see the approach of any danger. They usually place themselves in a very secure position indeed. When the rest of us would be fishing in or around Jim's pool, Richard and Edna would scour the Blown Wood with their glasses to see if they could spot Sika stags. Richard would use his telescope, Edna her 8 x 30 Zeiss monocular. Very difficult indeed to spot them but Richard and Edna usually managed to see them.

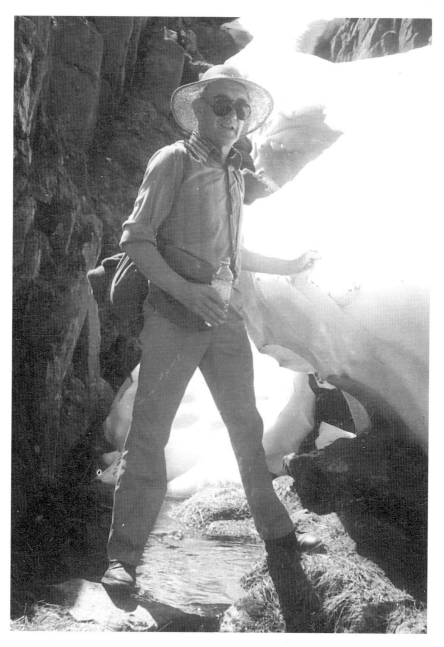

Where did you get that hat? Ronnie Ross at Torridon in July.

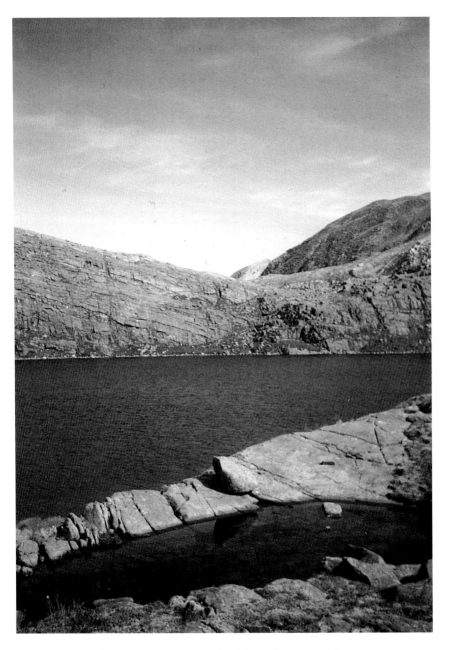

Objective attained. A high loch at Torridon.

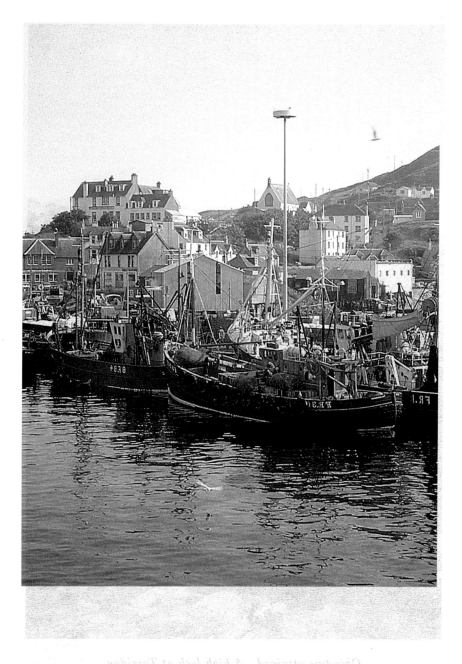

We leave Mallaig harbour.

Chapter Thirty Seven
To Rhum with the Deer Society

In 1972, there was a Deer Society Meeting on Rhum and we were delighted to attend. Rhum is one of the large islands in the Inner Hebrides with its near neighbour, Eigg. Rhum, however, is devoted to research on the Red Deer unlike Eigg which has crofting and tourism.

For many years Rhum was owned by the Bullough family of wealthy Industrialists who poured a fortune into the place. They built a huge structure of red sandstone facing Scriesort Bay and named it Kinloch Castle. It is a gigantic place, containing a Great Hall, ballroom, minstrel's gallery and much more. The Castle was surrounded by a beautiful garden in which a pool of heated sea water housed a stock of turtles.

Goodness knows where the red sandstone came from, certainly not from the island, so it must all have been imported. The Bulloughs had commissioned a series of gigantic oil paintings showing different views of the estate. These were displayed along the main gallery. You enter into the great hall, as befitting a castle. Errol Flynn would have nodded approval! Around this room at first floor level runs a gallery. Immediately ahead of you as you enter is a full size Steinway grand piano and the whole place furnished with pieces put in when the castle was built at the turn of the century.

An incredible place, then, in such a remote situation. When George Bullough, later to become Sir George, was 21 years of age in about 1900 it was decided that as a coming of age experience he would tour the world in the Bullough's elegant steam yacht, The Rhouma (old name for Rhum). No hurry, it was to take about two years. They don't do things like that these days!

Sir George married a French woman and her sitting room remains unchanged with French furniture and relics of Napoleon.

There was another lodge at the far end of the island, Dibbiedale Lodge.

The whole lot was eventually left to the National Trust on the understanding that Kinloch Castle was to remain untouched for ten years so naturally the Trust's great ambition was to pull it down! No such restriction was placed upon Dibbiedale Lodge so they couldn't wait and pulled it down anyway!

Fortunately, just before the ten years expired, they decided that it might, after all, be a good idea to save such a unique place, so Kinloch Castle gained a last minute reprieve!

Sir George died in 1939 so he missed the horrors and huge social changes of World War II...a good time to leave the stage.

The Bulloughs built a mausoleum on the west side of the island looking across the Atlantic towards America and that is where Sir George's remains lie.

His rifle was a .303 Holland & Holland double that he left to his stalker George MacNaughton who promptly sold it back to Holland & Holland for £50.

George was still there, going strong, when we first visited Rhum and what an interesting man he was. So much to tell us about the island and the deer.

A peculiar beast. Could it be a Red Deer/Giraffe hybrid?

The normal shooting seasons are not followed on Rhum as the objective is research. Deer are shot during every month of the year and, unlike normal forests, deer are shot throughout the entire age groups. There is a continuous process of analysis on parts of the carcass at mainland research establishments.

Correction! Deer, of course, are never "shot" on Rhum, they are "culled"! A team of experts live on the Island to carry out all aspects of research.

Rhum has its own species of ponies which are used to carry in the deer. Lovely animals, descended from the Spanish ponies that swam ashore from the ships of the Spanish Armada that were forced to flee northwards to escape their English pursuers, only to be wrecked on the west coast of Scotland. Well, that's the story and who was it that said "Never mind the truth, print the legend!".

We had crossed to Rhum on the "Western Isles", a converted fishing boat that ran a service to the Hebrides. We embarked on it at Mallaig and were warned that as the sea was quite rough it would be better to stay on deck. The reason for this was that down below in the cabin the inevitable smell of diesel combined with the pitching and rolling of the boat would make sea-sickness a certainty!

So wrapped in our waterproofs we all found seats on the deck. But it was both cold and windy and, yes, the boat pitched and rolled with a vengeance. Edna and her mother soon gave in and went down below, leaving Caroline, Ross and I on deck.

I love being on a boat at sea and the more it pitches and rolls the better I like it, going to the stem of the boat for a while to experience the full effect.

After a reasonable time I looked down below to see two pitiful figures, Edna and her mother, clutching plastic buckets to their chests and being thoroughly seasick!

As we went with the Deer Society our accommodation was in Kinloch Castle but this only applied to Edna and I. Where would Edna's mother, Caroline and Ross stay? The answer was with Ian Simpson, his wife Cathy and their three daughters at their house nearby. They made us all most welcome and it was a thoroughly enjoyable stay.

We all returned at a later date to stay with them again.

Ian was the boatman on the island. The Rhouma was now a sturdy fishing boat, diesel powered, and was used as a convenient means of transporting scientists and equipment to different bays along the Island. (This was not, of course, the original magnificent Rhouma which the Bulloughs fitted out and staffed as a hospital ship at their own expense during the Boer War.) We did manage a few trips to different bays and thoroughly enjoyed them.

So Rhum is an earthly paradise for those people intensely interested in Red Deer, isn't it? Well, not exactly, because there is a downside....The Highland Midge!

Midges are a drawback in any part of the Highlands but at Rhum they are the worst we had ever experienced anywhere. Scientists analysing the concentration of midge larvae at Rhum had come up with phenomenal figures per cubic inch of soil. Parties of school children camping at Rhum as part of a project studying deer suffered agonies from the attention of these infuriating insects.

During the hey-day of Rhum when the Bulloughs entertained their guests they were issued with broad brimmed hats complete with mosquito nets suspended from the brims to keep the midges at bay: Surely something of a deterrent to successful entertaining! If there is anywhere in the Highlands with a greater concentration of midges than at Rhum I can only quote Sam Goldwyn again and say "Include me out"!

The Bullough mauseleum, Rhum.

Another monster?   No, a wild goat in Lea MacNally's enclosure at Torridon.

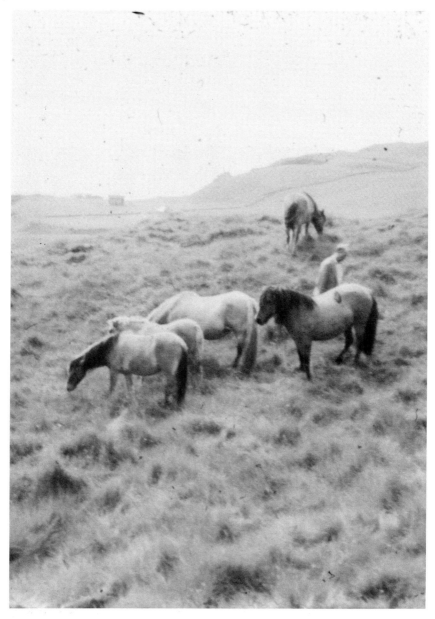

Some of the Rhum ponies. Reputedly descendants of those that swam ashore from the wreck of an Armada Galleon.

Chapter Thirty Eight
Rhum Hospitality

On our later visit to stay with Ian and Cathy Simpson and family we again enjoyed their hospitality. Each family on the island was given a weekly allowance of venison and Cathy made good use of it as imported meat and all other foods were so expensive. Because of this, food was on the table to be eaten, not wasted and the children were made to understand it. For the first time in my experience, if food that should have been eaten by the children was left it really did appear for them to eat next day. Yes, I know that you have seen this in television plays, but in real life?

Every week, as there was no television, they would have a film show in the village hall which was great fun for all. The locals were there, we Sassenachs and any of the youngsters camping on the island. We saw Steve McQueen in "Bullitt" there.

On the island at that time was Dr. John Fletcher: a doctor of Veterinary medicine. He was on Rhum for several years then he and his wife Nickie bought Reedie Hill Farm, Auchtermuchty, where they created their own deer farm. They not only supply the finest venison but have inspired others to do the same. In addition they supply live Red Deer for the creation of new deer farms, not just in England and Scotland, but throughout Europe. It was from John that we bought our initial stock of deer for Newton Park Farm in 1981 and since then all surplus calves have been sold back to him.

John's wife, Nickie has written a book on venison cookery, a most valuable asset in any kitchen. They are both numbered among the "good guys" of this world. John later wrote *A Life for Deer* about his life in the world of deer and running his Reedie Hill deer farm. It is a book that is essential reading for anyone interested in Red Deer.

George MacNaughton, with his years of experience, had much to tell us and among the many pieces of advice he gave us was this: You are making an approach to deer and, still a long way off, one of the animals looks intently in your direction. You freeze into the heather and after a minute or so, the hind resumes grazing. Obviously she noticed some kind of movement but failed to see you, or so you think.

George, however, maintains that on the contrary she *had* seen you, or seen a movement that she knew to be danger, and had simply resumed grazing with the intention of keeping a wary eye in your direction. Often, in such cases, it is impossible to get anywhere near within rifle shot because long before you do so the deer have all taken flight.

I'm sure that there is a lot of truth in this. When I first started deerstalking I was told that the eyesight and hearing of deer were both poor but their sense of smell was so acute that they could scent a man as far as a mile away if the wind was in the right direction. Having been able to observe Red Deer closely at Newton Park Farm I can confirm that contrary to what I had been told, their hearing is very acute indeed. On the Hill in Scotland it is never silent... there is always the sound of running water in the hill drains and, of course, the wind in the heather. The deer, then, have unusual sounds partially blanked out by the background noise so this, perhaps, is why the opinion has developed that their hearing is poor.

One of the lovely bays on Rhum.

With regard to sight, man is an alien figure walking upright on two feet so, to a deer, he is instantly recognisable but what if he is crawling through the heather and cannot be identified? The answer is that the deer are alert to *movement*. They have no need to completely identify who or what is causing this movement but any unusual or unexplained movement is a good enough signal for flight.

George was also involved with the process of shooting deer with narcotic darts so that the live animal could be examined and blood samples taken, before the antidote was administered and the animal released. These narcotic darts are very bulky and fired from a special rifle propelled by a blank cartridge, different loads for different ranges.

When they were first used at Rhum the dart could go clean through the animal, killing it! Eventually the technique was mastered and all was well.

Ross pats one of the Rhum ponies.

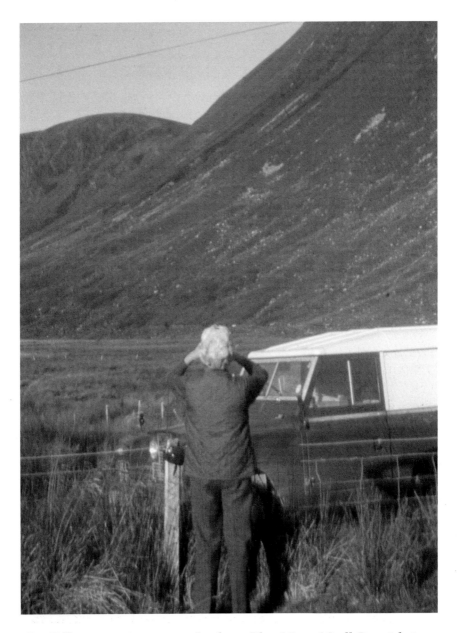

Sue Pilkington spies eastwards along Glen Mor. Meall Deanich is on the left.

Chapter Thirty Nine
With Jim Pilkington at Deanich

We had finally established the pattern of holidays at Deanich with a family holiday in August and then back in October for the serious stalking. This meant taking the children away from school in October for two weeks. Eventually the time came when we could no longer do this so it looked as if it was to be the end of our October stalking. Jim Pilkington, however, saved the day! He knew the situation and rang us up to ask if Edna and I would like to join his party for a week in October 1974. We were, of course, absolutely delighted.

Surprisingly, his brother Stephen who had spent so many wonderful days at Deanich and Alladale never returned, though he was most welcome to do so.

Although I never met Stephen he was, by all accounts, a "remarkable" character. He was married with one daughter and he and his wife had done some of their courting at Deanich and Alladale, as described in his book. He obviously was endowed with a quick temper and Susan Pilkington was to tell us of a time when she was staying at a forest where Stephen, too, was a guest. Something or other failed to suit him so bundling his wife and luggage into his car he raced down the estate track, almost running Sue off the road when she unexpectedly encountered him on a bend.

Jim was a keen and competent salmon fisherman and for many years had stayed with his friend, Sir Anthony Nutting while he fished on the Helmsdale. Jim always spoke highly of the Helmsdale gillies but, on one occasion, when Stephen was fishing on the Helmsdale, he had a violent disagreement with one of these excellent gillies and, once again, abandoned his stay and roared back home in a temper to Jim's considerable embarrassment.

Jim was a bachelor but during his stay at Deanich and Alladale he was always accompanied by a cousin's divorced wife, Susan

Pilkington. There was nothing romantic in this arrangement: They were the best of friends and Sue ran the lodge with unobtrusive efficiency. They always engaged the services of a cook who was usually a Sloane doing it as a holiday job.

The Pilkingtons didn't do things by halves and would be there from about September 1st to the end of October. Jim had a farm in Berkshire but did not run it himself so his whole year was devoted to field sports. After leaving Deanich and Alladale he would return home and spend the winter pheasant shooting or "picking up" with his beloved dogs. Early new year would find him shooting in Ireland, then back to Scotland for the start of the salmon fishing. Dublin Horse Show next then salmon again. August 12th would see him grouse shooting in Scotland and then, on September 1st, stalking again. We worked out that he only had about two weeks in the year when he was at a loose end!

We used to tell Jim and Sue that they were the perfect example of why *not* to get married. They seldom had a disagreement but when they did it was conducted with meticulous politeness. A raised eyebrow? Perhaps! But a raised voice? Never! Nothing nearly as vulgar as that.

We once saw a television play in which a superb actress played the role of a tall, brilliant hostess, no longer young and with a cut glass accent. She made a superlative job of it, but Sue Pilkington would have done it better.... and she would *not* have been acting!

Jim Pilkington and Sue made an incomparable host and hostess and all guests were made welcome to the n'th degree. All their guests had dogs and if you explained that your dog would only eat his Doggimix if it was mixed on the living room carpet and laced with three tins of Lyles Golden Syrup they would not have turned a hair or showed a glimmer of disapproval. They would, in fact, have been delighted to help and would have asked if three tins of Golden Syrup would be enough or could they fetch another one from the pantry?

So as an example of the perfect host and hostess they were the ultimate and there was much to learn from them.

Now everyone runs a Highland lodge in their own way and in our case it was either as a small family party or a larger party in August when Ross' friends from Repton School joined us. For Jim and Sue Pilkington, however, it was quite different. For a start all his friends would come to stay, spread over the weeks from September 1st to October 20th. Many of them were the friends who had stayed there with Jim and his brother Stephen in the 1930's but now, of course, their sons and daughters came too, so Deanich Lodge really burst into life.

It was very strange for us to arrive at Deanich Lodge as guests, rather than being in charge of the whole show. Jim and Sue Pilkington were incomparable hosts and we, in return, did our utmost to be exemplary guests. After all, we knew from experience all about running a lodge.

Before travelling up, we rang Sue to ask what supplies we could bring. She didn't need a lot, but did want some eggs. "How many?" we asked. "Oh", said Sue, "about ten dozen." So, in addition to a stock of supplies that we knew would be needed, fresh vegetables, for example, we had the ten dozen eggs on the roof-rack of our Mini Estate which we had decided to use for the journey. On the way we had stopped for a meal at Charnock Richard services on the M6. Having just started out again, we heard a tremendous bang...The tray of eggs had flipped over on the roof! The car was hastily stopped and the eggs checked....only two were cracked. Amazing!

Snow on the tops in October.

For a man who was obviously not short of a few bob, Jim's rifles were a peculiar selection. He still had his 7mm Mauser from his days as a young man but, in addition, he had a well-worn 7mm BSA with a telescopic sight. He also had a survival from World War One: A German 7.9mm Mauser cavalry carbine with an aperture sight and a stock that would not have looked out of place in a pile of firewood! He also had a .22 rifle with which inexperienced guests could practise. Jim would hand them the rifle and a box of "squibs" (i.e. .22 cartridges) and send them off to practise.

The only person I ever remember using the 7.9mm Mauser was Christopher Palmer-Tomkinson. Notwithstanding its unprepossessing appearance it shot straight enough and Chris made very effective use of it, often taking it to the Hill on his own and coming back with a stag.

A very old friend of Jim's was Mrs Tizer who owned the forests of Gordonbush and Kintradwell in Sutherland. She had an excellent Mannlicher with a telescopic sight and continued to stalk until well into her eighties. She would go out in the morning in the Land Rover accompanied by stalker and gillie. They would hope to get a stag within easy stalking distance on the way out. They would then stay in a remote bothy until it was time to go home, then repeat the process on the way back.

Early one year, Mrs Tizer said to Jim "I'm getting too old to stalk now, Jim, you might as well borrow my Mannlicher for the stalking season". So just before the start of the stalking season Jim rang her and asked when it would be convenient to collect the rifle. "How do you think I will manage?" she indignantly replied, having completely forgotten her promise to lend him the rifle. She used it again for that season and for a number of years afterwards. We were never to see it at Deanich.

By then she had been a widow for many years but her husband had, I understand, been with Jim at Eton. He was a man who loved to take very long shots and had commissioned a pair of 12 bore Purdeys with every barrel bored full choke; a most unusual arrangement. At the start of the War they were carefully cleaned and put in their superb leather and oak Purdey case and stored in the Gunroom at

Gordonbush. After the War the case was opened and the guns were gone! Someone had stolen them and they never showed up again.

This brings me to a peculiar theft suffered by Jim Pilkington. Before the War Jim had kept a game book which was not merely a bare record of his shooting, stalking and fishing but a complete description of his sporting days. After the War he opened the book to find it absolutely blank: Someone had carefully sliced out every page with a sharp instrument such as a razor blade. But why would anyone want to do such a thing? The man who stole Mr Tizer's Purdeys did, at least, have an understandable, if despicable, motive....He wanted to shoot a pair of Purdeys and wanted them free of charge. But Jim Pilkington's game book? Surely no use to anyone as the stolen pages could not be shown to anyone else again. It brings to mind the old Yorkshire saying: "There's nowt so queer as folk!"

The author, Edna, Sue Pilkington, Enid Du Pree and gillie with a stag on the Middle Ridge above Eisen-yarn-Corrie.

Christopher Palmer-Tompkinson and his wife were frequent guests of Jim Pilkington at Deanich as were his brother Charles and his wife. Their father had been at Eton with Jim and had been the Land Agent at Sandringham. He had become the British Skiing Champion in his younger days. Chris and Charles followed his example and were keen stalkers, too. I have an idea that either Chris or Charles also became the British Skiing Champion.

Chris is a remarkable character in the very best sense of the word, an amazing personality and the life and soul of any gathering. He would always turn up at Deanich with some new gimmick that would amuse or baffle us. He was as fit as a fiddle and the high hills of Deanich were no deterrent to him.

Of the generation who stalked at Deanich with Jim in the 1930's a few still continued to come as guests. John Puxley was one of them. By then getting on in years he was no longer fit enough to stalk but he loved being at Deanich where he had spent so many happy days as a young man. We first met him at Deanich in October 1972 and I remember him telling us that in his opinion no agricultural land in England was worth more than a rent of £10 an acre. This was low even then!

In the early 1930's the Puxleys had a 1,000 acre estate in the south of England but no-one would take it on. The Puxleys eventually found a Scottish farmer who would take it but it was on condition that it would be rent free for a period of years. They were glad to accept this as it meant that the land would be kept in good heart rather than revert to weeds. We found John Puxley to be a charming man and there was much to be learned from him.

Another friend from Deanich in the 1930's was Michael Wroughton who was, like John Puxley, at Eton with Jim. A big, powerfully built man but, unfortunately, his legs would never again take him up the Deanich hills. Another man of enormous charm, well endowed with wit and humour.

Bill Curling was another guest of the 1930's generation who came accompanied by his wife. Although of similar age to the others, Bill was still perfectly capable of walking the Deanich hills and shooting straight, too. If Bill got into position for a stag, even after a long stalk, that stag was always brought to the larder. Like all the others Bill was marvellous company with a fund of stories to keep us all roaring with laughter.

Two young people, brother and sister, were Rupert and Helen

Gosling. At that time Helen had been seconded to Princess Anne and her husband Mark Phillips for six months or so to organise their wedding presents and the essential "thank you" letters. Both of them were true outdoor people ready to tackle the steepest climb and the longest stalk. Both were unmarried at that time.

Rupert loved fresh air.... couldn't get enough of it! The living room at Deanich Lodge at the end of a day's stalking in October with the fire blazing and everyone swopping yarns about their stalking day was, as I have said before, the most comfortable place on the planet but not, of course, the warmest place on the planet, despite that blazing log fire. Rupert, however, always chose a place on the settee nearest to the door with the door slightly ajar! Rather him than me!

The Du Pree family were also visitors. Enid Du Pree was a widow but her husband, too, had been a friend of Jim's at Eton. The two boys, Richard and Peter, both farmed in the south east of Scotland and were both fanatically keen stalkers. Their father had bought one of the new .244 Holland and Holland rifles but neither of them liked it: "Too long". they said!

Jim Pilkington, the author, Sue Pilkington, and Richard Munro, ready to head for the Hill.

As well as stalking Red Deer they were both very keen Roe Deer stalkers. Neither was married in those days though Richard was to get married later. Two charming young men and, again, tireless stalkers.

When Johnny and Sheila Murray were first married they would stay in the small end of Deanich Lodge. Sheila would be the cook/housekeeper and Johnny would be on hand to stalk without the delay of travelling from Ardgay on his motorcycle. He would also be very helpful and would keep the fire and boiler going and supplied with wood.

The drying room at Deanich is a small room that houses two huge copper tanks heated by the boiler and in a Highland shooting lodge with guests arriving back from the Hill cold and soaking wet, a first-class drying room is essential. Back from stalking we would undress in the welcome warmth of the drying room, slip on dressing gowns, grab a cup of tea and head for that hot bath. A luxury you wouldn't exchange for a boatload of bawbees!

Seeing the stalking party away in the mornings Jim would say something like this: "If I were you, with the wind in this direction, I would head for the Strouban Path. At the top you should see deer and a shootable stag. If not, head for the top of the Strouban Ridge and spy again. There should be deer ahead but, if not, carry on past the White Stone and Reedy Loch and to the rim of Corrie Mor. But that is only *my* idea, you do *exactly* as you please!"

In the lodge with the Pilkington party, as I have said, there were always dogs. Dogs, in fact, always outnumbered guests. If there were ten guests there would be eleven dogs. When each guest arrived he would be accompanied by his or her dog and dog basket. After a day's stalking coming home wet and cold the first essential for us was a cup of tea followed by a hot bath, but not to the Pilkingtons or their guests. The first job was to dry their dog then to feed it and it was only after these jobs were satisfactorily completed that they would attend to their own requirements.

The dogs, in the main, got on very well but if one dog persistently irritated another the owner would tolerate so much and then issue the command: "Seeimorf". The long suffering dog could then retaliate and put an end to further annoyance.

Jim had a black Labrador bitch named Widge, short for wigeon and a German shorthaired pointer named Sam. (In Honda's earlier days they named one of their motorcycles the Pointer "after the famous racing dog!") Sam was supposed to be capable of both pointing and retrieving but I don't think he ever got that far. Widge, however, was an excellent retriever that Jim had trained and in the pheasant shooting season Jim was just as happy to pick up as to shoot. The other guests had all sorts of dogs but, in the main, the predominant choice was retrievers though the ladies liked smaller breeds.

Widge always accompanied Jim on the Hill and although stalkers, in general, are none too keen on dogs accompanying the stalking party Widge was never any trouble and always kept well out of sight of the deer.

Although my shooting as a guest of the Pilkingtons was perfectly acceptable there was one occasion when this was not the case. We were stalking on the South Side near the Strath Rannoch march and got into position for a shot. I fired at the stag who, although obviously hard hit, went on and was quickly out of sight below us on the undulating ground.

We quickly followed up and got into position from where we had last seen him with a good view of the slope below, but no sign of the stag. The good news was that the stag was obviously too hard hit to go far. The bad news was the problem of finding him to administer the *coup de grace.*

We spied the ground with our glasses and Jim Pilkington spied with his telescope. Nothing! We continued to look and look and finally Jim spotted a horn protruding above the heather and the horn was moving so the stag was alive....and alert!

We approached as carefully as we could hoping that we could get a view of him good enough to fire that final shot but as we drew closer he must have sensed us and was on his feet running directly away from us like a Derby winner.

I swung the rifle onto the stag but did not fire and Jim shouted in anguish, "For God's sake, shoot!" But I was sure that the stag would stop before going out of sight and, if not, I would have no choice but to fire. A stag running directly away from you, however, is a very poor target.

I followed the stag with the rifle sight and, at the last moment, he stopped. At that instant, I fired killing him outright with a bullet straight through the back of the neck....but it was a damned close run thing!

Fortunately I never did lose a stag wounded during my time with the Pilkingtons.

After staying for the first time with Jim Pilkington at Deanich we would ask him to join us for a week in August and he was always a most welcome and exemplary guest.

Starting for the lodge, well-pleased. Grimble.

Ready to start.

Ronnie Ross firing a .22 Brno at the target. His colleague, with telescope, spots for him.

Chapter Forty
Stalking by Sassenach and
Professional

In the early days of deerstalking with muzzle loading rifles and their curved trajectories, Scottish deer hounds often accompanied the stalking party, though I had always understood that none survive today. The breed is thought to be extinct, having died out during World War One. Certainly I have never seen one. They were not unlike a mixture of large greyhound and Irish wolfhound but, surprisingly, they hunted by sight, not scent. When you realise how quickly deer can get out of sight when disturbed, to have dogs that could not follow the scent seems an enormous handicap. But in the old days a shot would be fired and "Bran" and "Thunder" would be instantly slipped to follow their quarry. They would hold the stag at bay until the Rifle could catch up and administer the *coup de grace.*

In fact the chase with the dogs after a wounded stag was considered to be a vital part of the deerstalking scene and on some forests deerhounds were used to bring down "cold" deer, i.e. not just to pursue a wounded stag. On Culachy Forest there is a huge saucer shaped stretch of ground that was ideal for this purpose and dogs would be "slipped" at a stag on it. Lea MacNally has a photograph of a pair of Scottish deer hounds pulling down a stag at the conclusion of one of these hunts on Culachy. "Not a pretty sight", said Lea, and all of us would agree today.

I understand that dogs were still used to track wounded deer on some forests, certainly up to the 1960's, the most famous being Strathconan. But the dogs used were collies with their acute sense of smell, so they were far more suited to the task than the traditional Scottish deerhounds.

Nowadays, however, with the universal adoption of the telescopic sight the chances of losing a wounded deer are greatly reduced and, in any case, the Scottish Highlands must set a standard of marksmanship that would be hard to equal anywhere in the world.

It would be both pointless and distasteful if the Rifle did not shoot competently with clean kills being his overriding objective. If that standard cannot be achieved, then deerstalking is not for him.

I remember reading Ernest Hemingway's account of his wife shooting her first lion. Come to think of it, I have read two different accounts he has written about the same event, but lets take account number one! Whether it was his fourth or fifth wife, I can't remember but his name for her was "Miss Mary". So Miss Mary set out with Ernest and two guides to get a lion with her 6.5mm Mannlicher. Having hit the poor creature no less than five times she finally got it. This, I would have thought, was something to keep your trap shut about, not celebrate as some kind of achievement! They don't do it like that in Scotland!

Taking the shot.

Which brings me to air a personal theory with which you may, or may not, agree. It is this: Sassenachs shooting deer in Scotland would be far better off shooting with single shot rifles without telescopic sights, *provided that they had good eyesight.*

Yes, I can visualise you holding up your hands in horror and declaiming "The man must be mad." but let me explain: Please note that I use the word "Sassenachs".

The real business of stalking is hind shooting in the winter by the professional stalkers. They have to decide how many hinds to shoot to keep the numbers on the ground in proper control and have to shoot the poorest hinds, if possible. Hinds that, as far as can be judged, would have a poor chance of making it through the winter anyway.

To point out a stag for the "Sassenach" Rifle to shoot is comparatively easy...."That eleven pointer on the right or the switch in the middle." A switch is a stag either with no points at all or with brow points only. But to select hinds requires an expert eye. Having selected, say, three hinds out of a group of ten the stalker would shoot the first hind but then the rest of the group are instantly on the move.

So to quickly identify the other two requires tremendous expertise. It must be done, however, and the next hind shot. After that they have moved out even further and the last one must be accounted for.

Super stalkers. The rifle-shooting team from the Highland branch of the British Deer Society: Ron Aitken-Head, David Alison, Steven Mackenzie, Alec Murray, Marcus Munro, Alladale, Derek MacAskill, Glencalvie.

If the Sassenach thinks it is cold when it starts to snow on a stalking day in October it bears no comparison to conditions in midwinter. Then it is *really* cold in that snow-covered landscape. Not so bad while you are moving but if you have to stop and wait for a while you are quickly chilled to the bone so the stalk has to be made quickly with the minimum of time spent waiting.

The professional stalker has many hinds to shoot in very short days in midwinter so he must get as many hinds as he can account for in a day's stalking. He may well have to shoot fifty to a hundred hinds during that short hind stalking season.

For the professional, the stalking rifle is the tool of his trade and must give him the best opportunity of accounting for deer quickly, efficiently and humanely. In his case, then, the modern telescopic sight is essential. Having said this, however, Tommy Gordon, John Gordon of Glencalvie's father, for many years shot the large number of hinds required with a single shot .303 BSA rifle and iron sights.

So if a telescopic sight is right for the professional stalker today, why not for the Sassenach? Well, for the Sassenach, things are very different.

Let me say, from the start, that a telescopic sight does *not* make a bad shot into a good one. Ask many professional stalkers with experience of stalking with guests before the arrival of telescopic sights and they will invariably say: "In my opinion better shooting was done (by Sassenachs) before telescopic sights".

The Englishman who travels to Scotland to stalk is usually vastly inexperienced by comparison with the professional stalker and his perception of stalking is very different. The professional has to account for his numbers in, very often, harsh conditions. The Sassenach is there to enjoy the whole scene: The magnificent landscape, the sight of the deer and the challenge of the stalk. For him it is not a question of shooting as many stags as possible in a day but of the enjoyment of the stalking. To get one stag is a real achievement and two a tremendous bonus .... and expense!

So accompanied by the professional stalker he climbs to the first spying point to look for a suitable stag. If one is selected at a fair distance away the initial approach is commenced and as that distance is reduced the stalk begins in earnest. It may involve a wet crawl along the bed of a small burn or a glutinous crawl through a peat hag but, in any event, crouching and crawling cannot be avoided.

Next the approach to get into position for a shot at reasonable range, say 100 to 120 yards. Finally the shot must be taken with great care, as that first shot must be fatal.

So why, at this point, should I suggest a single shot rifle with iron sights? Well, for a Rifle with good eyesight, and it is assumed that good eyesight is essential for this purpose, iron sights should be perfectly adequate without relying on a telescopic sight. So why single shot? Because that, too, would impress upon him the absolute necessity of making that first shot count.

So that's my opinion. What do you think?

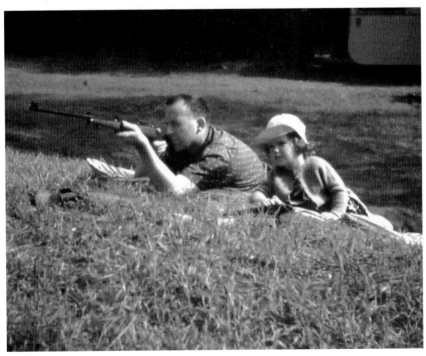

The author firing a .22 Brno at the target. Daughter Caroline, sans telescope, spots for him.

Richard and Marcus Munro, tip-top riflemen.

Chapter Forty One
Rifles and Riflemen, Ancient and Modern

A "remarkable" rifleman with a love of the Highlands was H. Mortimer Batten with a number of books on the Highlands to his credit. He wrote a series of articles in *The Motorcycle* during the War years, all with a Scottish theme. Stalking was, of course, very much in the picture. The "hero" of this series was "Old November", a venerable sidecar outfit - the sole transport of a Scottish stalker. Old November's exploits became familiar to the readers of *The Motorcycle* during those years.

After the First World War H. Mortimer Batten cruised the Highlands in his 1914 Grand Prix Car which was, I believe, a Peugeot. Generous hospitality saw that he was never short of fishing, shooting, and stalking. After the Second World War he emigrated to Canada: A strange choice for someone with a lifelong love of the Highlands but as he was a bachelor he had no wife or family to keep him in Scotland.

I have previously mentioned the single shot falling block Black Powder Express rifles favoured by most professional stalkers and many Englishmen, too. One of the most famous systems was the Farquharson Action. Farquharson was from Blairgowrie in Perthshire, a stalker turned poacher, not the other way round! He went on to write a book: *The Romance of Poaching in the Highlands.*

He was a superlative shot both with the stalking rifle and the competition rifle. Having designed his new falling block rifle action he reputedly carved it from a turnip before having one made. He had been a great friend of Alexander Henry, the famous Edinburgh gunsmith, but the design of the Farquharson action was the cause of contention between them and finally ended their friendship. Henry claimed that the Farquharson design owed much to his own.

The Alexander Henry falling block action was also very successful and was offered as one of the rifles in the trials to select a true breech loading rifle for the British Army to replace the makeshift Snider action which was used to convert the Enfield muzzle loaders to breech loading.

The Henry action was not accepted as the Government chose the Martini design, but the Henry rifling was. The breech action was designed by an Austrian lace manufacturer, Frederick Von Martini so the new rifle was called the Martini Henry. It was introduced in 1872 and was to continue in service until the advent of the British Army's first magazine rifle, the Lee Metford, in 1883.

In the days of Black Powder Express rifles the favoured rifle for the Sassenach was the .450 or .500 double rifle. Heavy rifles but, of course, the Sassenach had a gillie or stalker to carry it. Often the .450 was preferred with its slight reduction in weight and slightly flatter trajectory. But the choice for the professional was usually a .400 single barrel falling block Express; not only did he appreciate the even flatter trajectory and lighter weight, but he had to carry the darned thing!

When hind shooting the stalker would get into position to shoot at a group of hinds and would have two or three spare cartridges held between the fingers of his left hand, so in expert hands those stalkers could fire and reload with lightening rapidity. They could get those four shots fired as fast, or faster, than the man with the double rifle.

The single shot Black Powder Expresses of that era with their Alexander Henry or Farquharson falling block actions were beautifully made and a joy to use and handle. The largest calibre of the Expresses was .577 but made for shooting big game and considered unsuitable for Highland deerstalking. The smallest of the Expresses was the .360 and considered too small for Red Deer but, in the right hands and carefully aimed it could be deadly enough. Lady Idina Stewart was famous for her string of one shot kills with her .360 Express and, unusually, telescopic sight, in the late 19th century.

Nowadays it is well understood that your eye does not have to be right against the eye-piece of the telescopic sight. If this was the case the recoil of a powerful rifle would give you a tremendous whack! So the distance your eye has to be away from the eyepiece is known as the "eye relief". But in the l9th century the telescope had to be right against your eye so how did Lady Idina manage with the .360's considerable recoil?

I once had a .300 Black Powder Rook and Rabbit rifle made by the great Daniel Fraser of Edinburgh in the 1880's (with a telescopic sight) and although the .300 has a greatly reduced recoil it could, if held loosely, give you an unpleasant smack. To avoid this the eye piece is spring loaded so I wonder if Lady Idina's rifle had a similar sight? The sight on the Daniel Fraser has cross hairs but there are two horizontal ones for different ranges, presumably for this small calibre rifle, fifty yards and one hundred yards.

Not a stalking rifle, but a .300 Black Powder Rook and Rabbit rifle made by the great Daniel Fraser of Edinburgh, An example of a 19th century telescopic sight with spring loaded eyepiece.

It is difficult today, even impossible, to obtain any first-hand experience of stalking with the Black Powder Expresses but Lea MacNally knew an old stalker named Johnnie Kito who had stalked in those days. He had told Lea that the "best range" for the Expresses was eighty yards but I have often wondered exactly what he meant. Those rifles would shoot with a reasonably flat trajectory much further than that so I wonder if he meant that the "best range" was not for the rifle but for the "afterpiece"?   I would have thought that this was the most likely explanation.

One more word on today's telescopic sights. I'm sure that stalking as such is much less interesting because shots are inevitably taken at longer ranges. I remember when I eventually gave in and bought a David Lloyd rifle with its virtually immovable telescopic sight and Johnny Murray got me into position for a shot at a stag on the Middle Ridge. I pointed out that the distance was excessive. "But these rifles shoot "flat" to 300 yards." said Johnny. "Yes " I replied "but I have to be able to actually *see* the stag". My case rests, as Raymond Burr might have said!

The superlative 6.5mm (.256) Mannlicher.   This is the Jeffery Mannlicher used by the author.

At that time I had recently purchased a .243 David Lloyd rifle. David Lloyd's wife's family had an estate near Rosehall, Sutherland and he was a fanatical rifle shot and stalker. He had evolved the .244 cartridge that was adopted by Holland and Holland for their new .244 stalking rifle in the 1960's. This was the Holland & Holland .375 cartridge necked down to .244 giving a tremendous striking blow at a very high velocity indeed so it shot "flat" for an enormous distance. He then designed his own rifle.

If you laid down all the cartridges fired in Scotland to check telescopic sights in a year they would stretch from here to Timbuctoo! And back! Having zeroed in your rifle it would eventually suffer a knock on the Hill so you would have to start all over again.

So how to avoid all this fiddling about and, in addition, have a rifle that could be completely depended upon? A rifle that once you got into position for a shot you would know, without the slightest doubt, would not have gone "off song". The answer was a rifle that was, as near as possible, with a telescopic sight built in as part of the rifle.

So David Lloyd set to and designed such a rifle. The telescopic sight is screwed directly onto the action *so it cannot be adjusted.* It has been claimed that the David Lloyd rifles can be thrown onto a concrete floor without altering the adjustment of the sight.

So what if the sight *did* go "off target". The answer is that it doesn't, but if it did so it would have to be returned to David Lloyd for correction. My rifle, however, despite having taken some pretty severe knocks has never altered and has always remained 100% accurate.

In money terms, David Lloyd rifles are expensive. In *value* for money terms, they are a bargain. After all, what would you give to ensure that you did not lose a wounded stag? Yes, I agree, no rifle, even a David Lloyd, is an *absolute* guarantee but it is as near as you will ever get.

So the David Lloyd is the prince of stalking rifles. You can have a choice of calibres but all are made on the incomparable 1898

Mauser actions from World War Two German military rifles.... like my humble .303 BSA before them!

Lea MacNally knew an Englishman turned Highland keeper and stalker near Strathpeffer who had not one but two David Lloyds: A .243 and .270. He had decided to commission a third so one of the two would have to go.....was I interested? I was, indeed, and chose the .243 with 4X Zeiss Telescopic sight, a purchase I have never had cause to regret. Young and old pick up that rifle and shoot straight with it so with the David Lloyd in your hands you are absolutely confident that the rifle is right. The only thing that can go wrong is if the deer happens to move as you press the trigger or, of course, the all important "afterpiece". In the hands of Ross, Bill, Larry and his friends it was to prove its worth time and time again.

The incomparable David Lloyd rifle. Hand made with the telescopic sight designed as part of the rifle.

Marcus Munro of Alladale, winner of the British Deer Society Scottish Inter-branch Rifle Shoot. Ultra high velocity .22 hand-built by J Hare and Marcus Munro in Florida U.S.A.

Chapter Forty Two
Days on the Hill by "An Old Stalker"

There have been many books written about stalking, especially during stalking's hey-day, but almost every one was written by the Rifle, not the Highland stalker. An exception was *Days on the Hill by "An Old Stalker"*. This was the nom-de-plume of David Taylor who stalked on a number of forests, but ended up as second stalker at Glen Islay.

This is one of my favourite books on stalking but Lea MacNally did not agree. He found the book irritating and felt that the author was an embittered man. Well, I can understand this, because he had much to be embittered about! In my opinion the book gives a valuable glimpse of a stalker's life around the turn of the century.

The book was written in 1926 but describes stalking days long before that date. Many of the Rifles for whom he had stalked would have tried the patience of a saint!

One of his Rifles endlessly argued with him, especially when a stag had been missed. David Taylor wrote:

"There were times when he became altogether unreasonable. On such occasions I considered it prudent to walk away and leave him to follow accompanied by the man who accompanied us. The latter then had to listen to a detailed account of all my faults and shortcomings but this did not disturb me in the least. When I thought the gentleman had recovered his equanimity, I allowed him to overtake me. As a rule he never referred again to the stalk or excuses, but inquired as to what was to be done next".

One Rifle missed a stag then asked Taylor to go out next day to find the wounded beast. Realising that what was required was that Taylor should shoot a similar stag, he went out until he found a beast that would do, but took two shots to kill it. Back at the lodge:

"I was heartily congratulated and the other gentlemen in the lodge were brought into the larder to see the stag. Addressing them, the Rifle said:

"I knew he was hard hit and could not go far, but I can't understand how I hit him quite so far back, elevation all right too".

This was not the only time this "sportsman" used this trick, but the next time he was careful not to state the number of points the "wounded" animal possessed.

Rigby's advert for Express Rifles.

On another occasion the same Rifle asked Taylor to accompany him with his own rifle. Taylor wrote:

"The gentleman fired and I saw him hit a calf immediately over the stag's back. As I expected he (the stag) ran clear, affording plenty of time for a good aim, and I saw my missile take him in a vital part. Just at that moment the stricken calf fell. "You've got a calf" said my companion, "" Looks rather like it" I replied. The stag ran for about twenty yards and also dropped. "He's down. I knew he couldn't possibly go far" was the next remark addressed to me.

On going up to the dead stag the bullet hole had to be found. After it was located he said: " Isn't it wonderful how far an animal will travel with a bullet through the heart?" Matters now assumed a very pleasant aspect which they certainly would not have done had I declared the real state of affairs. I have since wondered if he really thought he hit that stag or was it only make-believe, or did he think he had outwitted me?"

There were many other ways in which David Taylor was sorely tried. For example, another Rifle always overestimated the weights of the stags he had shot. On one occasion, knowing this, the head stalker added half the difference between the real weight and the weight the Rifle would have estimated and this flattering weight was written on the card sent to the lodge.

Far from being delighted with this over-optimistic weight the Rifle insisted that a mistake had been made and decided to weigh the stag himself. As Taylor wrote: "The result was little to his satisfaction and it was difficult to determine whether he or the stalker bore the greatest appearance of humiliation".

Although many of the Sassenachs for whom Taylor stalked were poor shots and even poorer sportsmen, there must have been some with whom he got on well because not least of the appeal of stalking is the pleasure of the stalker/rifle relationship.

Posing for the camera at the turn of the 19th Century.

(Top) Ross with the Braelangwell children on the miniature Kawasaki. Adam on the tank, Steven and Claire.
(Bottom) Handsome Larry Cawood radiates charm.

Chapter Forty Three
By yon Bonny Bikes and by yon Bonny Braes

Caroline and Ross are older than Marcus and we used to take two motorcycles to Deanich for them to ride. The first time we tackled Richard Munro's home-made switchback road from Deanich Lodge to the Inverlael Hydro Road, those steep descents terrified Caroline until I explained to her how to switch off the engine with the handlebar button at the start of the descent. Gravity would then turn the engine over which acted as a brake and you took your thumb off just before the bottom of the hill. The engine would then burst into life ready to zoom up the next hill. She quickly grasped the technique and from then on thoroughly enjoyed zooming up and down the home-made road and, of course, the other roads and tracks at Deanich in fine style. Great fun for both she and Ross.

The Braelangwell children and Marcus Munro were immediately impressed by the joys of motor-cycling and they all became suberb riders when we eventually fixed them up with motorcycles.

With so many opportunities to ride off the road, they became superlative riders and of course, they started motorcycling so young. Leaps, climbs and near vertical descents became commonplace for them.

Marcus' friends were also infected by the biking bug and one of them, Christy Pavla, we fixed up at the right price, with a 50cc trial bike when he was sixteen. We used to irreverently call him Christy Pavlova and he too, became a superlative motorcyclist.

Years later, going to work early one morning with his brother in his car, he was heading along the straight road out of Bonar Bridge towards Lairg. The car left the road, crashed and they were both killed.

A dreadful tragedy. There were no witnesses, so why this happened will never be known.

Rachel from Braelangwell was another intrepid biker, long before she was sixteen and Adam started on a Honda monkey bike which we bought him when he was about seven or eight and was an excellent rider. He, too, could ride this little bike nonchalently over all kinds of terrain.

He was not, of course, allowed on the road, but sometimes rode on the wide, bumpy grass verges near Braelangwell. There was very little traffic on the road, especially out of season and on one occasion, Adam decided to take to the road. All went well until a police car pulled in behind him.

Adam rode to Braelangwell and got off the bike. One of the policeman went up to him and asked "How fast will that bike go?" "Seventy miles an hour." Replied Adam, inaccurately.

"I'm sure it was doing that round those bends" said the policeman "Now where's your mother?" "In the house." Said Adam with a wave of his arm.

So the policeman went to see Margaret to point out that Adam must *not* go on the road. Message received and understood. So Adam was careful to stay off the road...when anyone could catch him!

Ross aged 7 on a similar Honda monkey bike to that ridden by Adam Ross.

In my younger days I used to ride a Speedway JAP in grass track racing. Marvellous bikes...no gearbox, no brakes and 40 BHP instantly on tap when you opened the throttle of that alcohol engine. Power-sliding a motor-cycle is one of the most exhilarating forms of locomotion known to man...or woman.

When Steven of Braelangwell was about twelve, he had graduated to a 50cc Suzuki and one New Year he was riding it on the road. There was a stretch of ice, then a dry section, followed by another icy patch and so it continued.

Steven hit the ice and with a masterly display of balance and throttle control, he put the bike into a controlled slide. Just before the ice ended, he brought the machine upright to hit the dry section. The throttle snapped open and up went the front wheel in a wheelie. Down again just in time to hit the next patch of ice and the process repeated.

"Let me have a go" I asked, wondering if I could still master the technique. Well, I did manage some half-hearted.....all right, quarter-hearted slithery slides, but wheelies, with that patch of ice ahead? You must be joking!

Steven and Marcus went on to bigger and better machinery. Both were on the road at sixteen and they finally graduated to four cylinder Japanese monsters.

Steven flies through the air........

Richard Waddington with his 51lb salmon, caught in Norway.

Chapter Forty Four
We meet Richard Waddington

When Ross was in his teens in the mid-1970's his friends Bill Auden and Larry Cawood from Repton School would join us at our farm to shoot wood pigeons. They were all excellent shots. Stationed in a clearing in the woods as the pigeons flew in to roost they would pull them out of the sky.

As Bill and Larry were such good shots, why not ask them to join us at Deanich in August? Obviously they jumped at the chance. Introduce most Sassenachs to Scotland and you start a rapport with the country that never fades and this was certainly the case with Bill and Larry. Not only were they super shots but first-class fly fishermen who could cast an impossibly long line, so they were in their element.

With a larger party we took more stags in August and when the boys joined us their shooting was exemplary. So all the youngsters shot and fished and had an absolutely marvellous time. Jim Pilkington would arrive too and he was instantly accepted as "Jim" by them all and was always subjected to a barrage of questions on shooting, fishing and stalking, all of which he took in good part. His knowledge of the deer and deer forests of Scotland was unsurpassed and would be hard to match by any Sassenach.

"What do you know about Kinloch Teletubby Forest, Jim?" they would ask and Jim would know all there was to know about the place: How many stags, who owns it now, who owned it in the past, what the salmon fishing was like, how many acres and much more! Jim was questioned about everything from flies and fishing lines to rifles and Roe Deer.

All the boys, as expected, got on wonderfully well with Richard Munro, Marcus and Richard Munro's housekeeper, Sybil Ross. Plus, of course, everyone else in the glen they met.

By then the Deanich and Alladale sportings had been let to an unusual couple, Janet Ashton and Major Richard Waddington and we were to lease Deanich from them. Richard Waddington by then was an old timer but a remarkable man who had led an amazing life. He had invented a new type of salmon fly which was such a great success that many claimed it had revolutionised salmon fishing. Many salmon fishermen swore by their "Waddingtons".

Richard Waddington once said to me: "I have never had any money but I have always been able to do exactly what I wanted to do". Not a bad achievement! He had owned Rolls Royces, fished and shot everywhere, which brings me to an unusual story.

At the start of the War in 1939 two young Englishmen boarded a train in London. One of them was going to join his unit in Colchester and heading into the unknown leaving the security of his family and, perhaps, destined never to return.

The other young man was obviously in a different situation and was going on holiday with his guns and fishing rods on the luggage rack above him.

Like all Englishmen, after a friendly nod, they immersed themselves in their newspapers but after a decent interval they did start a conversation. The one going to join his unit pointed out how envious he was of the other man who was obviously going on holiday, only to be amazed to hear that he, too, was also going to Colchester to join the same unit. "But why have you got your guns and fishing rods?" spluttered the first Englishman in amazement. "Look here!" said Englishman number two "You never know when you will be invited to fish and shoot!"

Those two men were Bobbie Gilroy and Richard Waddington and I was able to remind them of this story, as told to me by Jim Pilkington, when I spoke to them together at Alladale.

During their time at Colchester they were being instructed by a Sergeant on the construction and use of the Bren Gun. Richard Waddington was clearly taking little notice so the Sergeant said to him sarcastically "It would appear, Sir, that you think you know more about these guns that I do!" "That's true" replied Richard "I used to sell the things!"

By the time we met Richard Waddington he was well into his

seventies but, surprisingly, he used to stalk and shoot perfectly well with Janet Ashton's rifle. She had a modern rifle with telescopic sights. The name escapes me but on the barrel was engraved "Regulated by Holland & Holland" so she always referred to it as her "Holland & Holland".

"Just get the stag in the telescopic sight" Richard Waddington used to say to Richard Munro "and you can't miss!" Believe it or not he could miss but, even so, he made excellent use of the rifle.

Another thing Richard Waddington said to me was: "Nowadays no Englishman can afford to shoot grouse. Soon no Englishman will be able to afford to shoot stags." We thought this to be a ridiculous prophecy at the time but the cost today really has become astronomical.

Richard Waddington was once called "The world's greatest salmon fisherman" and his permanent legacy to the world of salmon fishing is his Waddington salmon fly. This is a triple hook fly, resembling the tail fin of a small fish, with a shank of metal wire up to three inches long. Heron feather fibres complete the job. The lure looks like a small fish.

Like the controversial fisherman Jim Pilkington met in the 1920's, Waddington was also unconcerned about the colour of salmon flies. He said "It is the tone of the fly that is important, and for this reason, the colour of the wing of the salmon fly is of little importance".

During his glory years he was one of the best-known characters on the Scottish sporting scene, famous for both salmon and grouse. During those years, salmon fishing was at its zenith, far different from the drastically reduced catches of today.

He regarded the Spey as "the king of all Scottish rivers" He wrote that "compared to the Spey, the Dee is trivial, the Tay lacking in fish and the Tweed tedious".

Demobilised as a Major in 1945, he considered his future: "I was an experienced General Staff Officer, I had made war on foot, on ski, in Jeeps, in armoured cars, in boats, in ships, in landing craft and had been twice blown up. None of this would be of the slightest use in civilian life." He had served in six campaigns.

His first job, for two weeks, was as an unskilled mechanic, but he soon moved to Scotland, renting a house on the Spey. He then started work on a series of books, taking a new look at salmon fishing, the migration of Atlantic salmon and the most effective lures for catching them.

In addition to salmon, he was famous as the first man to make grouse-shooting pay. In 1947, with little or no money, he took the bold step of leasing the seventy thousand acre, Glenlivet Estate in Banff-shire. Their grouse moors produced only 120 brace of grouse per annum. Within five years, his efficient management and ferocious attack on vermin had increased the bag to 6000 brace a season.

He renovated the three lodges and let the grouse shooting and fishing to, among others, Nelson Rockefeller, Henry Ford, Texan oil millionaires, Royalty and heads of state. He was even far-sighted enough to create ski-slopes for winter sports.

He described his successful methods in *Grouse Shooting and Moor Management* (1959). During the 1950s, he claimed that he made a profit of £1 an acre from his grouse moors.

Richard Luis Owen Waddington was from an Anglo-Chilean family, born in January 1910. His grandfather was the Chilean ambassador in Brussels and his father fought the last known duel in Belgium in defence of the honour of his "rather wild" sister. He killed his opponent.

Young Richard was destined to have an eventful life. On the outbreak of World War One, he and his sister were sent to Chile to live with an aunt, returning in 1919. His father died shortly after his birth and his mother remarried James "Junk" Marshall, who owned a large estate in the Lake District, where Richard learned to fish and shoot.

Educated at Marlborough and Edinburgh University, married in 1931, then a series of jobs including pig farming and journalism, before the outbreak of war.

His best salmon was a fifty-one pound monster, on the Aaro in Sonjeford, Norway. He wrote, "this fish represented the fulfilment of a dream. It was caught on a fly of my own tying, played and tailed entirely alone and in a tremendous river, such luck only occurs but once in a lifetime."

His only unfilled ambition was to catch a 40 pound salmon in British waters, but he did come close at the Dog pool of the Inverness-shire Garry. He hooked a huge fish, which took him a tremendous way downstream until at last he had to hold fast and hope that fish would not break him. When the fish was landed, he thought "Here at last is my 40 pounder - but alas, he was only 38 pounds."

He was a complex man, who loved to solve mathematical puzzles in his bath, loved both classical music and jazz and owned a collection of early jazz records.

When he finally married Janet Ashton, it was only two years or so before his death. When we met them, Janet Ashton was, I suppose, in her mid-thirties and had been Richard Waddington's secretary for years. She was well spoken, dark-haired, slim and attractive in a non-glamorous outdoor-girl way. Many people expressed amazement that she had stuck to Richard Waddington for years as, on the surface, they appeared to be an ill-matched couple though as she was to marry him years later, they were, perhaps, not so very ill-matched after all.

Janet Ashton, presumably with Richard Waddington, had started in the Sporting Agency business letting stalking, grouse and salmon but, as far as I know, it was not a full-time business. Even so it did enable Richard and Janet to take Alladale Lodge for much of the stalking season and we had to negotiate with Janet for the Deanich stalking.

Ready to start. Ross, Edna and Caroline.

Richard Waddington's ex wife became Mrs McManus! No, she didn't marry me or any relation of mine but this is how it came about: Richard Waddington had, of course, been married in his earlier days but eventually that marriage ended in divorce. When he was in his fifties he married a young Swiss girl in her early twenties and they had a son, Richard, who was a schoolboy when we were at Deanich. He was a lively and likeable youngster who, unfortunately, had an artificial forearm though he managed wonderfully well with it.

Like so many of these marriages with a huge age gap, the marriage was to end in divorce and the son lived with his mother. She then married a Mr McManus and I understand that they ran a hotel in the Scottish Borders but, sadly, Mr McManus died and I know no more of the story.

After the marriage to the Swiss girl and before eventually marrying Janet Ashton, Richard did marry again in 1982 but I knew nothing of this until I read his obituary in the Daily Telegraph in November 1999.

Autumn approaches. West from Deanich Lodge with Inverlael cliffs in the far distance.

Japanese sika stag in its summer coat.

Horatio Ross.

Chapter Forty Five
Horatio Ross

One of the greatest shots of the 19th century was Horatio Ross. With gun, rifle or pistol he was impossible to beat and, in addition, he was one of the hardest riders to hounds in his day.

He stalked at Dibbiedale, which marches with Alladale, for many years. He then stalked the adjoining Kildermorie Forest and finally Wyvis.

He was born on September 5th 1801, the only son of Hercules Ross of Rossie Castle, Forfarshire. Hercules was a great friend of Nelson, hence the decision to name his son Horatio.

At age eighteen he joined the 14th Light Dragoons but after seven years, finding that work interfered with sport, he resigned his Commission, purchased a string of horses and took up quarters in Melton Mowbray.

Melton Mowbray in those days was where the madcap members of the hunting set gathered to gallop over the Leicestershire hunting country. So with the hardest riding and shooting set in England, Horatio matched his ability with his companions in all kinds of contests, often with huge sums of money wagered on the outcome.

Two exclusive shooting clubs in London were the "Red House Club" and the "Old Hat Club". Nowadays "old hat" is taken to mean old fashioned or out of date but the original meaning was very "top drawer". My mother always used it in its original meaning so the correct meaning had endured for a century or more.

Horatio was unbeatable at live pigeon shooting contests at these clubs: Live pigeons were released from a trap at, for example, twenty-five or thirty yards from the shooter and for a kill to be counted the bird had to fall dead inside a given boundary. In 1828 after shooting against the best shots in Great Britain and Ireland he won the Red House Club Cup, the blue riband of pigeon shooting, by scoring

76 birds out of 80 at thirty yards rise. The other birds were killed but fell outside the boundary. A performance that today's expert clay pigeon shots would find hard to equal. Remember, too, that Horatio Ross was shooting with a muzzle loader.

Live pigeon shooting. You will see from the puff of smoke at the breech that the guns were flintlocks.

On another occasion in the same year, after successfully winning at the Red House, Lord De Ros asked him if he could shoot equally well at live game. Horatio said that he would be prepared to shoot against any man in England and would allow Lord De Ros to select any man he chose.

The match was arranged for November 1st 1828 at Lord De Ros' shooting quarters at Mildenhall, Suffolk for a wager of £200 a side though much more than that was eventually wagered on it. The shooting was to be from sunrise to sunset at partridges and no dogs were to be used. The opponent chosen was Colonel Anson, superlative shot and tireless walker.

Colonel Anson started at a tremendous pace in an attempt to outwalk Horatio and although initially ahead by mid-day he was obviously tiring badly. As they were followed by a huge crowd the birds were very wild and shots had to be taken at fifty to sixty yards.

About fifteen minutes before the match was due to end Colonel Anson was one bird ahead but could walk no further so he proposed a draw. With £1,000 of his own money at risk and two birds to get in fifteen minutes, Horatio agreed.

Horatio Ross and Captain Rees Howell Gronow were considered to be the finest pistol shots in the world. Gronow had been goaded into accepting a challenge from an arrogant Frenchman and the duel took place in the Bois de Boulogne, Paris.

Once into position the Frenchman put his glove into a tree and asked Gronow which finger he should fire at. Gronow remained silent so the Frenchman said "Ah, we will say the little finger". He then levelled his duelling pistol and shot away the little finger.

Captain Hesse, Gronow's second said to him "You must do something to try and shake that fellow's nerve". Gronow then threw his hat in the air and put a bullet through the centre of the crown. Bowing to the Frenchman he said "Monsieur, voila votre destine!" Two minutes later the Frenchman lay on the grass with a bullet through his brain. Not long after that, Captain Hesse, Gronow's second, was also killed in a duel. Although many people attempted to match Gronow and Horatio Ross and get them together for a shooting match with pistols, Gronow would never agree and having killed two men in duels in France Gronow told Horatio that he could no longer stand the sight of a pistol.

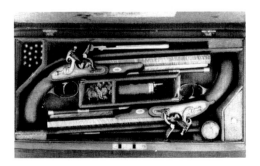

The pair of John Manton rifled flintlock pistols with which Horatio Ross shot ten brace of flying swallows before breakfast.

Strangely enough Horatio Ross never fought a duel or saw one fought yet he was asked to be a second no less than sixteen times. On each occasion, even though a resolution of the dispute seemed hopeless, his diplomacy and reasoning were always successful and the duel was always avoided.

On one occasion Horatio fought a contest, pistol against rifle at one hundred yards with Lord Vernon of Sudbury Hall, South Derbyshire. Horatio won against Lord Vernon's rifle. There is still a Lord Vernon at Sudbury and I wonder if he has any details about this remarkable contest? What, for example, is known about the makers of the weapons?

But one of the most outstanding feats of all time with a pistol was Horatio's acceptance of a challenge to shoot ten brace of swallows on the wing in a day. The contest was shot at his home Rossie Castle. They were long shots at swallows who had built their nest round the towers of Rossie Castle, three and a half stories high. He fired as the swallows were hovering, almost at a standstill, just before entering their nests and the contest was completed before breakfast.

Most surprising of all was that the pistols were flintlocks: A pair of John Manton rifled pistols. The pistols still survive and ended up in W. Keith Neal's unique collection.

To shoot with a percussion cap muzzle loader is virtually the same as shooting with a cartridge breech loader but with a flintlock there is a noticeable delay between squeezing the trigger and firing the charge so the use of flintlocks made this feat even more remarkable.

Horatio Ross was also a superlative target rifle shot having captained the Scottish Team for the Elcho Cup eleven times and having made the highest score for Scotland on two occasions when he was over sixty years old.

He was also one of the earliest photographers in Great Britain and became an expert photographer for those days. In 1839 Henry Fox Talbot perfected his method of producing photographs from a negative and some examples of Horatio's photographs are preserved in the gun case of W. Keith Neal's Prague rifle.

But regardless of his other abilities it is as a deer stalker that Horatio Ross is of greatest interest to us.

He claimed never to have attempted to achieve a huge bag of grouse in one day. His best daily total was sixty-five brace which you may well regard as a pretty good score. At deer, however, he really was the very best.

Jim Pilkington always said that he liked to spend the whole day on the Hill and so did Horatio Ross but, unlike Jim Pilkington, he was always up at 3am and not back to the Lodge until 7 or 8pm: "Walking, running or crawling all the time ". Even at the age of eighty he was still up at 3am to start the day's stalking and that was by no means his last year.

In 1828 he shot 87 deer on Fealar, one of the Atholl forests. This, of course, with a muzzle loading caplock double rifle. In 1837 he shot 75 deer in a season in Sutherland. In 1851 he shot 118 deer on Mar Forest and that, too, would have been with a muzzle loader. During that season he once shot thirteen deer in one day with fourteen chances.

For many years he took the Dibbiedale stalking in Strathcarron. Dibbiedale, which marches with Alladale, was a separate forest then but is now amalgamated with Glencalvie. Horatio later stalked Kildermorie which marches with Dibbiedale in the south. He then stalked Wyvis to the south of Kildermorie.

During his years at Dibbiedale, he and his family of five sons squeezed into Dibbiedale Lodge at the foot of Glen Dibbiedale. How they all managed it is a mystery, because the Lodge, unlike many grander places, was tiny, consisting of a sixteen foot square living room, one bedroom, and "two cupboards that contained beds".

When the two forests Dibbiedale and Glencalvie were bought at the turn of the nineteenth century by Mr Dyson Perrins, he had the old Lodge demolished and built a beautiful new Lodge, Loch na Chaorann (pronounced, believe it or not, Harn) together with a huge deer and grouse larder further north near the Kildermorie march. The two forests were then known as Dibbiedale; now they are known as Glencalvie!

The private road to the Lodge and down to Ardross near Alness was possibly the first tarmac road in Scotland ....certainly the first in Ross-shire. The roof was taken off in the 1950's and the whole place demolished in the 1990's.

Yes, you're quite right about Dyson Perrins, he *was* the Perrins of Lea and Perrins Worcestershire Sauce, which brings me, strangely enough, to ex-Prime Minister Harold Wilson. Harold Wilson was interminably teased by the Press for his liking for HP Sauce. Nothing wrong in that, you might say, but HP Sauce was considered to have a plebian image, a reflection on Harold's good taste! He protested that it wasn't true! His preference was for Lea and Perrins Worcestershire Sauce, but the Press did not believe him.

When Harold Wilson unexpectedly lost an election a mischievous reporter rang the HP Sauce company and asked how this would affect HP Sauce sales. "The brown sauce market is not subject to political fluctuations." replied the solemn spokesperson.

Today's owner of Glencalvie, Mr Peter Fowler, has built a superlative Lodge on the site of the old Dibbiedale Lodge, so now Glencalvie is stalked from the two Lodges, Glencalvie and Dibbiedale. W. Keith Neal showed me a superb cased double caplock rifle that had belonged to Horatio Ross. It was by a Prague maker and W. Keith Neal told me that this maker was considered to be "The Purdey of Europe".

When storms hit the Deanich/Alladale area with every hill burn masquerading as the Richenbach Falls, cutting off much of the ground and causing us to fall behind with our numbers, we would consider it acceptable to go out in the evening to cut off a stag as the deer came down from the tops. We would usually choose a corrie adjoining the Dibbiedale ground. A burn running down the centre of the corrie was the march and we would take up a position to give us a good chance by the side of the burn. I would always look across the burn and wonder where Horatio would have chosen to take up his position a century or more before. In his hands would have been the very rifle we had seen at W. Keith Neal's.

An enormous amount has been spoken and written about the distance a shot should be taken at deer in Scotland *with iron sights*. In my experience the stalker tries to get you into position for a shot at 100/120 yards if at all possible. Into position for a shot you ask your stalker how far out the stag is. "140 yards" he says. "140 yards" you say indignantly, "he's a 170 yards out if he's an inch!" *Wrong.* Having seen our deer at Newton Park Farm at *known* distances I can assure you that if your stalker says 140 yards he is estimating in your favour, not the other way round. That 140 yards is probably nearer 120/130.

But on the subject of distance Horatio Ross made it a rule never to fire at a stag unless he was certain of a kill so we will let him have the last word. He wrote: "I cannot accuse myself of having wounded deer, because I make it a rule never to fire at deer beyond the range of 150 yards, and then only if I had a good, steady view of the deer." He went on to say "however well men may shoot at a small mark on a target at a long distance, I venture to implore them to think of the misery and pain they may cause to poor deer for years by reckless shooting; and I beseech them to keep in mind, when getting near the end of the stalk, the words ...... *one hundred and fifty yards"*.

Horatio Ross died aged 85 on December 6th 1886 so to what did he attribute his remarkable health to such an advanced age? These are his own words: "It may be useful to others if I state what I believe to be the cause of preserving until so late a period of life the activity of a man of middle age. I attribute it in a great measure to my having always kept myself in a state of moderate training. I have always lived well and for many years have drunk nothing but light claret, one bottle per diem: But I have never omitted, wherever I was, in town or country, whether the weather was fair or the reverse, to walk regularly eight miles, and generally twelve miles, every day of my life, unless I had an opportunity of going out shooting. I have also for a great many years been very particular in taking a sponging bath of cold water every morning".

A handleable nine bore tubelock Joseph Manton for live pigeon shooting, reputedly made for Horatio Ross. Compare this with a nine bore caplock made for wildfowling by Thomas Heath.

Braelangwell Lodge. The "little end" on the left, "big end" on the right. Part of the Keeper's House on the other side of the road top left.

Chapter Forty Six
Hinds it is To Be

After a year or two of having the youngsters as our guests in August the idea struck us that we ought to take them hind stalking at New Year. Stags in September and October were out of the question because of school, but hinds at New Year would be fine because this would be in the school holidays. As hind stalking would be much cheaper than stalking stags, they would get much more shooting.

So hinds it was to be, but where to start? Deanich Lodge was not practicable for midwinter: Far too remote and in any case the water supply would be difficult as it would so easily be frozen. Another problem was that with a spell of hard weather and snow- storms you could easily be trapped in.

The answer was Braelangwell Lodge in Strathcarron for a number of reasons: Firstly it is much nearer civilisation as it is only about seven miles from Ardgay and as it is on much lower ground, water supplies would, surely, never be frozen (yet they were to be on one occasion!).

Most Highland lodges were, as described earlier, built in the stalking boom between 1850 and 1900 but Braelangwell Lodge is much earlier, built, I believe, about 1760. What its original purpose was seems to be unknown but, presumably it was built for a local laird as it is such a huge place.

The Braelangwell Estate is owned by the Godmans and is primarily a fishing estate with a good stretch of fishing on the River Carron so at the end of the season the lodge was shut up for the winter. It does have an area of stalking ground of about 3,000 acres marching with Amat and Forest Farm on the west and the old grouse ground, now largely wooded, to the north. The adjoining woodland on the roadside also produces some Sika stalking on the Braelangwell ground. So the visit to Braelangwell in "The Glen" over the New Year in 1978/79 was to bring a new dimension into our Scottish saga and was a resounding success. We have seen in every New Year since with Ronnie and Margaret Ross, the keeper at Braelangwell and his wife. All but two of those New Years up to 2002 we stayed at Braelangwell Lodge. One year we took Gruinyards Lodge on the other side of the river. Gruinyards is a much grander and more modern lodge built in the 1890's.

So were we at Braelangwell Lodge for the Millennium New Year 2000? Sadly, no, as the price for the Millennium had been multiplied by ten! We were, however, still able to see the New Year in with Ronnie and Margaret at their keeper's house opposite the lodge. We had taken a house near Bonar Bridge and we were back at Braelangwell Lodge for New Year 2001 when the rent reverted to the normal price.

Gruinyards Lodge with Stephanie in the foreground.

It is always an adventure to drive to Scotland but never more so than in midwinter. In that first year, we stopped at Charnock Richard on the M6 for breakfast as usual but by the time we reached the Lake District the landscape was snow covered; it was a foretaste of things to come! I did all the driving: On we went through the Borders and eventually to Dunblane. The run on the east side is never as interesting as on the west but this time there was no shortage of interest!

Through the Borders there had been snow storms of varying intensity and snow on the road but from Dunblane onwards the roads were covered in hard packed snow and the snow- storm had settled in with a vengeance.

I don't mind driving on snow because after snow and ice covered roads on a motorcycle, which I am used to, it is so much easier in a car, but that confidence is not necessarily shared by my passengers. In any case I have the steering wheel to hang onto!

So on we went through all those dreary villages: Aberader, Aberuthren, etc. to Perth. That run from Perth to Inverness, about one hundred miles or so, is interesting even in fine weather and in snow the landscape is magnificent. But would we be able to get over Drumochter Pass, the highest point of the journey, or would the road be closed? On we went in the teeth of the storm but, yes, the gates on the approach to Drumochter were open so we managed to get over.

At Drumochter and, further on, at Slochd Summit the deer were right down to within rifle shot of the road, driven down by the storm. Once over Drumochter, however, the storm eased a little so on we went through Inverness and Dingwall.

The final obstacle that could beat us was the drive over Struie Hill. At Evanton the storm had intensified and snow was hitting the windscreen like horizontal stair rods. But, once again, the road was still open so we were eventually over the Struie and heading down to Ardgay unscathed.

Our first of many visits to Braelangwell, of course, and our first real meeting with Ronnie and Margaret. Yes, we had met them briefly during our time in the Glen but not with a chance of getting to know them. Braelangwell Lodge is in two parts: The big end and the little end but for our party we only used the little end. The big end has a huge kitchen, the little end only a small one but we managed well enough. In addition to the boys our party consisted of Edna and I, Caroline and Ross. We had taken the hind stalking on Alladale and

Deanich so there was to be tremendous scope and as much shooting as the boys could handle.

Bill Auden, Larry Cawood and Ben Hingley had travelled up in Larry's father's long wheelbase Land Rover which was to be a tremendous help during our stay.

The hind stalking at New Year 1979 was a resounding success and this was to continue unchanged through the 1980's with virtually the same *dramatis personae*. Stephanie Orton, Ross' girlfriend, whom he was to marry in 1988 joined us for New Year 1985 and has been with us in the glen every New Year since.

Work and marriage meant that the boys eventually dropped out, but we have never done so and although we no longer took the Alladale and Deanich hindstalking from the late 1980's we were still able to see the deer there every New Year and get a shot or two at Braelangwell, Forest Farm and Amat.

The New Year party games continue, with Stephanie taking over more and more. She has arranged all the quizzes for years.

Margaret Ross of Braelangwell. "A marvellous person in every way". So said her former teacher.

(Top) Dinner at Braelangwell. L to R; Margaret Ross, the author, Steven Mackenzie, Stephanie and Edna.
(Bottom) Braelangwell Lodge in the snow.

Ready to start Hind-stalking by Alladale Lodge Deer Larder. Left to right: Larry Cawood, Caroline, Ross and the author.

Chapter Forty Seven
Highland New Year

We had arrived at Braelangwell Lodge on 30th December 1978 and were in the Highlands at New Year for the very first time. For New Year's Eve we went to a celebration at Foulis Ferry, on the road to Tain. Larry drove us in his father's Land Rover. We enjoyed ourselves and were back at Braelangwell Lodge before midnight as we had been asked by Ronnie and Margaret to see the New Year in with them.

We have been especially fortunate to know Ronnie and Margaret and count them as very special friends. Some folk allege that real hospitality starts north of Perth. Yorkshire folk say it starts at Yorkshire despite their county motto of "If ever tha' does owt for nowt, see tha' does it for thissen."

The south of England is not famous for New Year hospitality and I am absolutely certain that this is not because of the character of the people but that in these days of nuclear families, the opportunity for people in a community to mix is greatly reduced.

But regardless of any theories there is no question at all that hospitality flourishes in the Highlands. Margaret Ross' hospitality is unsurpassed. Despite not having known us before that New Year, Margaret made us so very welcome and has continued to do so. Margaret is attractive and well-educated with an Edinburgh University degree. Among her many accomplishments she is an absolutely superlative cook.

She has four children: Rachel, Steven, Claire and Adam. At that first New Year, Rachel was almost ten, Steven was six, Claire was almost two and Adam was the baby aged eight months.

Ronnie Ross is the Braelangwell keeper, stalker, river keeper, guide, philosopher and friend to every Sassenach who visits Braelangwell. There are many marvellous characters in the Highlands but it would be hard to find anyone who could compare with Ronnie. Not only does he know his job from A to Z but he is a consummate diplomat quite capable of charming the birds from the trees, let alone having the ability to have any Sassenach metaphorically eating out of his hand!

A superb fisherman, excellent rifle shot and a raconteur *par excellence.* All the virtues and abilities of the finest Highland stalker are embodied in Ronnie. Difficult guests? Never known one! If they were, in fact, difficult, Ronnie would be far too polite to know it.

In reality, of course, some of Ronnie's guests would try the patience of a saint! But not Ronnie's!

Ronnie Ross with a salmon at Braelangwell.

At Christmas time at home television is barred: We see far too much of it during the rest of the year, so our friends come round in the evenings to our programmes of party games. Charades, give us a clue, quizzes, pencil and paper games, and much more. So with all of us at Braelangwell plus the Ross family it was party time all over again with one important addition...Sardines!

A rambling Highland lodge is the ideal place for Sardines and the Ross family were introduced to Sardines together with all the other party games. With so many places to hide, Sardines was hilarious. Yes,

I agree that Sardines are at their best with a mixed party of teenagers and the delicious opportunities for stolen kisses but, even so, they are thoroughly enjoyed by all ages.

So with overcoats on and armed with torches, everyone trooped out in turn to attempt to find and join the first two who had been sent out to hide. On one occasion we just could not find the two who had originally been sent out, only to discover them eventually hiding in the roof rafters above the drying room in the "big end" of the lodge.

The highlight of the New Year at Braelangwell was Margaret's party. The big drawing room in the "Big end" would be cleared and everyone in the glen would be invited. Margaret would lay on a tremendous hot and cold buffet... venison, salmon, beef with all the trimmings and mouth-watering sweets. I would challenge the finest and most expensive hotel to equal Margaret's buffets. Surpass them? Impossible!

In the early years music for dancing would be provided by Willie MacDonald and his fiddle, but later, John Gordon, the Glencalvie stalker, would arrive with his electric organ and the whole joint would be jumping.

If TV wanted to film a typical Highland gathering at New Year, one of Margaret's parties would be ideal.

Margaret Ross and Margaret Macleod would sing and Johnny Murray would sing his party piece, *Springtime in Alaska.*

Singing my Sassenach song.

"It don't mean a thing if it ain't got that swing." One of Margaret and Ronnie's New Year parties. Left to right; Murray MacLeod of Tain, Rachael Braelangwell, Linda Gordon, John Gordon at the organ, Willie Moffat of Lubchoinnich, Margaret Ross.

Highlanders are not at all inhibited about standing up to sing in front of such a large gathering, but Sassenachs? Not the kind of thing they are ever called upon to do.

I decided, however, that inhibited or not, I must steel myself to take part, so I rattled off a few verses to the tune of *The Laughing Policeman*. The verses were all about the members of our party and the people in the glen. So here is an example. Larry Cawood was a student of Cirencester Agricultural College, known locally as "Aggies":

The citizens of Driffield salute their favourite son
His name is Larry Cawood and he's full of Yorkshire fun
Those Aggies tried to beat him and put him to the test,
But at birds and booze and blarney, our Larry is the best.

Out stalking with a German, Ron heard him shout "Mein Gott,
Sieg heil und Squashy Sauerkraut, I'll shoot der ruddy lot!"
He fired off all his bullets, without a single break,
He missed the stags and hinds and shot a knobber by mistake.

Then, everyone would join in the chorus between verses:

Oh what a funny story, I'm sure you all agree
'Cos Tony Blackburn heard it first and passed it on to me
The first time that I heard it, I very nearly died
As it was I laughed and laughed and laughed until I cried.

The last verse usually went something like this:

We've been away to Germany, we've been away to Spain,
Ate monkey stew in Timbuctoo, but wouldn't go there again,
Where'ere you go in this wide world, I don't care where or when,
You'll never beat the quality of the people in this glen.

A visit to the pantomine at Inverness was also not to be missed, where we Sassenachs enthusiastically booed the baddies, cheered the goodies and shouted "He's behind you!" when the ghost appeared.

Looking west along Glen Beag to that magical mid-winter landscape beyond Deanich Lodge.

Chapter Forty Eight
The Hill in Mid-Winter

The deer, of course, had been driven into the glens by the snow, as most of the vast area of the Alladale and Deanich forests was impossible for the deer to graze. We were soon to find out that hind stalking is a very much colder business than stags in September/October.

For stags we had always worn heavy walking shoes and due to the wet conditions underfoot your feet were always wet and cold but for midwinter different footwear was required. Hunter Wellingtons were the obvious choice so that even if your feet were cold they would, at least, be dry. Edna, however, would have none of it. She was not going to walk in Hunter Wellingtons because of their lack of grip. She decided to stick to her normal walking shoes despite the fact that it would be 30 degrees colder than in October.

On our first day's stalking Edna and I, with Johnny Murray as stalker, started out from the back of Alladale Lodge in deep snow. In no time at all Edna's feet were wet through and freezing but on we trudged through the snow. About a mile or so from the Lodge one of her well-worn shoes snapped in half... So there we were far out on the Hill with one of poor Edna's shoes out of action in deep snow.

"Well, Johnny" I said "I did my best to persuade her to come in Hunter Wellingtons but you're married and you know how illogical women can be". "You're quite right" said Johnny "if black was white they'd say it was green!"

Johnny has a remarkable sense of humour and his one liners would always have you rocking with laughter. So we set to and managed to tie up Edna's shoe somehow to enable her to get back to the lodge: The hinds were safe from us that day!

On another occasion, Johnny and his gillie heard a rifle shot from a different stalking party on an adjoining forest, followed by a second shot a few moments later: a bad sign! One shot should have been enough! They exchanged glances.

A third shot followed, then a fourth. "Ah, well" said Johnny "while there's lead in the air, there's hope!"

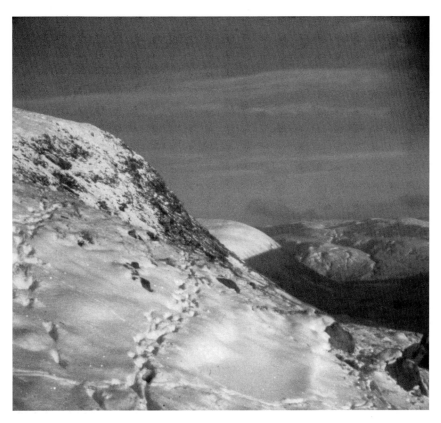

Hinds just out of sight at Corrie Crocher. Are the stalkers getting within shot?

Johnny was once with a stalking party who were absolutely determined to have a marvellous holiday, with no holds barred. Whisky flowed unceasingly. "They never went to bed on the same day that they got up" said Johnny "and you could have become an alcoholic in a week!"

Johnny had been a confirmed bachelor and was no longer young when Sheila had arrived to act as cook for the Pilkingtons at

Alladale some years before. She decided that she was going to marry Johnny ...and did so!

Sadly the marriage did not last. Even so, however, the marriage transformed Johnny in a way that surprised us all so even after the marriage ended some good came of it.

Johnny had been the ponyman when we first went to Deanich but he knew the ground like the back of his hand and eventually graduated to stalker. He was a good, careful stalker, never prepared to take chances so he was an excellent man to be with on the Hill, especially with those trademark one-liners!

During the years spent hind stalking at Deanich and Alladale our party of enthusiastic young men thoroughly enjoyed the stalking but I left most of the shooting to them. I was perfectly happy to accept the role of afterpiece's assistant and never shot more than a hind or two during the whole time. They would get far more out of the shooting than me, so that was fair enough.

In addition to their Deanich and Alladale stalking, Ronnie Ross would take the boys stalking on Forest Farm and Braelangwell. Jack McNichol, the Amat stalker, had the task of shooting Japanese Sika in the planted and enclosed forestry areas. He very kindly asked us to shoot there and Ross and I did so.

This kind of shooting was new to me and I really enjoyed it. We would carefully advance through the woodland, into the wind. Jack's rule was neck shots only so that no venison would be spoiled, but this was fine. We had many rewarding days at Amat. When Jack retired, Alan Dean, the Amat keeper and Steven Mackenzie, who was there at the time, would also give us a shot at Amat.

Towards the end of our stay one year we were trying to get in for a shot near the bottom of Corrie Crocher (Croaker to you), just before Meall Deanich. Richard Munro was stalking for Ross and I was the afterpiece's assistant! The ground was snow covered and we were involved in a seemingly endless, wet, cold crawl through deer tracks in the long heather, and no, we never did get a shot at that hind! I decided that it would be a good moment to compose a choral tribute to Richard and Sybil. The tune I chose was little Jimmy Osmond's *Long Haired Lover from Liverpool.*

When we had finally said our goodbyes to Richard and Sibyl we all sang the Alladale song.

> *We've had a super-dooper holiday at Alladale*
> *and enjoyed it every day.*
> *We've had some ding-dong stalking with Richard Munro*
> *and there ain't no better way.*
> *We've enjoyed your Highland hospitality*
> *and we would like to say:*
> *We'll all be back to see you all again,*
> *because you can't keep us away.*

Looking east along Glenmore from Deanich Lodge towards Corrie Crocher.

The Argo at Alladale.

(Top) Feeding the stags at Alladale in mid-winter. The author talks to the old stag and feeds him potatoes to gain his confidence.
(Bottom) Still talking, the author takes off his deerstalker and moves towards the stag.

Chapter Forty Nine
Never Say Never

With wildlife you can never say never. If you do, then something will occur to prove you wrong!

Red Deer temperaments vary widely, just like humans. Deer tend to come down into the glens at dusk, but at Deanich in August we used to see a stag consistently coming down in the evening long before dusk and staying quite near the lodge. He was not fed, but he just seemed to have an affinity to man. This happened for several years and then he graduated to Alladale Lodge, where he was fed by Sybil, together with other unusually tame deer.

He was named "Herbert", not a very appropriate name I agree! Herbert, on occasion, would go into the keeper's quarters at Alladale if given half a chance! Surely you could be forgiven for saying that no wild stag would ever be brave enough to do that.

One winter's day, when we were hind-stalking, the Argo throttle cable broke and I was repairing it. Potatoes had been carried in the Argo for deer feed so, for Herbert, there was the smell of food. As I worked away, Herbert came next to me and scrabbled with his forefoot at the floor of the Argo, hoping to scrape up some potatoes....a sight hard to match anywhere in Scotland: Man and stag toiling away side by side!

On another occasion, we were out with Marcus Munro feeding the deer in mid-winter at Glenmor, Alladale. One old Royal stag was little more than skin and bone. Had he been seen during the season, he would undoubtedly have been shot, but somehow he had managed to elude the rifle.

Marcus and I decided that he would never survive the winter. Only one tooth left in his head and he had become tame enough, or hungry enough to take a potato from your hand. He was, remember, a truly wild stag who had never approached human habitation, not one of the Alladale feeders.

"If deer at Newton Park Farm were as tame as this" I said to Marcus "they would want to put their noses against your forehead. Would he do the same?" "I don't know" said Marcus "I've never tried!" with a look that clearly said "We've got a right one here!"

So I talked quietly and reassuringly to the old stag, feeding him some more potatoes and gaining his confidence. Taking off my deerstalker, I bent towards him, still talking to him and the old-timer did put his nose against my forehead...a wonderful moment that astounded Marcus and his assistant stalker Innes MacNeill. Not much they hadn't seen in the world of deer but this was unique.

The old stag is finally brave enough to put his nose against the author's forehead.

I am a great believer in the effect of the human voice on animals, tame or wild! Shout "Gerraravit!" and they will immediately make no mistake about the message! On the other hand, talk quietly and reassuringly and they will know that you mean them no harm.

My most remarkable example of this was at Newton Park Farm. I was working on a piece of machinery on the upper floor of the long barn, when I noticed a coal tit standing on the floor looking at me, only a few feet away. The bird had not been there when I arrived.

Small birds can sometimes find their way in, but fail to get out. No food or water for them in an alien environment. This bird was clearly distressed, with its beak opening and closing, no doubt lack of water rather than food.

So I chatted away to him quietly and reassuringly as I carried on with my job. He listened to me with his head on one side. Had he moved back a few feet further he would have been out of my sight under a pallet, but he made no attempt to do this.

After about fifteen minutes, he flew away to perch on one of the roof trusses forty feet or so away. I carried on working. About fifteen minutes later, I looked round to find him back again exactly in the same spot, though I had not seen him arrive.

Again I chatted to him as I worked and again he listened. Finally, still talking, I slowly moved towards him and he allowed me to pick him up in my cupped hands. He accepted this, making no attempt to struggle, so I took him downstairs, made him a "nest" in a bale of straw and put him into it. Ten minutes or so later he flew away strongly.

So what do you make of it? The most amazing feature is that the bird, after flying away, came back to be near me in exactly the same place. Note that it was summertime and in any case, we do not put food out for the birds.

I could be absolutely mistaken, as Jim Pilkington might have said, but in my opinion, the bird, finding itself in a completely alien environment, came over to be near another living creature. When I made the correct soothing sounds the bird sensed that there was nothing to fear from me. Anything more than that would be pure speculation....but what do you think?

Feeding the stags at Deanich in wintertime looking east along Glen Mor.

Chapter Fifty
The Seers

I don't suppose that Seers are thick on the ground in your neck of the woods but, as the millennium approached, predictions were in vogue. Nostradamus, many centuries ago, made streams of predictions in convoluted verse but the problem is that they are so vague and complex that they are meaningless. An event occurs, Nostradamus is consulted and, *lo*, a prediction is found that, with a generous slice of imagination, can be assumed to match it. "Nostradamus predicted that" say the pundits but only *after* the event, not before.

Nostradamus predicted that in 1999 the "Prince of Darkness" would descend and destroy the world, but it did not happen! I am afraid that it is not given to mortal man to be able to predict the future, but many have chanced their arm.

One of the most famous Seers in our part of Scotland was the Brahan Seer, Coinneach Odhar Fiosaiche (Sallow or Brown Kenneth, the soothsayer) of the 16th century and he is still quoted today. Pronounce Brahan as a Cockney would pronounce brown.

Brahan is an estate near Dingwall and Coinneach Odhar, pronounced coo-in-yach oar, worked there.

He made many predictions, among them: "Long lines of carriages without horses will run between Inverness and Dingwall and Skye". The railways?

And of the healing waters of Strathpeffer: "Uninviting and disagreeable as it is now the day will come when it shall be under lock and key". This, of course, has happened.

He also predicted that a terrible disaster would befall the world when the river Ness should be spanned by five bridges. The fifth bridge was constructed a few days before the outbreak of World War Two.

He predicted that the glens would be emptied of people and

replaced by sheep: A prediction that was only too true. "The big sheep will over-run the country and the disheartened clans will flee before it across the sea to islands as yet undiscovered. The land will pass into the possession of strangers and be so desolate that no cocks will crow in the glens north of Dromochter. The price of sheep will rise and then fall and in time they too will disappear and be forgotten." All this has happened.

"Ships will anchor at the summit of Ben Wyvis." Helicopters, perhaps?

His most chilling prediction, however, is still in the future: "The deer and other wild animals in the huge wilderness will be exterminated and browned by horrid black rains. The people will then return and take undisturbed possession of the lands of their ancestors." Nuclear fallout is the only answer to this one but, of course, we don't believe in seers anyway, do we?..... do we?

At a gathering of the local gentry he had been invited, presumably to demonstrate his remarkable gifts. Lady Seaforth's husband was in Paris at the time and Kenneth unwisely declared that he was being unfaithful to her. The furious and humiliated Lady Seaforth had him burned to death in a tar barrel. Curious that he could not have predicted this!

A memorial to him can be seen at Chanonry Point near Fortrose in the Black Isle where he was rolled down the hill in that burning barrel. Or could that have been another "Brown Kenneth" accused of witchcraft a century earlier? You decide!

There are, however, still Seers in Scotland and in the Ardgay area the modern-day Seer is Swein MacDonald. Local people are divided in their opinion of Swein MacDonald's mystical powers: Some say "A load of rubbish." others say "I'm a believer!"

I must say that I have always been on the lookout for a good, second-hand crystal ball. All I need to see is tomorrow's newspaper with the racing or stock market results but my search, up to now, has been unsuccessful!

How anyone can solemnly declare "I'm a Pisces so that means

I'm witty, far-sighted, warm-hearted, intelligent and with a love of rice pudding", baffles me!

Wasn't it G.K Chesterton who said that "When men cease to believe in God, they don't believe in nothing, they believe in anything."

After the start of World War II one of the national newspapers conducted a survey to see if any of the astrologers who wrote in the daily papers had predicted this monumental happening that would affect so many lives.....not one had done so!

Another thing that amazes me is that in today's technological age when man's achievements have risen to hitherto unimaginable heights, the belief in astrology continues. The ancients who believed in astrology also believed that the earth was flat! My case rests!

A stag cleans his antlers.

Croick Church by Ardgay in the 1920's.

Chapter Fifty One
The Glencalvie Clearances

One of the hundred or more parliamentary churches built by the great road-builder Thomas Telford was at Croick, Strathcarron. It served the ninety people who lived at Glencalvie which was owned at that time by William Robertson of Kindeace. In 1842, two years before his death, Robertson decided to clear them all out so that the whole area could be offered as one large sheep run.

The trifling details of the eviction were left to James Falconer Gillanders, his factor, the third generation of a family of factors. He cleared off his employer's tenants, then leased the land himself and made a mint! His grandfather had been Lord Seaforth's factor on the Long Isle and had worked hard for his employer... and himself! He accumulated £20,000 (well over one million pounds in today's money) and bought himself an estate in Easter Ross.

His son followed his example and became Lord Seaforth's factor. He also lined his own pockets successfully, allegedly being better off than many Highland estate owners.

Grandson James, however, the man who evicted the Glencalvie tenants was the most successful of all: Like Patrick Sellar he was "respected by his superiors, admired by his peers, loved by his family and hated by the people."

Writs of eviction were issued against the Glencalvie people at Whitsuntide 1845 and *The Times*, hearing of it, sent up their reporter Thomas Campbell Foster to investigate. He was later to report on the Irish famine for the *The Times*.

He was appalled by what he saw and staying at the inn at Ardgay wrote:

"Those who remember the misery and destitution into which large masses of the population were thrown by the systematic clearances (as they are here called) carried on in Sutherlandshire some 25 years ago under the direction and on the estate of the late

Marchioness of Stafford - those who have not forgotten to what an extent the ancient ties, which bound clansmen to their chiefs were then torn asunder - will regret to learn that the heartless course, with all its sequences of misery, of destitution and of crime, is again being resorted to in Ross-shire."

He had just been to see the scene of the evictions, where all the crofts were empty other than one, in which an old soldier, Hugh Ross, lay dying. All the people stood by, the women in their plaids and shawls, the men in their plaids. They were singing the 145th psalm *The eyes of all things wait on thee, giver of all good.*

Two days later they moved to Croick churchyard constructing makeshift tents from tarpaulins, blankets, or anything they could utilise for the purpose.

There were 27 children under ten, seven of whom were ill, a few unmarried men and women but most were married couples over forty years old.

The *Times* reporter went to see them and they crowded round him, shaking his hand, but there was little he could do to help, other than to report their desperate plight. A few of them scratched despairing messages on the windows of the church where they survive to this day.

He was infuriated that such people who had always paid their rent punctually had been heartlessly evicted but, of course, to the proprietor nothing mattered but money....and there was more of it to be obtained by letting the lot to a single tenant to graze sheep. The owner, Major Charles Robertson was not even in Ross-shire at the time to see the misery caused by his instructions.

Most of the Glencalvie tenants were of the Ross family, described in the writs as "Ross alias Griesnich" (shoemaker). These writs are still to be seen in the toll booth at Tain in a room above the cells of the old gaol. A fortnight later the families had left the Croick churchyard and Gillanders claimed that he had resettled six of them. The *Times* reporter followed them and reported that some of them "got a piece of black moor near Tain 25 miles off, without any house or shed, out of which they hoped to attain subsistence. Another two families were given turf huts near Bonar Bridge, but the rest are hopeless, helpless"

There is no trace today of their occupation on "the black moor", where the unfortunate Rosses were abandoned and for the rest of the people....scattered to the four winds, some, no doubt, to the Glasgow slums and others more fortunate, across the ocean to Canada.

Steven Mackenzie fishing at the head of the Morrell Pool, Braelangwell. William Ross' wife was clubbed into this pool during the Gruinyards clearances.

After his "successful" clearance of Glencalvie James Gillanders had married his boss's daughter, Miss Robertson, never a bad career move! In 1854, he undertook the task of clearing the nearby Gruinyards estate, which is on the opposite side of the river to Braelangwell.

This time, however, the tenants did not submit peacefully, though their opposition was of course, hopeless. When the Sheriff's Officer arrived with the writs of eviction, they were snatched off him and burnt. He and his assistant were stripped of their clothes and driven from the glen.

Three weeks later, things were very different: the Sheriff-substitute and the Procurator-Fiscal arrived with new writs and 35 constables, stopping at the Mid-Fearn Inn to drink "several bottles of ale, porter and whisky."

At Gruinyards, they were met by sixty or seventy women, backed by less than a dozen men and boys. "Clear the way...knock them down." Shouted Sheriff Taylor, and there was a fierce baton charge. Journalist Donald Ross wrote:

"The police struck with all their force...Not only when knocking down, but after the females were on the ground. They beat and kicked them while lying weltering in their blood. Such was the brutality with which this tragedy was carried through, that more than twenty females were carried off the field in blankets and litters, and the appearance they presented, with their heads cut and bruised, their limbs mangled and their clothes clotted with blood, was such as would horrify any savage...Dirty work must be done by dirty hands, and a cruel business is most generally entrusted to cruel hearts and ferocious dispositions."

At Braelangwell, William Ross's wife tore her apron into strips for bandages and was clubbed into the water for her trouble...into the Morrell pool where the Braelangwell and Gruinyards guests now peacefully fish for salmon.

Four women and a boy were hauled to the Tollbooth in Tain and locked in the cells. Later one of the women Ann Ross and a boy, Peter Ross, were taken to Inverness to face trial.

Lord Justice Hope, interrupting a shooting holiday on his son's estate in Sutherland, told them that the law must protect all persons, high and low and all persons, whatever their feelings, or perverted notions of right and wrong, must submit to the authority of the law.

"Neither they, nor their neighbours can be allowed to suppose that they can live in this kind of wickedness and rebellion spent against the law. They must be taught submission on the very first instance."

Ann Ross was sentenced to twelve months in prison and the boy to eighteen. And the fate of the evicted tenants? Not known, but once again, scattered to the four winds.

Although this is not Glencalvie, this is the kind of dwelling that the Glencalvie crofters would have inhabited. Note the tiny field with its crop of oats.

Strath Chuilonaich in winter.

Chapter Fifty Two
Forest Farm Stalking

Carry on past the telephone box at The Craigs in Strathcarron and rather than turning left for Amat, Glencalvie and Alladale, continue straight on for a mile or so. On your left you come to Croick farmhouse, occupied during the days when we were hind stalking by James Moffat and his wife Katie. This was the farmhouse for Forest Farm which stretches along Strath Chuilonaich (rhymes with cool-enough).

Just past Croick farmhouse is Croick Church. Visitors from all over the world come to Croick Church in the search for their ancestors after the clearances in the glen and a few years ago an Australian TV team turned up to film there.

Just past Croick church the single track road ends, barred by a gate. From then on an estate track continues along Strath Chuilonaich with the river on your left. About five miles on you come to the remote shepherd's cottage of Lubchoinnich (pronounce it Lub-co-nich) with its few farm buildings. At that time it was inhabited by the two shepherds on the Forest Farm estate: William Moffat, James Moffat's brother and Alan MacLean.

That, for practical purposes, is the end of the line though it is still possible to continue on by Land Rover right across country to join the road near Oykel Bridge in Strath Oykel.

Forest Farm was never considered to be a deer forest as it was, primarily, sheep ground but as it adjoins the forests of Alladale and Corriemulzie (the Mill Corrie) on the west there were always deer on the ground. It was always good for about 25 stags and at least that number of hinds.

For many years Forest Farm was owned by the Campbells but Colin Campbell of Ardgay eventually sold it to Mr. Wilson who was the owner when we first stayed at Braelangwell.

Some years ago Forest Farm was bought by a consortium headed by Julian Smith for a huge sum of money. They planted much of the glen with a mixture of native trees i.e. Scots pine, birch, etc. in the character of the original Caledonian forest. I understand that although they paid an enormous sum for the property a large sum was claimed later in Forestry grants.

Mr and Mrs Moffat were faced with a huge reduction in their sheep ground and as they were, in any event, nearing retirement they moved out and bought a cottage, Sgodachail near Braelangwell. (Give up on this and pronounce it Scooch-hall!). Their son, Robert, who lives in a house at The Craigs, still farms sheep on the ground that remains unplanted with trees at Forest Farm.

Ronnie Ross had the responsibility of hind shooting on Forest Farm and very kindly used to let our young people come along with him for a shot at the hinds. After a day's hind shooting they would often be grateful, when overtaken by darkness, for a welcome warm at the Lubchoinnich fireside and a dram ....or two.

Get caught on the Hill in the dark in midwinter and anything can go wrong! Only too easy to stumble into a hole and break a leg miles from anywhere.

On one occasion Bill was out stalking with Ronnie and darkness came with no sign of them. We were getting very worried indeed, though Margaret, used to unpredictable hours in stalking, didn't turn a hair.

Finally we heard the sound of Ronnie's pick-up and to our great relief Bill and Ronnie finally came in and sat down. Ronnie assured us that all was well so we collectively breathed a sigh of relief. Up until then Bill had been silent. "Did you get a hind, Bill?" we asked. Bill raised an imperious arm then extended three triumphant fingers. "Three" he replied. No need for us to have worried after all!

Bill is a marvellous shot anyway and he loved the David Lloyd rifle, being convinced that with that rifle in his hands he couldn't miss....nor did he. How we wished that Bill would miss a hind just to prove that he was still human, but Bill continued his unbroken run of one-shot kills.

Finally, to our great relief, he did manage to miss, though he never made a habit of it!

On one occasion we saw from the road an injured hind on the Amat ground at The Craigs so we asked the keeper, Jack McNichol, if we could shoot it. He readily agreed.

That year Bill had adopted a white oversuit for hind stalking and it was a great success. Off went Bill in his white suit and we all had a view of the whole thing from the road as the hind was about 500 yards out. The white suit against the snowy landscape, a patchwork of white and black. Suddenly Bill disappeared! He had fallen into a deep hole that had been bridged over by snow. All we could see was a pair of hands, still holding onto the rifle and waving it above the ground. Hilarious for us though not for Bill! Although Bill was shaken up the rifle remained unscathed and Bill went on to successfully shoot the wounded hind.

In the living room at Braelangwell Lodge. Steven, the author, Margaret, Claire, Adam, Ronnie, Bill and Rachel.

Walter Winans, American millionaire, with his full stocked Mannlicher.
Surely the finest shot of all time at running stags.

Chapter Fifty Three
Walter Winans

Walter Winans was an American millionaire who thought big! Towards the end of the 19th century he leased over 200,000 acres from sea to sea which included the forests of Kintail, Patt, Luibnadamph, Killilan, Glomach, Glenstrathfarrar, Glen Cannich, Fasnakyle and Craskie incurring a rental of about £20,000 a year (about a million pounds in today's money). This, remember, was just for the rental so what were his other expenses? A well-known photograph of one of his deer drives showed almost twenty stags killed. There were 17 ponies and a supporting staff of 35 people. No way could that lot come cheap!

To afford sport on this scale must have inspired an enormous amount of envy among his contemporaries and, in addition, his skill as a rifle shot didn't help! Winans was, without doubt, a marvellous shot at running deer and could shoot running stags as far away as 200 yards.

How this was possible with the enormous forward allowance necessary, I cannot begin to understand, but Winans prowess at running deer was well witnessed and recorded. He wrote "How can a man learn to hit when encountered unexpectedly or in rapid motion if he never shoots a rifle except with both elbows resting on the ground." So for those rifle shots who only shot at a standing deer from a good rest, Winans reserves his contempt.

He went on to write "Few men who go deerstalking have killed a deer moving, even at a walk, while fewer still are those that can kill a right and left when the stags are running past at the speed of a race horse and bounding into the air." and with that statement we are forced to agree!

Another great shot at running deer was Viscount Castleross who wrote a gossip column in the Daily Mail in the 1930's, At his estate in Ireland his party trick was to have deer driven past him when he was concealed from their view. As the herd raced past he would fire a single shot and two deer would fall dead, hit by the single bullet. He had fired at the precise moment when two stags had come into line, side by side and, yes, it did amaze all his friends who had been brought along as spectators.

In the days of Henry VIII every man was obliged by law to practise *daily* with bow and arrow, quite a problem in those days when so many workers had little or no leisure time at all. Winans agreed with this idea and considered that in the early 20th century such shooting should be reintroduced. He wrote: "I drew attention to the dangerous consequences to a nation through excessive devotion to games, such as cricket, golf and football. Many partisans of these games were indignant at my remarks, but public opinion now endorses my doctrine of the absolute necessity that every able-bodied man should be able to handle a rifle".

He suggested that it would be a good idea if a machine could be produced to throw a ball of about cricket ball size about twelve feet into the air for rifle practice at a moving target.

Walter Winans and his entourage start out for the hill.

The running deer target at Bisley was a great favourite of his and, in addition, he suggested that the moving figure of a soldier at two or three hundred yards should also be introduced.

For stalking in Scotland he was very keen on camouflage, not only recommending different coloured jackets and knickerbockers but even different coloured stockings! He even went as far as to dye a white pony to make it less conspicuous on the Hill.

The kind of check favoured by the Jazz singer George Melly would have suited him because he favoured big checks for the Hill though not in town! He also liked to have colours that would blend in with the changing landscape as autumn advanced, attempting to match the changing tints of the season by getting more yellow and red into his clothing.

He had his waistcoat buttoned to his neck and on his right shoulder buttons were sewn to take his telescope when he was crawling...so he didn't spend *all* his time shooting running stags! He wore very long jackets with very long sleeves which were normally turned up but could be turned down to cover his hands if it was cold. Surprisingly, he didn't wear plus-fours, knickerbockers or breeks but "breeches cut off just above the knee, as worn by Swiss peasants, leaving the knee bare" with the result of being "less apt to give rheumatism, as the knee dries as soon as it gets wet, instead of having clammy bits of cloth against it all day."

A right and left at running stags. by Walter Winans.

It must have been hard going *working for the Yankee Dollaaar* in Walter Winans service. He advised employers to "be suspicious of too long a "spy" for deer on the part of a stalker. It may only be his lazy way of passing the time.... once I caught two stalkers who did not think I understood any Gaelic, "spying" the oats in each others crofts and comparing their progress, when they were supposed to be spying for deer".

But, of course, his first love was shooting driven deer and this was very much out of favour in the late 19th century so Winans was out of step with many of his stalking contemporaries.

One of Walter Winan's successful deer drives.

Grimble, who wrote the first stalking "Bible", listing the deer forests of Scotland met Winans several times and wrote that Winans "on one occasion frankly told me that he was physically not strong enough to undertake the fatigue and hardship of stalking; that his hobby was shooting driven deer and in order to indulge this for five or six days a week for six weeks in succession it was necessary to have an extent of ground so vast that virtually the deer could not be driven off it. Looking at the matter in this light, the writer sees no reason why Mr Winans should not be left in peace to enjoy his sport in his own way and he certainly pays very liberally for the ground he rents".

Winans was also a competent artist and the *Shooting Times* described one of his pictures as a breath of mountain air and "Mr Winans must be congratulated for the striking lifelike scenes he has created. *They're Away* is simply marvellously good ....a remark which fully applied to *A running shot*, possibly the best illustration of deer we have ever seen".

So in addition to his skill with the stalking rifle, he was also a creative artist.

Nothing was left to chance when Walter Winans planned a deer drive and in his book *The Sporting Rifle* published in 1908 he drew his plans for different drives. Flags and bugles were used to control or stop the deer drive.

In his book there is one statement with which I am in complete agreement: Referring to deer driving he wrote: "This is an unfortunate combination of words to describe moving deer towards the shooter. It has led to the "driving deer into a narrow place from which they have no escape" style of abusing those who indulge in this form of sport. If the writers of such nonsense themselves tried to *drive* deer, they would find how impossible it is. Deer will not be "driven"; if they think that they are being forced they will break back, however thick the beaters are....instead of being called "deer-driving" it ought to be called (coining a word in the German manner) deceiving-the-deer-into-going-where-you-want them to."

Walter Winans arrives home after a day's conventional stalking, not driving.

The best spying position. Grimble

Stalking for a quiet shot William Scrope

Chapter Fifty Four
William Scrope

William Scrope (pronounced Scroop) was the man whose book *The Art of Deerstalking*, published in 1838, had an immense influence in promoting the new sport of deerstalking. Many others were later to write better and more informative books, but his was the first.

He was one of the gifted amateur naturalist/sportsmen who were well known in the 19th century and did not have to trouble with work to earn their bread and butter. He owned property in Wiltshire and Lincolnshire together with the Pavilion at Melrose, his holiday home in the Scottish Borders. He enjoyed the friendship of his neighbour Sir Walter Scott.

Deciding to try his hand at deerstalking he asked Sir Walter to write to the Duke of Atholl on his behalf. Sir Walter described him as: "An English gentleman of family and fortune...I am enabled to say that Mr Scrope is not only a perfect gentleman, and incapable of indulging his love of sport otherwise than as becomes one, but that he is a man of highly cultivated taste and understanding as well as much accomplishments".

This superlative recommendation gained him access to the Atholl forests which continued for the whole of his stalking career. He took Bruar Lodge and continued to return year after year.

Thormanby wrote: "The Duke had constituted Scrope a sort of amateur head game-keeper, and the fortunate painter-sportsman, luxuriously housed in Bruar Lodge, found himself practically uncontrolled master of a vast tract of moor and mountain forty miles long by eighteen broad, comprising 135,458 acres, of which 30,000 were devoted partly to grouse and partly to deer, whilst 52,000 thousand were reserved solely for deer".

Scrope ensured that the Duke was kept supplied with grouse

and venison and his friends, too, were not forgotten. Having once sent a haunch of venison to Sir Walter Scott he received the following reply: "Thanks, dear sir, for your venison, for finer or fatter ne'er roamed in a forest, or smoked in a platter".

Scrope set out deerstalking in a business-like manner. He liked to start out at dawn with three or four gillies. He usually took three rifles to the Hill, carried by one of them.....what a heavy and unwieldy load! Another was in charge of the deer hounds and the others to stalk or be despatched to distant parts of the ground to "move" deer towards the stalking party.

There was no shortage of excitement with heart bursting races to cut off deer, steep climbs and even steeper descents, almost always against the clock. If in a position to fire at several stags in a group he would fire with the first rifle, throw it down and repeat the process with the second and third rifles. He wrote that he "generally flung down each rifle as soon as he had discharged it - rock or moss, it took its chance".

His rifles were of excellent quality made by the famous London gunmaker, Charles Moore and several still hang in the great hall of Blair Castle, still in good order despite the scars on their stocks due to their having been thrown on the ground time and time again.

The forest joust   William Scrope.

The most popular calibre at the time was 16 bore i.e. .662 inches. They fired a one ounce round ball encased in a cloth patch to ensure a tight fit in the bore to grip the rifling. A modest charge of black powder was the propellant but the amount of the charge was limited: Too heavy a charge and the ball would "strip" i.e. not grip the rifling.

But Scrope's well-made rifles would be quite accurate, particularly up to 100 yards. Beyond this the bullet drop would have been a problem. With a *known* distance the sight could easily be adjusted to suit but it is notoriously difficult to estimate distances in the vast landscape of the Highlands.

But the main problem was the striking power of that solid ball, bearing no comparison to the striking power of the later Black Powder Expresses or the later cordite rifles. Even with a reasonably well placed bullet, a long chase with the deer hounds was often inevitable and, in fact, considered to be part of the enjoyment of the stalk. The deerhounds Bran, et al were often essential to bring the wounded stag to bay.

With such a vast area at his command the disturbance that the dogs inevitably caused was of little consequence, not so with the smaller acreages today.

Scrope was the first man to write and describe stalking methods which are much the same today: To spy the ground with a telescope to find a shootable stag. Next to plan an approach, taking into consideration the wind direction and the lie of the land. Keeping out of sight of the deer by taking advantage of any cover and, if necessary, crawling through bog or burn until finally getting into position for a shot at about 100 yards. So today's stalker has very much in common with Scrope, a century and a half ago.

Scrope found that the companionship of the stalkers, or foresters as they were then called, and the gillies was an enormous part of the appeal of deerstalking. Just as we, and generations of Rifles before us have done. In his book he is generous in his praise of John Crerar, Peter Fraser and their companions.

Scrope had enjoyed a classical education at Eton and Oxford and Sir Walter Scott regarded him as "one of the very best amateur painters" that he had ever seen. In Scrope's books he was responsible for the landscapes and persuaded his friends, such as Charles and Edwin Landseer, to put in the deer and the dogs. Even today Scrope's paintings have stood the test of time though much of his writing seems strange or even silly to us today.

Unfortunately Scrope's enjoyment of stalking was all too short, lasting only ten years as he was fifty years old when he first went to Atholl in 1822. In 1838, when his book was published, his stalking days were already six years behind him. In his dedication to the Duchess of Atholl he wrote that although years had passed;

"But the glories of the Highland landscape, though faded from my view, are dear to my remembrance, and I look back, as from out of a cheerless glen, upon those distant and sunny scenes of my life".

The book is written in the third person with Scrope describing himself as "Tortoise" and his companion as "Lightfoot".

Looking for a wounded deer William Scrope.

An enormous amount has been learned about deer since Scrope's time but, making allowance for this, much of his view of the deer and the Hill remains remarkably relevant. Like so many others, then and later, he was wildly incorrect about the age to which deer lived. He, too, thought that they could reach 200 years of age.

For many readers the sensible parts of Scrope's book can be read and enjoyed and the absolute nonsense skipped. Particularly excruciating are his reporting of Highland speech, for example "Hout-tout! Clish ma clavers. I'm ower auld-farren to be flayed for bogles". Did he really expect his readers to believe that the Atholl foresters, who would have been Gaelic speaking, really talked like that?

On the other hand I recently read a book about fishing in Scotland, set in the 1960's, in which the fictional fishing gillie's speech is a cross between Harry Lauder and Ooor Wullie! A touch of the Scropes, perhaps!

But despite all criticisms, Scrope is to be congratulated for being the first to write a book packed with descriptions of the deer and the Hill which brought deerstalking to the attention of a much wider public. There is no doubt that his book spurred many to travel to the Highlands and enjoy that magnificent landscape.

Shots from Cairn-cherie William Scrope.

The Monarch of the Glen.   We cannot have a chapter on Landseer without a picture of his best-known painting but take no notice!   He produced far more realistic paintings than this.

Chapter Fifty Five
Landseer

Although Scrope and Charles St. John provided the spur to deerstalking by their books, Edwin Landseer gave it further impetus by his paintings.

Harold Wilson will always be identified by "The pound in your pocket has not been devalued". Bruce Forsyth by "I'm in charge". Edwin Landseer by his painting *The Monarch of the Glen*.

These are your instant reactions. *The Monarch of the Glen* is a hopelessly over-romanticised depiction of a Highland stag that has condemned Landseer as a treacley Victorian painter whose appeal could only be to the Victorians. A man with no idea how to paint Highland wildlife.

I must admit that I, too, shared this all too instant view until I saw a pencil drawing of a group of hinds by Landseer. This brought me up with a shock!.... He really did know deer and how to depict them without sentimentality. If, however, the customer in Victorian times wanted an idealised picture then Landseer was perfectly capable of providing it. Even so, much of his work was very much more realistic than *The Monarch of the Glen* and he could, without doubt, convey the spirit of the deer and the Hill.

Landseer started out by painting pet dogs for wealthy clients and first went to the Highlands in 1824, right at the start of the deerstalking era. He was a handsome young man, twenty two years old.

The objective of his visit was to study the deer and the Hill, staying ten days at Blair Castle as a guest of the Duke of Atholl, then on to Bruar to stay with William Scrope.

At Bruar he started deerstalking and although enthusiastic enough he was never a very reliable shot. Even so, that stay on the Atholl Forest gave him a clear picture of the whole stalking scene which was to inspire so many of his paintings.

Often, when into position for a shot, he would quickly hand over his rifle to the forester and haul out his sketch pad instead! Landseer, like so many Sassenachs since, was captivated by the Highlands and would soon visit every year.

Return from stalking by Landseer. Now that's more like it! Look at the Deer Hounds.

Georgiana, second wife of the sixth Duke of Bedford, was described by the diarist Le Marchant as a "bold, bad woman with the remains of her beauty". She loved Scotland and every year in late summer she would travel to her holiday home, The Doune, in Rothiemurchus. Later, to be right among the hills, she had an encampment built far out in Glenfeshie. It was in a magnificent location by the River Feshie and surrounded by towering mountains.

The encampment consisted of a group of simple huts, wood and turf on stone foundations and although the Duke did not share the Duchess' love of Scotland, Edwin Landseer did and was a frequent visitor to the encampment.

Although the Duchess was old enough to be Landseer's mother they became very close: So close, in fact, that the Bedford family accepts that he was the father of at least two of her ten children.

Naturally enough their long association gave rise to speculation and scandal. The Duke died in 1839 and Landseer was eventually to propose to the Duchess, only to be refused. No doubt the title "Duchess of Bedford" was considerably more attractive than "Mrs Landseer"!

Landseer decorated the dwellings with frescoes and sketches during the 1830s but, sadly, the Duchess died in 1853 and then the whole encampment fell into disrepair, no doubt hastened by a dispute over the ownership of the land between neighbouring landowners: Grant of Rothiemurchus and the Mackintosh of Mackintosh.

When Queen Victoria visited the desolate but inspiring site in 1860 she was enchanted by the beauty of the view: "The scene of Landseer's glory".

Hero and Leander Sketch in the Braemore visitor's book by General Crealock.

General Hope Crealock who wrote and illustrated the monumental tome *Deerstalking* visited the place in the 1860's. He managed to find one sketch that was still recognisable so he was able to copy it, ensuring that some record of these remarkable works survived.

To this day the deer come down at night to graze over the ruins of the foundations and the place is still called "The Duchess of Bedford's".

Glenfeshie was the inspiration for several of Landseer's paintings including *Waiting for the deer to rise*. The three men waiting for the deer were Horatio Ross, stalker Charles Mackintosh and gillie Marcus Clark whose nickname was Callum Brocrair, the foxhunter, renowned for his strength.

On one occasion Horatio Ross, shooting rapidly, killed five stags. He would have made it six but in the heat of the moment a bullet was rammed down the barrel of the muzzle loader before the powder charge. One of the stags was an exceptional beast and Horatio said to Malcolm Clark that he would give £20 if the carcass could be brought back to the lodge intact without being cut up. "It should not cost the Captain that sum", said Malcolm and hoisting the 18 stone beast onto his shoulder he carried it down to where it could be loaded onto the pony. It was then taken to be finally unloaded at the Doune in the presence of the Duchess of Bedford.

Landseer's fame gave him an entry into many Highland deer forests and he was often invited to stay with the Breadalbanes where he stalked at Black Mount, another inspiration for his paintings. John McLeish, the stalker in the 1840's, described Landseer as a "Braw wee mannie" who "carried a braw rifle".

On one occasion a stag had been wounded on Ben Toig but when pursued by the deerhounds to Loch Tulle they finally brought it to bay. Although Landseer had not been stalking he managed to race out from the lodge to see the stag brought to bay by the deerhounds. The gallant animal managed to kill two dogs before being finally shot. One of Landseer's most famous paintings was based on this: *The Stag at Bay*.

The Deer Drive was another painting inspired by a deer drive on Black Mount. This was when Lord Tweedmouth and Lord Dudley killed nineteen stags in one drive on a pass between Larig Dochart and Altahourn.

He was also a frequent visitor at Ardverikie (some of the original hind stock at Newton Park Farm came from Ardverikie). He painted the walls of the lodge with frescoes, as at Glenfeshie. Ardverikie Lodge was burnt down on October 11th 1873, the day Landseer was buried but, fortunately, the paintings had previously been photographed. The new Ardverikie Lodge is the fictional Glenbogle Lodge in the television series "Monarch of the Glen".

General Crealock's opinion was that these original sketches were ideas for some of Landseer's great paintings and were "more truthful and lifelike than the finished pictures done later". See my own remarks at the start of this chapter.

A bad end. Another Braemore sketch by General Crealock. I liked the ravens.

But Landseer's most important contact had to be Balmoral. He had painted several Royal portraits and in 1850 was invited to stay at Balmoral where he was asked by the Queen's Private Secretary, Sir Charles Phipps, to "come well provided with drawing materials" at the Queen's request.

He sketched the Balmoral stalkers and gillies and painted several pictures of the Queen at Balmoral. His most famous picture of all, as I have said, was *The Monarch of the Glen*, inspired by Balmoral and painted in 1851. It was originally one of three paintings commissioned by the Government for £1,500 and was intended to be hung in the House of Lords refreshment room. Before the painting was finished, however, the House of Commons withdrew its funding and *The Monarch of the Glen* was sold to Londesborough at a price of 350 guineas or 800 guineas ....opinions differ! It was an excellent buy because thirty years later it was sold for £6,510 and eighteen years after that for £7,245. It went to Lady Pringle who refused many offers including one of £10,000. This illustrates the appeal of the picture to the Victorians.

So what is it worth today? I have no idea! No doubt it would have plummeted in value in the early twentieth century but I would have thought it would have risen again now. Out of fashion it may well be, but I would much sooner have it than Damian Hurst's dead sheep!

Much of Landseer's work really does convey the spirit of the Hill, the drama of deerstalking, the majestic setting and the poignant drama of the death of a noble animal. A reappraisal of *all* his work today is long overdue.

His influence, during his lifetime, is impossible to estimate but was, without doubt, very considerable when the new sport of deerstalking was gaining in popularity. In 1874, a year after his death, an exhibition of his work attracted 105,000 visitors. A sale of his own collection during the same year realised £69,000 and he left an estate of £160,000. To get some idea of today's values multiply by fifty so you will see what an immensely successful painter he was.

A Titian Breaks Bay. Another over-idealised picture of a stag, so beloved of the Victorians. General Crealock.

An Easy Chance. Grimble.

Chapter Fifty Six
The Stalking Bibles

There have been three attempts to list the Deer Forests of Scotland. All, no doubt, already out of date by the time they reached publication but, nonetheless, a worthwhile attempt in every case and a most important record.

The first of these "Bibles" was compiled by Augustus Grimble, a practical and enthusiastic stalker or, more precisely, Rifle. In 1888 he wrote a most informative volume entitled *Deer Stalking*. This described his stalking experiences and also gave valuable advice on all aspects of deerstalking. His enthusiasm still shines through over a century later and the book is well worth reading today. Most of his stalking had been on the forests of Corrour, Gaick, Invermark and Lochmore, four excellent forests.

In 1896 he wrote his first list of the best known Deer Forests and in 1901 he amalgamated both books in what can only be described as a "massive tome". This book was entitled *Deer Stalking and the Deer Forests of Scotland*. Once again, this book is packed with interest.

He gives the story of many of the forests, for example, when they were first afforested and the subsequent owners or tenants. Events of special interests connected to the forests, too, are recorded and historical incidents as well. A book well worth reading today. This was written, remember, right in the hey-day of stalking before the First World War was to change everything.

The next "Bible" was written by Alexander Inkson McConnochie: *The Deer and Deer Forests of Scotland*. Once again, well worth reading today. It gives a list of the forests with descriptions of them, their acreage and a brief account of their history. The latter part of the book describes notable stalking days with, finally, an account of the deer. Much of this information is now far out of date but it does make amusing reading.

The last "Bible" was *The Deerstalking Grounds of Great Britain and Ireland* written by the great stalking enthusiast, George Kenneth Whitehead in 1960. This is by far the most extensive work to date: Over 550 pages, packed with information, and with all the major deer forests listed and described. Their acreages are given together with a brief account of their history. The best stags shot on the forest are listed, given their number of points, length, breadth and span together with date shot and by whom.

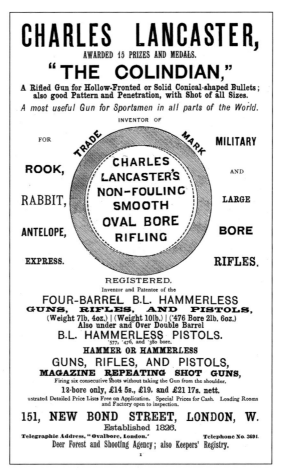

Excellent choices for the sportsman in 1895.

A Rich Gude Spy. Grimble.

"Haul that halyard."

Chapter Fifty Seven
The Cruise of the "Hornpipe"

In 1980 we chartered the *Hornpipe* to cruise the Western Isles of Scotland for two weeks. The *Hornpipe* was a 62ft long ketch of 45 tons owned and built by Ted Dinsdale Young.

So in late July we set off for Scotland. In the car were Edna and I, Ross and his friend from Repton, Marcus (Pod) Hill. Our trailer was loaded to bursting point: Suzuki 50, Kawasaki 90 and the rest of the trailer crammed with luggage of every kind.

We had breakfast at Charnock Richard on the motorway just after 8.30am. Petrol was at the shocking price of £1.49 per gallon, the highest price we had ever paid. The price in the Derby area was £1.30/1.35.

Our Allegro Estate was also crammed full with luggage but, even so, it buzzed along happily at about 70mph, though slower on the hills. Caroline and her current boyfriend, Nigel Hunter from Harrogate, were due to meet Mr and Mrs Hunter for breakfast in the Lake District and then carry on to Scotland.

They were the first to reach our usual coffee stop at the Dinwoodie Lodge, Lockerbie to leave a note. When we got there at about 11.50am we got their note and found that they had left 15 minutes before.

Once Glasgow was behind us we enjoyed that marvellous run over the Grampians. Less traffic than usual for the time of year due to the high cost of petrol, or so we all thought then! Afternoon tea at the Craigdhu Hotel, Ballachulish about 4.30pm then dinner at the Spean Bridge Hotel with Caroline and Nigel who arrived soon after. Price £30 for the six of us. On then to stay with Miss Campbell at Dundreggan (the Field of the Dragon) in Glen Moriston. Bill Auden and Larry Cawood had already arrived so the luggage was unloaded from the trailer, (but not the bikes), and loaded into Larry's father's Peugeot Estate, ready for the boat next day.

An early start next morning for a spectacular run through wild, west coast scenery to Loch Hourn, about twelve miles long and one of the longest sea lochs in Scotland: The gleaming white *Hornpipe* lay at anchor on the millpond-calm loch....a wonderful sight we will never forget.

Ted Dinsdale Young saw us and rowed across to meet us. Then we had a marathon haul, ferrying our luggage across to the boat. At last we were on board. Ted pressed the starter and the 100hp six cylinder diesel engine thundered into life. The *Hornpipe* glided away for the start of our voyage... a memorable moment!

Ted knew all the forest ground on either side of the long loch so was able to tell us all about it as we sailed along. As we started to come towards the mouth of the loch and the open sea, the *Hornpipe* started to pitch and Edna, always a poor sailor, started to feel queasy. From the mouth of the loch we continued to Mallaig where we stopped for fuel and water.

Roofless house on the Isle of Lewis.

Once clear of Mallaig, all we part time sailors, under Ted's instructions, hauled up the sails to experience a remarkable sensation: The boat took on a life of its own: canvas taut, ropes straining in an incredible combination of speed and power. The boat became a huge powerful creature, heeled over and racing forward as she pitched and rolled.

Everyone was delighted, elated, except for poor Edna who was soon down below in the cabin feeling desperately seasick. I am told that seasickness occurs in two stages; first you are afraid that you are going to die.... Next you are terrified that you won't! We headed for Loch Scriesort on the Isle of Rhum, ghosting in to our anchorage with me at the wheel while Ted and the boys lowered the sails in the calm of the sheltered loch. Edna was helpless with seasickness in her bunk so Caroline prepared the meal for us all.

But the calmness of our sheltered anchorage was not to last: During the night a gale blew up and the *Hornpipe* rolled and swung in a huge arc, tugging at her anchor chain. The wind hissed and rattled in the rigging and the anchor chain clanked against the side of the boat in sympathy. Sleep was impossible for any of us and Edna continued to be ill throughout the night.

Morning dawned with the gale unabated and to make things worse there was driving rain. Too rough even to go ashore. In the afternoon, however, we were able to get Edna ashore at last.

We went to see Ian and Cathy Simpson with whom we had stayed during our last visit to Rhum to see the deer. Ian ran the Nature Conservancy boat, the Rhouma, the original name for Rhum. They made us most welcome but with a house full they were unable to put us up this time. On then to stay at the Castle in the hope that Edna's seasick pills would take over.

Fortunately I do not suffer from seasickness but those who do, tell me that it is indescribably dreadful. Edna suffered agonies ...and she had the rest of the holiday on the boat ahead of her as chief cook and bottle-washer.

She did, however, manage to get a night's sleep at last followed by a simple breakfast in the Edwardian opulence of the dining room at Kinloch Castle. We paused, for a moment, on the way out to savour the amazing atmosphere of the Great Hall. Then out into the pouring rain to get to the Jetty at 9.30am. Edna was now dosed with her Stugeron anti-seasickness pills and, with fingers crossed, hoping that they would work. Tracey Edwards, the indomitable yachtswoman, suffered from seasickness until she discovered Stugeron.

At the jetty in the pouring rain there was no sign of life on the *Hornpipe* though we waved and shouted! Finally they did see us and sent the dinghy powered by an outboard motor, only to have it run out of petrol half way across!

The gale had blown itself out so the sails were hoisted and we sailed out of the bay with a south west wind on our beam. It was mixed weather with rain squalls but spells of sunshine. North of the Sound of Sleat the *Hornpipe* went like a racehorse on two spinnakers. As we approached Loch Ailsh, however, a rope caught the boarding ladder and knocked it overboard!

Spinnakers lowered and engine started we motored back to find the ladder, but without success. Round again to hoist the main spinnaker...a marathon task requiring everyone straining on the ropes, with the ropes even cutting into hands. "I never want to see another spinnaker as long as I live." said Ross.

Nigel against a dramatic backdrop.

Next task to hoist the rear or mizzen spinnaker but despite heroic efforts by everyone, the attempt failed. Another try and this time when almost fully hoisted the spinnaker snapped!

Through the narrows then into Loch Ailsh and with a change of direction the spinnaker lowered, thank goodness, and main sail and jib set.

Throughout all this Edna, by a miracle, was not seasick and it looked as it the Stugeron tablets were doing the trick. Fingers crossed even harder!

From the Kyle of Lochailsh along the Inner Sound of Raasay heading for a tiny sheltered bay a mile or two south of the village of Applecross. This was the only testing area for torpedoes in the British Isles and there was a Naval establishment on the Isle of Rhona, just north of Raasay. As we were turning into our little bay a Naval vessel approached us. I took over the wheel and Ted exchanged a shouted conversation. They warned us to keep clear of the torpedoes that they were just about to test. Ted hastily took the wheel to prevent us running onto the reef!

Peacefully at anchor at last, as calm as if we were on a canal basin. Edna and Caroline then whipped up a truly magnificent meal, eaten by all with tremendous gusto! As the *Hornpipe* was at such a peaceful anchorage we all had the benefit of a good night's sleep.

Ted in pensive mood.

Next morning we awoke to a glorious day. Five seals lay basking on the rocks until disturbed by Bill and Larry going for a swim. We all had a marvellous breakfast and were then away again with everyone in splendid spirits.

Our objective that day was Loch Torridon to see Lea and Margaret MacNally. We proceeded along the coast and then turned into Loch Torridon, hauled in the spinnaker and hoisted the jib, mainsail and rear sail. The wind was now on our beam but sheltered by the land so the *Hornpipe* just ghosted along through Loch Torridon, and Loch Shieldaig and finally to anchor by the hotel in Little Loch Torridon.

We went ashore in the tender and paid a surprise visit to Lea and Margaret MacNally at the Visitor Centre, Torridon and their nearby house, "The Mains". Lea was bombarded with questions by the boys, all taken in good part until, all too soon, it was time to head back to the Hornpipe.

So the days continued happily. We all took turns at the wheel, discovering that to steer a sailing ship was very different from steering a Mini! Move the wheel and it seems an age before the ship answers to the helm: Not a problem when you are out in open water but very different when approaching land.

Ted, of course, took over for the difficult bits!

We sailed along the east coast of the Isle of Harris and came to the place where Bonnie Prince Charlie in a longboat rowed by his loyal Highlanders was being pursued by a Government ship. They were heading for the tiny hamlet of Rodal and as you approach you face a line of cliffs. There is, however, a gap in the cliffs and Bonnie Prince Charlie's longboat slipped through the gap with the Government ship helpless and unable to follow.

We approached this same line of cliffs at high tide, essential for the *Hornpipe* to have enough depth of water to get through. Ted headed for the gap which seemed impossibly small to us but by spinning the wheel from side to side the Hornpipe sailed through.

Once through you are in a superlative, circular natural harbour, a most beautiful spot. The *Hornpipe* was anchored and we went ashore in the tender. The boys fished from the seaward side of the cliffs and we walked inland.

Cruising along the coast of Harris we would say "Where shall we moor tonight, Ted?" Ted would get out the charts and we would chose a bay or inlet.

One day we chose "Peter's Port". An excellent choice as earlier in the year we had visited St. Peter's in the Black Forest, Germany and St. Peter Port in Guernsey. This would complete the trio.

That evening we ghosted along the inlet to Peter's Port. There was hardly a breath of wind, no habitation and only the seals to stare at us in surprise. A beautiful evening and a wild, peaceful landscape. Finally Peter's Port came into view: An ancient jetty and an equally ancient warehouse....and that was it! No human dwelling of any kind.

Once ashore we walked round this lovely coastline and came upon a tiny, sheltered bay. Lying peacefully at anchor was a beautiful boat, new or nearly new, painted in brilliant colours and built in Hebridean style with high stem and stern. We wondered who owned and sailed this lovely boat as there was no sign of human habitation that we could see.

So much to see during our trip on the *Hornpipe:* Basking sharks, lots of seals, gannets dive bombing for fish, seabirds of every kind from Manx Shearwaters to Arctic Terns. Arctic Terns make the incredible journey from Pole to Pole every year.

The Hornpipe leaps ahead.

We had gone fully equipped for sea fishing and were very successful. Our lures consisted of hooks attached to long streamers, an unlikely combination but, in the event, they were surprisingly effective. Bill and Larry were keen fishermen but Nigel was not! On one occasion we were in the big bay at Gairloch and Ted was persuaded to let the *Hornpipe* drift across the bay with the engine at tickover while we fished from the side of the boat.

Nigel was persuaded to have a go and he reluctantly took the rod. The technique is the very antithesis of the finesse required to cast a dry fly onto the surface of a Hampshire chalk stream. You lower the lures then jiggle the rod up and down like a pump handle. I will never forget the look of astonishment and delight on Nigel's face when he hauled up his line to find he had hooked two huge Colefish! A moment he will never forget.

Nigel was a worthy young man from Harrogate, Yorkshire and a fellow student of Caroline's at Nottingham University. He was studying mining engineering.

At Guisley, near Bradford, in the 1930's, Harry Ramsden had started a modest fish and chip shop, eventually to become *The Biggest Fish And Chip Shop In The World.* In those days it was the one and only Harry Ramsden's. Naturally I asked Nigel about this famous Yorkshire attraction but he was unimpressed, whereupon I told him that it was my lifelong ambition to visit this unique Mecca of fish and chipdom!

Whenever I met poor Nigel I would torture him about Harry Ramsden's. He must have had the impression that I was holding him personally responsible for the place! I would go on and on about my lifelong ambition and he would get more and more indignant, never realising that I was teasing him!

I once said to him: "Did you know, Nigel, that Shakespeare often mentioned English place names?" He confirmed that he did. "But did you know that Yorkshire was featured in one of his plays?" I asked. This was new to Nigel so I told him that the quotation went like this:

"When shall we three meet again
In thunder, lightning or in rain.
On yonder misty mountain top
or at Harry Ramsden's fish and chip shop!"

Goaded beyond endurance he came up with his funniest line ever and   snapped: "You've been innoculated with a gramophone needle!"

And, no, in case you ask, I never did get to visit that one and only Fish and Chip Mecca at Guisley.

So the days continued happily on the *Hornpipe* with so much to see as we sailed along the east coast of Harris,

Ted never slept! He always just dozed, ever on the alert for anything unusual, anything that would put the boat in danger.

On one occasion, moored in a sheltered inlet off Harris when we were all asleep we were abruptly woken by the thunder of the diesel engine as it ripped into life. The wind had strengthened during the night, the *Hornpipe* had dragged her anchor and was being driven onto the rocky shore with potentially fatal consequences!

Ted had instantly woken from his doze and sprang into action so disaster was averted.

Finally the time came when we had to head back for Loch Hourn and disembark, but what a wonderful experience it had been for us all, something we will never forget.

We then went on to Deanich for our two week stay with the mixture as before!

"Land Ho!"

Bighouse Lodge, Caithness.

Chapter Fifty Eight
The Caithness Floe Country

For two years from 1981, we took the stalking at Bighouse for the end of the season. Bighouse is on the north coast of Scotland on the Sutherland / Caithness border, facing the Pentland Firth. This was further north than we had ever stalked before so it was all new country to us - the Caithness Floe Country. This is flat ... and wet! The last of the high hills are the pair of mountains, large and small, called colloquially the "Benny Grahams".

Bighouse is situated at the mouth of the River Halladale, a fairly short salmon river. The lodge is a huge building on a series of "half floors", a strange arrangement. You would walk up to the first floor then the next floor started half a floor up. This arrangement continued. I never remember seeing another building quite like it. It was built originally as a barracks after the earlier 1715 uprising.

It was, of course, very much un-modernised so it was old fashioned and neglected. Jim Pilkington had known the man who had owned it for many years. There were faded photographs on the walls taken during his time shooting big game in Africa.

There was a huge living room and the kitchen was on a floor below. The stalker, Wallace Lyon, was a very pleasant man indeed who had, for a number of years, worked for one of the big breweries at Burton upon Trent. He was based at Alloa in Scotland (always reminds me of Hawaii) and used to drive the huge beer lorries between Alloa and Burton. Caroline and Ross affectionately named him "Tommy Tiger". His mother looked after the lodge.

His uncle had been the Bighouse stalker but had unfortunately cut himself with his knife either when cutting up meat or gralloching. The wound went septic and killed him!

Tommy Tiger told us that his uncle would wait for hours to get a shot at a seal at the mouth of the river, usually with success.

They had an Argo at Bighouse and Tommy Tiger used it with a masterly touch: He really was an expert with it. We would all squeeze into the Argo for the start of our trip to the Hill, sorry, flat! One beat in particular I remember with great pleasure: There was a substantial hillock that you could approach in the Argo then climb to the top of it. From there you had a wonderful view of the ground for well over 180 degrees. We would spectate from this excellent position and watch Tommy Tiger and Ross stalking, with a view of the whole scene. On this wet, squelchy expanse there was very little cover so to get in for a shot meant crawling for long distances, often with only a peat drain for cover. Tommy Tiger, however, was an excellent stalker and a stag would come back on the Argo every time.

With such terrain at Bighouse it was a wonder that the deer hadn't developed webbed feet as it was so different from traditional deer country, but there were deer enough to provide good, interesting stalking.

Tommy Tiger instructed Ross and I how to make a Lorryman's Knot. You could, when it was tied, haul on it to tighten it yet to release it was simplicity itself. A very useful knot for so many purposes. Ross has never forgotten how to tie it..... I have!

Close-up of a ruined tower with Edna and Caroline beside it.

So we had most enjoyable stalking for two seasons at Bighouse. The Caithness Floe Country was chosen for the planting of thousands of trees for investors in the 1960's and 70's. Terry Wogan was among the investors. There were very valuable tax advantages but whether or not it will prove to be a worthwhile long term investment, time will tell.

Abandoned on one of the stalking areas right out on the Hill was a "Weasel". Weasels were large U.S. Army tracked vehicles powered by a Ford Vee Eight engine and in the immediate period after the War they were *the* answer to getting out on the Hill to stalk and to transport stags and hinds. They eventually wore out but in their day Andrew Allen was *the* Weasel exponent.

Andrew Allen is a Highland contractor constructing roads, erecting fences and allied work. He is famous throughout the Highlands for his skill with the stalking rifle and during his career has accounted for over 22,000 stags and hinds to his own rifle. I have never met him, though have spoken to him on the telephone. He has enclosed a large area at his home where he breeds Red Deer.

Pass of the Cattle, Applecross. A dangerous drive in the early days of motoring, still formidable today.

Annie-Rose, Cameron, Dave Riley and Rosie the dog two days after Dave and Rosie found Cameron in the woodland.

Chapter Fifty Nine
Cameron and the Dinosaurs

Marcus and Jennifer Munro of Alladale have two children, Cameron three and Annie-Rose, two. In October 2000 on a family outing to the Falls of Shin Visitor Centre near Bonar Bridge, Cameron went missing while his mother fastened Annie-Rose into the car. With the river in spate on one side and thick woodland on the other, the prospect looked grim.

Jennifer crashed through the trees, frantically calling his name, but without success. At 4.30 pm, she raised the alarm. Local shops were scoured for torches as volunteers raced in to help the search.

Nothing found and with heavy hearts, they agreed to meet the next day at 7.00 am. By 7.15 am, 280 searchers from miles around had signed in: Bonar Bridge, Ardgay, Dornoch, Helmsdale, Tain, Lairg, Inverness and everywhere in between. More still were to come together with three mountain rescue teams, two helicopters, police and police dogs.

Steven Mackenzie was amongst the volunteers who formed a line, shoulder to shoulder, 300 yards long and advanced into the woodland. They went on for half a mile, terrified of what they might find. After half a mile, they considered that no three year old could have walked that far and the unspoken conclusion was that he must have been abducted or fallen into the river.

Dave Riley from Kingussie, a retired policeman and an experienced member of the Search and Rescue Association, was out with his ten year old collie, "Rosie" (the same name as Marcus' mother, who died when he was eight.) Dave had been involved in searching during the Lockerbie disaster and during his career he had been successful in the past, but with the grim proviso that he had never found anyone *alive.*

About 8.30am, with unimaginable delight, Dave and his dog found Cameron. Cameron had found a natural "igloo" of tumbled tree roots and had settled down in its shelter to sleep for the night. Amazing enterprise in wilderness survival for a three year old.

Rosie, of course, was barking excitedly. Cameron's first words to Dave were "Tell your dog to shut up!" Dave took off his coat to wrap round the little fellow: "I don't want that" said Cameron. "I've got a coat!" He was, thank God, warmly dressed.

But what was absolutely amazing, was that Cameron had not been afraid. In fact, Dave was amazed how chirpy and cheery he was. When asked what it had been like, Cameron replied "Dark!"

He had been looking for dinosaurs, found two, a big one and a little one, but chased them away with his stick. You and I would have called it a twig but, no matter, it did for the dinosaurs!

Cameron and Marcus were then taken to hospital at Inverness by helicopter, where Cameron devoured four pieces of toast and was pronounced fit and well.

So all ended well, thank God, and Cameron, having made it onto the television news and the front page of the *Daily Telegraph*, got home safe and sound. When Marcus was very small, we soon realised that he was a chip off the old block. Now we know that Cameron is too!

Cameron's third birthday, September 2000. Jennifer, Annie-Rose, Marcus and Cameron by the old keepers lodge in Glen Alladale.

Guest of Honour Cameron opens the Dinosaur Exhibition at Glasgow University.

(Top) The 16 point stag Freddie has been shot by Steve Crooks' narcotic dart and is now comatose.
(Bottom) Steve, helped by his daughter, saws off Freddie's horns.

Chapter Sixty
The Deer at Newton Park Farm

Surely nothing conveys the spirit of the Highlands more evocatively than the Red Deer. Having enjoyed the enormous privilege of seeing them on the Hill for many years we decided that it was time to bring some of them down from Scotland to Newton Park Farm so that we could have a living reminder of Scotland at our home in Derbyshire.

They had to be pure Scottish stock, of course, caught as wild deer in the Highlands. Doctor John Fletcher was the obvious choice to supply us and we approached him in early 1981 to obtain our small herd.

John supplied us with a stock of ten hinds and one stag, all true Highland stock caught up from Cognafearn and Ardverikie.

Before they arrived we had to have a suitably fenced area and decided upon two adjoining paddocks of about six acres in total on the west side of the farm buildings. One paddock would be used for hay to provide winter feed. When the hay was cut we could release the deer into the whole area or put the deer into the hay paddock to rest the other one. A water supply from the buildings had to be piped into the paddocks and a water trough put in each.

A large shed in the north paddock would be utilised to install ring feeders for the hay bales in winter and would also provide shelter from the weather, though the deer were to utilise the shed for shade in summer rather than as protection from the elements.

As the deer were wild-caught there was no exact knowledge of their age but, on average, estimated at about five years.

In the Highlands a hind will bear a calf in June but probably, but by no means invariably, not be in good enough condition to conceive a calf for the following year so the calf crop is usually about 50% of the hind stock. The calves have to face the bitter Highland winter and the weaker calves - and hinds - will not survive. Nature is a ruthless master. So I would estimate that on the average Highland forest the calf stock that survives will be about 30%. This is, I agree, a rule-of-thumb estimate and some more favoured forests will provide better results than this.

True to form, however, our first season's crop was five calves from ten hinds but at Newton Park Farm the winter is much kinder and the hinds have access to unlimited hay plus a daily supplement of sugar beet pulp, so all five calves survived. Once our hinds were established they would provide close to 100% calving and although the odd weak calf would not survive it would die within a month or so of birth. Winters would not kill calves here.

You cannot, of course, just turn wild Red Deer into a normal field and expect fences or hedges to keep them in. You must have fencing two metres (6ft 6") high. The fencing is high tensile steel wire.

We were told that if deer were really alarmed they *could* jump over our two metre fencing but had never experienced it until about two years ago. Attempting to herd the deer to separate the calves our stag, thoroughly alarmed, did jump the fence followed by a hind. Fortunately it was only the internal fence so no harm was done.

A better view of Freddie's antlers.

There are, of course, foxes in the woods at Newton Park Farm and for a decade or more I could have assured you that foxes do not take deer calves. Could have, but would have been mistaken because I know, from experience, that you can never say "never" when discussing wild life. There are many pundits, for example, who will assure you that foxes never take lambs but their knowledge is theoretical rather than practical: Just try telling that to a Hill shepherd!

But for a decade or so at Newton Park Farm no deer were lost to foxes. There were enough rabbits to provide a food supply for them. One year, however, myxomatosis returned, as it does, and with food short the foxes turned to deer calves and two or three were taken. The problem is that after the birth of a calf the mother will leave it, only returning at dusk to suckle it, so the obedient calf, lying in position as instructed by his mum, is at the mercy of a hungry fox. Since then, however, some rabbits have returned and this is no longer a major problem though an odd calf is sometimes taken in June.

What a marvellous moment it was when John arrived with our deer at dusk and they leapt out of his truck. Yes, they do leave the truck with a tremendous bound!

For weeks after their arrival their ears were never still and they appeared to revolve like propellers. There were so many different sounds that they had never been used to on the Hill. Eventually, however, they adapted to this new range of sounds.

"It's not like seeing them on the Hill." says Edna. "No", I reply, "but it's better than not seeing them at all".

They have, in fact, given us an enormous amount of pleasure and as we can observe them so closely there is very much to learn. Their faces, for example, are all different, just like humans. Their shape, too, varies, "Not a lot" as Paul Daniels might have said but there is a difference.

But the chief difference is in their temperaments: Some are bullies, some are mild, some adapt very easily to man, some don't! All, of course, accept us as an essential part of the scene and we really are "one of them".

Some hinds accept being patted, some never do but *all* of them will put their noses against your forehead to investigate you more closely. As for physical strength, there's no contest! They are much stronger than a man. Just try to pull the feed bucket away from them when they push against you. Not only are they stronger but they have four legs to push with!

A great pleasure in a summer evening is to watch them over the garden wall. Some of the hinds will be on their feet grazing, some lying down. The calves are not as playful as lambs but are playful, nonetheless. A couple of calves will get up and race round the paddock then come back to their starting point and flop down. One or two more will then take over to race round and the process is repeated.

On the far side of the paddock, just outside the wire, you will sometimes see a fox sitting on his haunches like a dog, observing the proceedings with great interest, watching and waiting. Get a shot at him? Not a chance! He makes sure that he is safely out of harm's way!

Some of the hinds.

John Fletcher and his wife have built up a successful business supplying fine farmed venison but a most important part of the business has been selling live deer to farms not only in this country but all over Europe. Every year he has taken our surplus deer calves but for winter 1999 he was unable to do so as the strength of the pound or, more correctly, the weakness of the Euro had brought this trade virtually to a standstill. Will it eventually come back? Goodness knows! We had hoped that John would have taken our year 2000 calf crop before the end of the year, but due to pressure of work he was unable to do so, putting off collection until March 2001 - then came foot and mouth making collection impossible. So what will we do when the next calf crop arrives in June 2001? Assuming we escape foot and mouth disease? Don't know!

With the stags so tame we have no alternative but to have their horns sawn off at the end of summer and before the rut. It doesn't hurt them a bit as the horns are completely grown and free of velvet. The stag is shot with a narcotic dart. He becomes semi-conscious so you are able to saw off his horns. The antidote is then administered and all is well. Yes, I agree with you, I don't like to have the horns sawn off but there is simply no choice! During the rut in late September, early October, the stags are consumed with rutting fever and as they have so little fear of man in enclosed conditions they could be dangerous and see man as an intruder. We have never had a stag who has shown any tendency to attack man but, as I said before, you can never say "never".

In any case when the deer are being fed with sugar beet nuts at the feeding troughs a stag could easily bring his head down quickly and inadvertently stab you with his horns. In addition to that a stag will swing his horns to push the hinds away from the feeding troughs to deny them their share of the food.

So when you say "I much prefer to see a stag with his full set of antlers". I couldn't agree more! So now you know why this is not possible with *enclosed* stags.

Deer calves are born in the Midlands at the same time as in Scotland. The first calves arrive in late May and most are born by mid-June. You can, of course, get later calves and an odd calf can be born in August though this is unusual. In the Midlands, such a calf will have no problems of surviving the winter but in Scotland it would not be strong enough to do so.

As I have said before there can be no more beautiful sight in nature than a Red Deer calf. Its red coat is spotted with white dots to provide a natural camouflage. The spots gradually fade over the following weeks.

We ear tag the calves using different colours for stags and hinds and, of course, different numbers. The mothers put their new- born calves down and "tell" them to stay there until the evening.

For up to forty eight hours you can approach the calves and carefully hold them so that you can ear tag them. Usually the mother hind will take no notice but, on occasion, a hind will race towards you then abruptly halt, stiff legged, only a few feet away. I say that they will not actually attack you but Edna and Ross consider discretion to be the better part of valour and, as you know, you can never say "never"!

The rut, too, starts at about the same time as in Scotland and in late September it is uncanny to hear the roar of a Highland stag echoing across the Derbyshire countryside.

The Monarch of the Trent Valley. Donkey Spice with her ears back will see off all the deer including Freddie the Stag.

The living room at Braelangwell Lodge, New Year 2001.

"Should auld acquaintance be forgot
And never brought to mind?
Should auld acquaintance be forgot
And auld lang syne?

For auld lang syne, my dear,
For auld lang syne.
We'll tak a cup o' kindness yet,
For auld lang syne."

Post Script

"The only place Dad ever wants to go is Scotland." So say Caroline and Ross and they're not so very far wrong.

Nothing can compare with the high hills of Scotland, the Red Deer and, not least, the Highlanders.

We have had some marvellous times and met some wonderful people. Wouldn't have missed a minute of it!

The world has changed since we first headed for Scotland in our Austin A90 Atlantic, back in 1954 when inflation was only a pup!

For most of us in those days, there was no television, central heating, fitted carpets, double-glazing or foreign holidays.

In addition to that, video recorders, personal computers, fax machines, mobile 'phones and the Internet were far in the future. There have been tremendous social changes, too.

But, despite it all, the high hills of Scotland remain unchanged and the Red Deer survive, regardless of all the pressures on them and the loss of so much of their winter feeding grounds.

So here's to the Highlands, the Highlanders and the Red Deer.

Long may they endure.

Sources

ADAM SMITH, JANET, **John Buchan** (Hart-Davis 1965). Modern biography.

AKEHURST, RICHARD, **Game Guns and Rifles** (Bell 1969). Excellent brief history.

ANDERSON, MARK L., **A History of Scottish Forestry** (2 vols, Nelson 1967). A work which must be read, containing an enormous amount of information.

BAKER, SIR SAMUEL, **Wild Beasts and their Ways** (2 vols, 1890). Big game hunting all over the world.

BREADALBANE, ALMA G., **The High Tops of Black Mount** (Blackwood 1907). A stalking classic by one of the greatest lady stalkers.

BROMLEY- DAVENPORT, W., **Sport** (Chapman and Hall 1885). Highly individual book on field sports.

BROWN, IVOR, Balmoral: **The History of a Home** (Collins 1955). Worthwhile description of Balmoral.

BUCHAN, JOHN, **John MacNab** (Hodder and Stoughton 1925). Evergreen stalking adventure in the Highlands.

CAMERON, ALLAN GORDON, **The Wild Red Deer** of Scotland (Blackwood 1923). Most informative and in many ways well ahead of its time.

CHALMERS, PATRICK R., **Mine Eyes to the Hills: An Anthology of the Highland Forest** (A. and C. Black 1931). An excellent anthology well worth reading today.

COLQUHOUN, IAN, **The Future of Deer-Stalking** (1925). Well worth reading.

CREALOCK, LT-GENERAL. HENRY HOPE, **Deer-Stalking in the Highlands of Scotland** (Longman's 1892). Posthumously edited by his brother Major General John North Crealock. This is one of the most important books on deer stalking by a man who was also capable of producing magnificent drawings of the Red Deer. A compelling account of his stalking days.

CUMMING, ROUALEYN GORDON, **Five Years of a Hunter's Life in the far interior of South Africa** (Mid 19th Century). Highland Stalker and the first African white hunter.

CUPPLES, GEORGE,, **Scotch Deer-Hounds and their Masters** (Blackwood 1894). An account of an important breed now long forgotten.

DARLING, FRANK FRASER, **A Herd of Red Deer** (Oxford 1937). A scholarly account of observing and virtually living with the Red Deer throughout the seasons. Essential reading for anyone interested in the Red Deer of Scotland. He also wrote **A Herd of Red Deer**. (Collins 1937). An important study well worth reading.

EDWARDS, LIONEL, and WALLACE, HAROLD FRANK, **Hunting and Stalking the Deer** (Longmans 1927). A knowledgeable anthology, essential reading.

ELLANGOWAN (J.G. BERTRAM), **Outdoor Sports in Scotland** (W.H.Affen 1889). A period piece which does, of course, convey the spirit of the times though with many fallacies.

FLETCHER, JOHN **A Life for Deer**. (Victor Gollancz 1988) Essential reading by a remarkable deer vet and deer farmer.

FRASER, HUGH, **Amid the High Hills** (A. and C. Black 1923). One of the best anthologies, very well written.

GATHORNE-HARDY, A. E., **Autumns in Argyllshire with Rod and Gun** (Longmans 1900). An excellent account of days on the Hill.

GREENER, W.W., **The Gun** (Cassell 1881). Monumental tome outlining the history and development of the gun.

GRIMBLE, Augustus, **Deer-Stalking** (Chapman and Hall 1886). Still eminently readable today. Surprisingly undated advice and reminiscences. Also **The Deer Forests of Scotland** (Kegan Paul 1896). The first comprehensive account of the deer forests of Scotland combined with the author's first book. Essential reading.

HALL,ROBERT, **The Highland Sportsman** (Simpkin Marshall 1882). Excellent guide to Highland sport.

HART-DAVIS, CAPTAIN H., **Stalking sketches** (Horace Cox 1904). Interesting collection of stalking reminiscences, illustrated by the author.

HARTING, J. E., **British Animals Extinct Within Historic Times** (1880). Important historical survey.

HARTLEY, GILFRID W., **Wild Sport and Some Stories** (Blackwood 1912) Excellent collection of stalking memories in Scotland and Ireland including a ghostly account of men in black carrying a coffin.

HORN, PAMELA, **Pleasures and Pastimes in Victorian Britain** (Sutton Publishing 1999) Compelling account of leisure activities in the nineteenth century. Everything from cricket to deerstalking.

LENNIE, CAMPBELL, **Landseer: The Victorian Paragon** (Hamish Hamilton 1976) Life of the greatest Victorian Highland wildlife painter.

LONDONDERRY, THE MARCHINESS OF, Henry **Chaplin: A memoir** (Macmillan 1926). Her father's life but does include some stalking stories. **Retrospect** (Muller, 1938) Her autobiography which includes some stalking interludes.

McCOMBIE SMITH, **The Romance of Poaching in the Highlands of Scotland** (Eneas Mackay 1904) About the great rifle shot and inventor of the Farquharson Rifle action and his contemporary Alexander Davidson.

McCONNOCHIE, A.I., **The Deer and Deer Forests of Scotland** (1923). One of the most important stalking "bibles'. Essential reading for anyone interested in the deer and the Hill. **Deerstalking in Scotland** (1924) Stalking reminiscences. **Deer Forest life** (1932) More valuable reminiscences.

MACDONALD, DUNCAN GEORGE FORBES, **Cattle, Sheep and Deer** (1872). Not a well thought of author as the book is considered to be inaccurate.

MACKENZIE, EVAN G., **Grouse Shooting and Deer-Stalking** (Love and Malcolmson 1907). Shooting and stalking reminiscences.

MACKENZIE, OSGOOD, **A Hundred Years in the Highlands** (Edward Arnold 1921). Excellent account of life in the west of Scotland in the nineteenth century.

MACNALLY, LEA, **Highland Year** (Dent 1968), **Highland Deer Forest** (Dent 1970), **Wild Highlands** (Dent 1972), **The Year of the** Red Deer (Dent 1975), **The Ways of the Eagle** (Dent 1977)
British Deer Society Cup 1967, 1972 and 1980 for his colour photography of deer. "Some of the finest Red Deer photographs I have ever seen". (MacNeish of the Northern Times.) Outstanding accounts of the deer and the hill by one of the most dedicated stalker-naturalist-photographers of all time.

MACRAE, ALEXANDER, **A handbook of Deer-Stalking** Foreword by the great stalker Horatio Ross (Blackwood 1880). Sensible, practical, handbook on stalking still true today.

MALCOLM, GEORGE, **The Population, Crofts, Sheep-Walks and Deer Forests of the Highlands and Islands** (Privately printed by Blackwood, Edinburgh 1883) It also contains **A Defence of Deer-Forests** by Donald Cameron of Lochiel.

MARTIN, THEODORE, **The Life of His Royal Highness the Prince Consort** (Two vols, 1876). Historical record with some mentions of Scottish stalking.

MILLAIS, J.G., **British Deer and their Horns**. (Henry Southeran, 1897). Excellent description of deer heads, beautifully illustrated by the author and with much information about the history of deer-stalking.

MITCHELL, JOSEPH, **Reminiscences of My Life in the Highlands** (Two vols, published privately 1883). Excellent memoirs of a distinguished engineer.

OLD STALKER, AN, **Days on the Hill** (Nisbet 1926). Most stalking reminiscences of the nineteenth century were written by the 'Rifles', not by the professional stalkers themselves. This book is valuable because it was written by a professional Highland stalker, David Taylor. One of my favourite books but Lea MacNally never liked it.

PARKER, ERIC, **English Wild Life** (Longmans 1929) Eric Parker's books are always well worth reading and this is a most interesting survey.

PEEL, E. LENNOX, **A Highland Gathering** (London 1885). Readable account of sport with rod, rifle and gun.

PILKINGTON, STEPHEN, **With a Gun to the Hill**. (Herbert Jenkins 1948) The book that started it all off for me!

PORTLAND, THE DUKE OF, **Fifty years and More of Sport in Scotland** (Blackie 1933). Another very worthwhile book about Scottish sport with much stalking. **The Red Deer of Langwell and Braemore**, 1880-1934 (Blackie, 1934). Not a lot of text but mainly photographs of outstanding heads.

PREBBLE, JOHN, **The Highland Clearances** (Secker and Warburg 1963). Brilliant account of the Highland Clearances by lifelong Scottish enthusiast, John Prebble.

RITCHIE, JAMES, **The Influence of Man on Animal Life in Scotland** (Cambridge University Press 1920). Much historical information and well worth reading.

ROSS, JOHN (Editor), **The Book of the Red Deer** (Simpkin Marshall 1925). Fascinating collection of accounts of stalking in Scotland and elsewhere.

RUFFLE, THE, **The Sporting Rifle in Britain** (Batchworth Press 1951) A modest book of 105 pages, but essential on any stalker's bookshelf.

ST JOHN, CHARLES, **Natural History and Sport in Moray** (Edmonton and Douglas 1846). One of the true stalking classics which includes the famous account of the stalking of the Muckle Hart of Benmore. A Tour in **Sutherlandshire**. (two vols, Edmonton and Douglas, 1849). An amazing account by a Victorian naturalist. **Natural history and sport in Moray**, reissued in a number of new editions under the title **Wild Sports and Natural History of the Highlands. Charles St. John's Notebooks** were edited by Admiral H.C. St John and published in 1901.

SCOTT, WALTER, **Waverley** (published in 1814). The first of the famous Waverley novels.

SCROPE, WILLIAM, **The Art of Deer-Stalking** (Edward Arnold 1838). The book that started the stalking boom - still readable today. Reprinted many times since and some editions entitled **Days of Deer-Stalking**.

SINCLAIR, SIR JOHN, **The statistical account of Scotland** (21 vols, 1791-9). Enormous collection of historical fact submitted by various parish ministers. Generally known as The Old Statistical

Account, to distinguish it from The New Statistical Account, published in 1843. Much information but heavy going!

SMITH, MRS E., **Memoirs of a Highland Lady** (John Murray, 1898). A view of life in an all but forgotten era. Life in Rothiemurchus, 1797-1830.

SPEEDY, THOMAS, **Sport in the Highlands and Lowlands of Scotland** (1884) Another very well known account of Scottish sport.

STEVEN, H.M. and CARLISLE, A., **The Native Pinewoods of Scotland** (Oliver and Boyd 1959). Essential reading for anyone interested in the evolution of the Scottish landscape.

STEWART, JOHN SOBIESKI and C.E., **Lays of the Deer Forest** (two vols, Blackwood 1848. Vol. 1 contains poems in Gaelic and English. Vol.2 is an eccentric opinion of deer-stalking with dogs in Scotland up to that time. The authors claimed direct descent from Bonnie Prince Charlie though he had no legitimate issue.

SURTEES, VIRGINIA, **Charlotte Canning** (John Murray 1976). Entertaining biography, well worth reading.

SUTHERLAND, THE DUKE OF, **Looking back** (Odhams 1957). Autobiography with accounts of Sutherland stalking.

TAYLOR, JOHN. (The Water Poet), **The Penniless Pilgrimage and Other Pieces**. (1618). The story of his Highland travels.

THOMPSON, FRANCIS, **Victorian and Edwardian Highlands from old photographs**. (BT Batsford Ltd 1976). Marvellous photographic record that must be read.

THORMANBY (J.W. Dixon), **Kings of the Rod, Rifle and Gun** (two vols., 1901). Excellent account of many of the characters who made sporting history. The chapter on Horatio Ross is essential reading.

THORNTON, COLONEL T., **A Sporting Tour through the**

Northern Parts of England and Great Part of the Highlands of Scotland (Vernon and Hood 1805). An account of wondering over vast areas of country and shooting anywhere he wished, long before the deer stalking era started in the 1840's.

VICTORIA, QUEEN (Edited by Arthur Phelps), **Leaves from the Journal of our Life in the Highlands** (Smith Elder 1868). Descriptions of Scottish visits and Balmoral life.

WADDINGTON, RICHARD, **Grouse Shooting and Moor Management**. (1948) One of the most notable figures in Scottish sport.

WALLACE, HAROLD FRANK, **British Deer Heads** (1913). Illustrated record of an exhibition organised by Country Life. **Happier Years** (Eyre and Spottiswood 1944). Autobiography with many stalking reminiscences.

WHITEHEAD, G. KENNETH, **The Deer Stalking Grounds of Great Britain and Ireland** (Hollis and Carter 1960). The first of the stalking bibles in the post-war era. Packed with information, facts and figures. Essential reading.
The Deer of Great Britain and Ireland (Routledge 1964). A further essential reference work.

WINANS, WALTER, **The Sporting Rifle** (Putnam, 1908). Memoirs and advice by the American millionaire who leased a huge tract of Scotland and practised deer driving on a vast scale.

YOUNGSON, A.J., **Beyond the Highland** line (Collins 1974). Fascinating account of three eighteenth century travellers, Burt, Pennant and Thornton.

The Journal of the British Deer Society has also been an invaluable source of reference.

By the same author
One Man's Motorcycles
1939 - 1949

270 pages, 150 illustrations

Yes, a motorcycle theme, but there is much more than that: Boyhood in Rhyl during the depression-driven 1930's. Engineering apprenticeship in Dickensian conditions in Derby, then aero-engine development at Rolls-Royce.

Starting in the motorcycle business after the War, buying, selling, restoring and racing motorcycles of the 1920's, 30's and 40's.

Along the way this book tells the story of the motorcycles and the characters who rode them against the backdrop of those times.

It is written to appeal equally to motorcyclists and the general reader in the hope that they will refer to it time and time again.

In the pages of this book you will meet Dick Seaman, Reg Parnell, Titch Allen, founder of the Vintage Motorcycle Club, Murray Walker and many others.

The price of this book, for a signed copy, is £14.50 including post and packing at current rates.

Available from:
M. E. P. Publishing
Newton Park Farm
Newton Solney
Burton on Trent
DE15 0SS
Tel: 01283 703280